# FLAWED EXPECTATIONS

MONSIGNOR MICHAEL J. WRENN
KENNETH D. WHITEHEAD

# Flawed Expectations

## The Reception of the
### *Catechism of the Catholic Church*

IGNATIUS PRESS    SAN FRANCISCO

Cover design by Roxanne Mei Lum

To His Eminence
John Joseph Cardinal O'Connor, D.D., Ph.D.
Archbishop of New York

On the occasion of the fiftieth anniversary of his ordination to the sacred priesthood, December 15, 1945; and in
gratitude for his own commentary on the *Catechism of the
Catholic Church* entitled *A Moment of Grace*.

# Contents

# Foreword

No one would deny that the *Catechism of the Catholic Church* is a priceless gift to all of us who stand, as we do, on the threshold of the third millennium. The tremendous welcome that this magnificent instrument of the deposit of our holy faith has received worldwide attests to its timeliness and significance. In the Archdiocese of New York, for example, all of our catechetical efforts, whether in school, nonschool, or adult-education programs, are presently being designed whenever necessary in the light of the vast treasures that a careful and prayerful reading of the *Catechism* can profitably yield.

The authors of *Flawed Expectations* are, above all, concerned with seeing to it that a proper reception and authentic interpretation be given to the *Catechism*. They have set forth, in great detail, a number of unfortunate negative reactions to the *Catechism* that have appeared in several commentaries published in the United States and elsewhere.

They deserve a resounding bravo for their efforts in analyzing tendencies that are counterproductive to the *Catechism*'s sole intent to assist the faith of God's people to become living, conscious, and active through the light of instruction. I find *Flawed Expectations* highly troubling, in that, however relentless its criticism may seem, too much of the criticism rings true and is well documented. Moreover, much of the criticism was foreseen even before the publication of the *Catechism*, so that the authors of this text are often merely verifying the actualization of what was anticipated by others.

9

Archbishop Eric D'Arcy, of Hobart, Tasmania, for example, in speaking of the need to produce classroom-type catechisms for different countries and cultures, in line with the *Catechism* itself, predicted:

> This is an exhilarating prospect. It offers faith-educationists their greatest opportunity in four hundred years. Nevertheless it bristles with difficulties, and in the English-speaking First World those are particularly acute. One of these cuts deeper than all the others: many of our most dedicated faith-educationists do not believe the *CCC* to be a providential initiative at all. They simply do not believe in a faith-education which is sympathetically doctrinal and systematically addressed to the cognitive powers —intellect, reason, imagination, memory.

I myself, in lecturing in advance of the formal publication of the *Catechism*, suggested that putting the *Catechism* to work would be a monumental task for bishops, quite apart from any fault that anyone might find with the publication itself. I quoted, for example, from our Holy Father's apostolic exhortation *Catechesi Tradendæ*. Speaking of catechesis in general, he observes: "Catechesis is intrinsically linked with the whole liturgical and sacramental activity, for it is in the sacraments, especially in the Eucharist, that Christ Jesus works in fullness for the transformation of human beings." He goes on, then, to include the homily within the context of sacramental activity:

> Respecting the specific nature and proper cadence of this setting, the homily takes up again the journey of faith put forward by catechesis and brings it to its natural fulfillment. Accordingly, one can say that catechetical teaching, too, finds its source and its fulfillment in the Eucharist, within the whole cycle of the liturgical year. Preaching, centered upon the Bible texts, must then in its own way

make it possible to familiarize the faithful with the whole of the mysteries of the faith and with the norms of Christian living.

Now, the most favorably inclined bishop, theologian, or catechist, however receptive toward the *Catechism*, finds the Pope's expectations of catechesis a tremendous challenge. If the *Catechism* is to be the foundation or the basic source-book for meeting the challenge, the work ahead was cut out for us long before its publication. Nor has the challenge diminished since.

I make these observations here, not to parry the thrust of *Flawed Expectations*, but simply to suggest that its authors' findings are substantially in accord with what many had anticipated before the *Catechism* even appeared.

If at times the authors' prose is charged and if they seem to be prepared to joust, this can, undoubtedly, be excused because of their zealous devotion to and defense of the *Catechism* and all that it portends for the future of the Church.

May *Flawed Expectations* assist catechists in becoming aware of those counterproductive theological and catechetical tendencies that the *Catechism of the Catholic Church* was originally intended to correct.

+ JOHN CARDINAL O'CONNOR
Archbishop of New York

# *Preface*

As many basic courses in Christianity regularly point out, our word "apostle" comes from the Greek *apostolos*, meaning "one sent out"; the word is related to the Greek verb *apostellein*, "to send out". Thus, Jesus himself originally sent out "the apostles whom he had chosen" (Acts 1:2). "You shall be my witnesses", he told them, "in Jerusalem and in all Judea and Samaria and to the end of the earth" (Acts 1:8). Or again: "Go therefore and make disciples of all nations . . . teaching them to observe all that I have commanded you . . ." (Mt 28:19–20).

The successors of these original apostles of Jesus, the bishops of the Catholic Church, have in our day not ceased to carry on this essential work of "teaching . . . all that I have commanded". Most recently, and perhaps as compellingly as any generation of bishops for centuries, they have carried out this work of teaching by commissioning, preparing, and issuing the new *Catechism of the Catholic Church*, an authoritative, comprehensive, and wholly up-to-date statement of what the Catholic Church holds and teaches, as it has been guarded, interpreted, developed, and handed down in the Church with the help of the Holy Spirit from the time of Jesus until the present day.

The current head of the bishops of the Catholic Church, Pope John Paul II, searching for the appropriate term to describe what this *Catechism* means for us and for our children, has several times returned to the word "gift"; it is a gift for both the Church and the world, according to the Pope. It lays out for us the teachings of Christ for the sake of our sanctification and salvation; we cannot go wrong following this guide. In bringing out this great work, the Catholic bishops have thus, once again, proved themselves quite literally to be the authentic "witnesses" to Jesus "to the end of the earth" that he intended and commissioned them to be.

After twenty centuries, the Church of Christ is a somewhat more complex organization than was the case in the days when the bishops were the heads of small communities of believers in Christ, among whom they perhaps personally lived among and ministered. While every bishop today continues to be "sent out" in the name of Christ, he is obliged, in the nature of things, to "send out" many others in his turn.

The Church's educational and catechetical enterprise today, for example, is vast and complex, consisting of many people, institutions, entities, and layers between the bishop, who is the primary teacher and overseer, and those who are being directly catechized in the faith, whether they are children or adults.

In addition to the catechists who are directly engaged in teaching the faith, whether professional or volunteer, there are pastors and priests; there are school principals, administrators, and teachers; there are directors of religious education (DREs), whether at the diocesan or parish levels (not to speak of all the personnel and offices and committees engaged in educational and catechetical endeavors at the *national* level!).

In addition, there are the graduate schools and catechetical institutes that form and train those who teach the faith, just as there are the professors and theologians who staff these higher-education institutions involved with catechesis. There are also the authors and editors and publishers of religion textbooks and other religious-education materials.

Not least, there are the myriads of volunteers who staff the average parish CCD program; some studies have indicated that over 90 percent of our catechists in the classroom are volunteers.

Properly speaking, all these people occupying such offices and carrying out such functions in the Church's educational and catechetical enterprise are "sent out"; they, too, are "apostles", even if only perhaps at secondary, tertiary, or even lower levels. The bishops do not, and cannot, teach the faith by themselves. Certainly the pope cannot do it by himself (although Pope John Paul II sometimes gives the impression he is *trying* to!).

With the issuance of the new *Catechism of the Catholic Church*, the Pope and the bishops have now admirably fulfilled one of their basic functions. We have the book; it is easily available; it is hard to misunderstand—you would almost have to work at misunderstanding it, if that were your aim. The Church's full teaching is now systematically laid out in the *Catechism* for anyone who wants to take the trouble to find out what it is.

There can no longer be any serious question, for example, about *what* it is that has to be taught in the Church's formal catechesis; for what it is that has to be taught is now all carefully laid out, in the *Catechism*.

The basic question now is whether or not what is now so lucidly and completely set forth in the pages of the *Catechism* will be effectively conveyed and transferred into the minds and hearts of Christ's followers and potential followers, in this generation and in generations to come. The question is, in other words, whether the *Catechism* will be properly and effectively *implemented* at various levels in the Church.

Or, to put the question in yet another way: Now that the *Catechism* is out, how is it being *received*? Is it being accepted, read, studied, used? Or is it in some places perhaps being neglected, ignored, put on the shelf, or even actively opposed? Where it is being accepted, is this sometimes mere lip service? Are there those who continue to hold a different idea of what catechesis should be than what the *Catechism* lays out? Will the new *Catechism* really make any *difference* in the Church's current teaching of the faith on the pastoral and practical levels? What is the long-term outlook for the *Catechism*?

Two of the principal architects of the *Catechism*, Cardinal Joseph Ratzinger and Archbishop Christoph Schönborn, have identified the reception of the book as one of the most important issues concerning it:

> The deeper reception of the *Catechism* in the life of the Church still lies ahead. Preaching and proclamation have yet to discover in it an aid to comprehending and communicating the faith as a living organic whole. Furthermore, the *Catechism* is meant to assist theology, which has become sterile and cold on account of overspecialization and rationalistic desiccation, to realize anew "the admirable unity of the mystery of God" (John Paul II in the Apostolic Constitution on the *Catechism*), in order to recover joy in the beauty of the faith and wonder over its vital energy.
>
> Catechesis must be encouraged to recognize that its paramount task is the transmission of the knowledge of the faith. For all believers, the *Catechism* is a "sure norm for the teaching of the faith" (ibid.), which is designed to help them know their faith better, to live it more profoundly, and to hand it on with firmer conviction.[1]

---

[1] Joseph Cardinal Ratzinger and Christoph Schönborn, *Introduction to the Catechism of the Catholic Church* (San Francisco: Ignatius Press, 1994), 7.

The principal aim of this book is to focus on the basic question of the *reception* of the *Catechism*, particularly (but not exclusively) in the United States; and particularly among the people, functions, and levels in the Church with formal responsibilities for catechesis, that is, for transmitting the authentic faith of the Church to others. There can be no doubt that the *Catechism* has already been accorded an enormously favorable popular reception, in the United States as well as around the world; the sales of the book alone indicate that. But what kind of reception is it getting among those with responsibilities for teaching the faith?

For example, what does the average religious educator think about the *Catechism*? What is the average religious educator being *told* to think about it? Does it appear that this authoritative, comprehensive, and entirely usable new summary of the Church's authentic teaching is generally being received among professional religious educators with docility and gratitude, if not enthusiasm? Will it henceforth be made the basis of what is being taught?

After all, religious educators, too, have not ceased being "sent out"; they, too, are supposed to be "apostles". The faith they teach is the Church's faith, not just their own; and the *Catechism* sets forth this faith of the Church. What do they think about it? How are they using it?

Or yet again: What do today's Catholic *theologians* think about the *Catechism*? They are the ones who usually train the religious educators, and the latter, in their turn, often tend to look to professional theologians and experts for guidance and inspiration. They often do so more naturally, more quickly, and more easily than they might look even to their pastors or bishops, as a matter of fact. This is probably inevitable in an era and in a culture that generally looks to professionals, to experts, for guidance and that also depends heavily upon published materials, courses, outlines, discussion questions, videos, and the like for instruction. Thus, it is a simple fact that the guidance religious educators receive from their pastors and bishops often comes to them via theologians and experts, or via the catechetical conferences and publications where these same theologians and experts often appear.

Of course all the theologians and experts are supposed to be "sent out" by the bishops too, and not just theoretically. On the evidence, though, how many of them today do see themselves as sent out by the bishops as "apostles" of Christ by the commission of the Church? And that means, not incidentally, by the commission of the current actual leadership of the Church, not that of some ideal "Church" existing in their own minds.

Are there, in other words, any "reluctant apostles" out there among those with responsibilities for teaching the faith as far as the new *Catechism* is concerned? Especially among the ranks of professionals in the Church, are there any whose vision of the faith, for whatever reason and under whatever influence, is different from the vision now firmly embodied and clearly set forth in the *Catechism*? Would any such differences, if they exist, be likely to produce "reluctant apostles", now that the *Catechism* has been so solemnly and firmly mandated as the Church's basic document for teaching the faith?

These are the primary questions this book will be dealing with. They are important questions, because the answer to the important question of whether or not the *Catechism* will be able properly to do the work for which it was intended and designed may depend, at least in part, upon the answers to some of these other questions.

At the present time, the picture is still a very mixed one;

in many ways, the *Catechism* has already proved to be a resounding success. However, much, very much still needs to be done in order to ensure that the whole *Catechism* enterprise can successfully build on its own very promising beginnings.

It is in the hope of being able both to help clarify what still needs to be done and to assist in the process of doing it that the present authors have been motivated to prepare this book on the reception of the *Catechism*. After having reviewed a significant number of the materials currently being issued in connection with the implementation of the document, especially commentaries, it is our contention that the *Catechism* is not being everywhere received in the manner in which both the Catholic bishops and the Catholic people had a right to expect, especially considering what the *Catechism* is and what it represents. Indeed, upon examination of some of the typical products supposedly aimed at implementing the *Catechism*, we can only conclude that these expectations are in some very important and even crucial respects seriously flawed expectations—hence, our title.

Since what is at stake here is so serious, it is not sufficient for someone merely to allege that the *Catechism* is not being everywhere properly received. It is necessary to *show* this where it happens to be the case. This we have undertaken to do in the chapters that follow our general introduction to the subject of the *Catechism*, the why and how of it, which comprises our first two chapters.

We do not apologize for the detail into which we have felt obliged to go in treating the way in which some have been receiving the *Catechism*. This detail has been necessary in order to prove our points.

Of course, the picture is not wholly negative, and we have also tried to give credit where credit is due. The *Catechism* has been available in English-speaking lands only for about a year as we write, and in spite of obstacles, and, especially, the lukewarmness and even opposition to the *Catechism* that we have found, especially in some of the Church's professional circles, we remain convinced that this *Catechism* is nevertheless going to be at the very heart of a renewed evangelization of the world in the course of the twenty-first century.

In any case, the whole subject is surely one of the utmost seriousness. The Church's bishops did not labor for nearly seven years to produce the *Catechism* only to have its message minimized or downgraded by some of the very people responsible for implementing it.

In the end, of course, it is the reader who will have to be the ultimate judge with respect to how well this book succeeds in its aim of showing how the *Catechism* is in fact being received. Nobody can deny, however, that the subject is a vitally important one.

# CHAPTER ONE

# Why the Church
# Needed a New Catechism

## I

One of the most remarkable religious phenomena in the decade preceding the advent of the third millennium of Christianity was the promulgation and publication of the *Catechism of the Catholic Church*, the first major catechism setting forth what the Church holds and teaches issued in more than four hundred years. Solemnly presented to the whole Church by Pope John Paul II on December 7, 1992, the Pope described the document on that occasion as a "gift which the heavenly Father gives to his children today, offering them with this text the possibility of knowing better, in the light of his Spirit, the breadth and length and height and depth of Christ's love (cf. Eph 3:19)." The new *Catechism* is "authoritative", the Holy Father said very plainly on this same occasion of promulgating it, and it "faithfully reiterates the Christian doctrine of all times".[1]

---

[1] Pope John Paul II, "*Catechism* Is Truly a Gift to the Church", Sunday, December 7, 1992, reprinted in *Reflections on the Catechism of the Catholic Church*, comp. Rev. James P. Socias (Chicago: Midwest Theological Forum, 1993), 39–40.

The *Catechism of the Catholic Church* quickly became a best-seller in country after country, as successive translations of it appeared. Within a year after its publication, over three million copies of it in nine languages had already been printed and distributed.

In the United States, advance orders for the *Catechism* mounted up to well over a half million even before the English translation finally became available in June 1994. Thereafter, copies numbering well over two million were quickly sold. A rather surprising number perhaps, considering that the book was a hefty 803-page tome, immediately recognizable by its light brown cover and distinctive motif of an ancient shepherd with his crook, watching over his sheep.

Inside, the text of the *Catechism* consisted of no fewer than 2,865 separate numbered paragraphs, extensively indexed and cross-referenced to each other and containing numerous footnotes, quotations, scriptural references, cross-references, and indices. At first sight, none of this appeared to promise very smooth or easy reading; indeed the book's whole aspect seemed positively forbidding—hardly an item for the bedside table. Or so anyone might have thought.

Experience quickly proved, however, exactly the contrary. The book turned out to be ideal for the bedside table, among other places; it proved to be a book one could read in, read through, study intensively, or look things up in. The 1985 session of the Catholic Church's Synod of Bishops in Rome, which had originally called for the preparation of a universal catechism, had said at the time that what was needed was a reliable "point of reference" for Catholic teaching. In promulgating the finished product, Pope John Paul II had also styled it a "reference text". Both terms proved to be very apt descriptions of the book at least in one of its aspects.

But it was considerably more than just a reference book, as the mass sales of the volume almost immediately proved.

In this country, the *Catechism* was published in a uniform edition by a consortium of some sixteen separate publishers licensed by the United States Catholic Conference, to which the Holy See had given exclusive rights to publish and distribute the book in the United States. The total sales of the book had to be counted as especially phenomenal when we consider that the hardcover edition sold for $29.95 and the trade paperback edition for $19.95. Nevertheless, eager buyers of the book quickly materialized nearly everywhere. And this was before the U.S. bishops awarded a contract to one of the country's major commercial publishers, Doubleday, for a mass-market paperback selling for less than half of the hardcover price. This paperback edition was to be available on newsstands, as well as in drugstores, supermarkets, airports, and similar places where people who never go near a bookstore might see and buy *this* book. Large numbers of the original sales of the *Catechism* had in fact been mail orders rather than bookstore sales. Sales of the book evidently extended far beyond those who frequent bookstores.

The mass-market paperback had a more striking cover, with a silver-lettered title (although the familiar shepherd motif appeared on the title page inside). In outward appearance, this paperback did not seem out of place with the thrillers, mysteries, and romances often displayed on the same book racks. Considering its subject matter, of course, it was remarkable that such a book could be found on these racks at all.

The mass-market paperback contract was expected to make the *Catechism* one of the best-selling religious titles in history. From the moment it appeared, the book broke most of the rules for religious publishing, and yet it was still able to achieve its huge sales. Moreover, the book continued to sell steadily. Between April and July 1995, over four hundred thousand copies of the mass-market paperback were sold in the United States. Worldwide, the result was pretty much the same. By the summer of 1995, well over eight million copies of the book in some twenty languages had been sold.

In short, a publishing phenomenon. Where did all these buyers come from, people suddenly interested in "Catholic doctrine", of all things? Catholic doctrine, in many if not most quarters of the modern world, had seemingly long since been relegated to the category of things considered passé, if not fundamentally incredible and simply to be dismissed. A book seriously setting forth Catholic doctrine, as if it might be something of interest to anyone, had to be a phenomenon. In the minds of many, it could surely only be some kind of inexplicable holdover from the ignorant and static past, if not something right out of the Middle Ages. What was happening?

As good an explanation as any for the instant and phenomenal popularity of the *Catechism of the Catholic Church* was provided by one of the principal architects of the volume, Cardinal Joseph Ratzinger, prefect of the Congregation for the Doctrine of the Faith in the Church's Roman Curia. "People want to know for themselves what the Church teaches and what she does not", Cardinal Ratzinger wrote.

This seemed to be especially true in today's world because, for a variety of reasons, there had already been for some years no little confusion in the air about what the Catholic Church really does teach and what she does not. Sometimes confident assertions about what the Church teaches seemed to depend on who was talking; other times the fact that the Church holds or teaches something might well be admitted—but then, in effect, immediately dismissed as of little or no importance, if it did not square with what was considered "modern knowledge" or, let us say, with "what modern Catholics believe", according to various polls and surveys.

The very idea that the *Church* might have a teaching of her own, which, in the final analysis, *was* the Catholic teaching, and necessarily so, was an idea that sometimes tended to get obscured in the peculiar climate of today's world. In this climate, there was a kind of confusion, as Cardinal Ratzinger pointed out, that was too often "generated by the vicissitudes of theological hypotheses and by their often highly questionable diffusion in the mass media".[2]

Modern theologians, it seemed, were apt to come up with ideas that were not always necessarily the Church's ideas. Moreover, it soon became very clear, the modern mass media, perhaps even understandably, generally like to publicize such variant ideas almost in the degree to which they diverge from established Church doctrine.

The situation the German Cardinal was alluding to, then, was something that had become rather well known: the Catholic faith in the modern world was widely understood to be in a state of crisis. The truths and indeed the relevance of many of the Church's ancient beliefs were increasingly being subjected to widespread denigration and even denial, often from inside as well as from outside the Church. This crisis of faith, as many knowledgeable people had come to realize, had been slowly developing in our society virtually

---

[2] Joseph Cardinal Ratzinger and Christoph Schönborn, *Introduction to the Catechism of the Catholic Church* (San Francisco: Ignatius Press, 1994), 18.

since the eighteenth-century Enlightenment, if not before. The Catholic Church, with her hierarchy, definite teachings, and firm discipline, had for a long time seemed relatively immune to the acids of modernity that were otherwise steadily eating away at the foundations of the civilization of the West and its Christian ideals.

But the appearances of the Church's solidity, or, at any rate that of some of her members, were in some ways deceptive. It would soon come out that many Catholics were, in fact, often as affected as anyone else by the powerful and self-confident, even though increasingly morally decadent, secular culture of the day. Catholics were by no means immune to the aggressive viruses of modernity.

The crisis of Modernism in the Catholic Church at the beginning of the twentieth century had demonstrated that members of the Church were not entirely impervious to the corrosive effects of modern skepticism, relativism, and even outright unbelief. One French priest and scholar, Alfred Loisy, who had started his career with the aim of benefitting the Church by means of modern historical and biblical scholarship, had ended up rejecting both his priesthood and his Church and disbelieving all the articles of her Creed except the purely "factual" one that affirms that Jesus had "suffered under Pontius Pilate". This kind of development, where the initial adoption of certain seemingly neutral modern ideas could sometimes lead to radical disbelief in Christ and his message, constituted an object lesson that was hard for the Church to ignore.

The Modernist crisis also demonstrated how the Church has typically and necessarily identified and rejected ideas contrary to her faith. This has been true down through history: the Church rejects alien doctrines the way any organism rejects foreign bodies. The Modernist crisis, however, also revealed that faith, in the modern climate, could no longer be very effectively defended merely by authoritative condemnation of those modern ideas that undermined and contradicted it. Often these ideas appealed to certain Catholics, who then introduced them into Catholic discourse in the guise of "bringing the Church up to date".

In this kind of "updating", it was not always clear at first that certain ideas *did* undermine and sometimes even contradict Catholic doctrine. Some of these ideas might have seemed to be perfectly assimilable to Catholicism at first. Given their strength and popularity in the world around the Church, moreover, such ideas were almost bound to infect members of the Church, at least in some measure, sometimes without their being fully aware of it.

What was needed to face up to the challenge of modernity, therefore, was not merely the condemnation of those modern ideas at variance with the Church's faith and vision but a restatement and a reaffirmation of what the Church really did believe in the face of the modern challenge. What was needed was a fairly radical effort that really *did* bring the Church up to date in a drastically changed world, but that did so on truly Catholic terms.

## II

It was the providential task of the Second Vatican Council of 1962–65 to restate essential Catholic teachings in a modern context and to reform a number of Church practices along the same lines. Vatican II was expressly convened in order to deal with the prospects faced by the Church and the Catholic faithful in a modern world that, despite some appearances, was essentially in the process of abandoning historic Christianity and of dropping any of the Ten Commandments that did not appear to fit the modern view of things.

Vatican II thoroughly revised many aspects of the Church's life and practice, while providing, especially in its great Constitutions on Divine Revelation (*Dei Verbum*), on the Church (*Lumen Gentium*), and on the Church in the Modern World (*Gaudium et Spes*), crucial restatements and applications of many of the Church's ancient beliefs. These restatements and applications were made in order to enable the current and subsequent generations of Christians to meet the challenge posed by an ongoing and often destructive modern culture, which continued to exert powerful influences both inside and outside the Church.

The sixteen documents issued by Vatican II, properly understood and utilized, do provide the Catholic Church with an indispensable doctrinal and intellectual foundation and means to challenge and counter the typically destructive ideas of today's modern culture. Moreover, the popes have been neither lax nor slow in building on the legacy of Vatican II in their encyclicals, apostolic exhortations, and other documents issued since the Council.

Following Vatican II, however, what immediately ensued was not a betterment but rather an aggravation of the symptoms of the modern crisis of faith, one that sometimes assumed rather dramatic proportions. Religious Modernism, for example, had not so much been destroyed as simply driven underground by the stringent measures that Church authorities had initiated against it, beginning especially with the encyclical issued by Pope St. Pius X in 1907, *Pascendi Dominici Gregis*. Many Catholics, and among them, precisely, educated Catholics, including clerics and religious, remained profoundly affected by certain currents of modern thought and culture. Right along, such people formed a strong Modernist and, later, what we may call a Neomodernist, element inside the Church. Often, these people tended to be in academic or teaching positions; and thus they were able to disseminate their ideas and attitudes among those whom they were teaching.

Neomodernist elements in the Church did not see themselves as subversives; they tended to see themselves as trying to make the Church more "credible" to the modern world, as they often stated it (of course, the original Modernists had generally pictured themselves in the same light). If only the Church could divest herself of some of her traditional ideas and practices that now seemed antiquated, outmoded, and even quaint, they thought, then the Church would be much more likely to attract "modern men" into her ranks. In some cases they may even have been correct about this.

Ominously, however—and like the original Modernists —some of these Neomodernists viewed already established and firm Church *doctrines* as out of date and as hindrances to the Church's relationships with the modern world and with other Christians. The very idea that authentic, established Catholic doctrines *could* be downplayed or dispensed with in such a fashion denoted a careless attitude toward, if not an actual ignorance of the nature of, Church teachings: none of this boded at all well.

Later, such a careless attitude toward, or ignorance of, established Catholic teachings would facilitate the rather uncritical introduction into Catholic life and discourse of alien ideologies such as radical feminism, extreme environmentalism, liberation theology, and the like. Indeed, the surprising thing, perhaps, was how tenaciously some of these alien ideologies were able to catch on among some supposedly professing Catholics in the postconciliar era.

One of Pope John XXIII's principal motives in convoking Vatican II in 1959 had been what he called *aggiornamento*, or bringing the Church up to date. Of course this jovial Pontiff always understood *aggiornamento* within the framework of his own traditional Catholic faith and deep piety. For people infected with Neomodernist ideas, however, the whole concept of bringing everything up to date provided an ideal climate in which to introduce some of *their* ideas and agendas and desired reforms. Vatican II had decreed all these many changes? Very well, there were a few other items that needed to be changed as well!

It was in this fashion that various changes were in fact introduced into the Church's life and practice that were thought or said to be in "the spirit of Vatican II" but that could nowhere be found either in the sixteen documents of Vatican II or in the Church's official postconciliar enactments.

Indeed, it sometimes seemed as if everything in the Church were up for grabs, that there were no limits on what might be "changed". At any rate, many voices, including, unfortunately, many clerical voices, some in positions of importance and authority, were asserting that this was the case; and, certainly, very many Catholics were acting as if it were. Psychologically, the stage was set for the rejection even of some firm Catholic teachings that had been handed down in the Church with the assistance of the Holy Spirit and authoritatively proclaimed by the Church's teaching authority. Formerly, it had been nearly universally understood by professing Catholics that certain authoritative Catholic teachings could never be changed or repudiated; but in the midst of all the other changes, this traditional understanding itself became obscured.

Then, in 1968, when Pope Paul VI issued his encyclical

*Humanæ Vitæ*, reiterating the Church's moral condemnation of artificial birth control, he was not merely laughed to scorn outside of the Church. For the first time in anyone's memory or imagination, large numbers of Catholics, including theologians and others in official positions in the Church, openly and publicly rejected a solemn teaching document from the Vicar of Christ. A *Time* magazine cover story of the period, featuring what it called "the pope's unruly flock", gave some idea of the confusion into which the Church, along with many questions concerning her established faith and morals, had fallen. The contrast with the Church of just the day before, which had exhibited such rocklike coherence and stability, could not have been more marked.

Catholics, then, it turned out, had not remained unaffected by the powerful intellectual and cultural currents of the modern age, many of which were inimical to the Catholic faith, indeed, to any supernatural faith. This was not always immediately or completely perceived, however. Within the Church, what we may call the Church's professional and knowledge class, including especially theologians and biblical exegetes, now often seemed to be more influenced by what all Catholics once, in good Johannine fashion, had commonly called "the world" (cf. 1 Jn 2:15–17) than they were by the Church's teaching authority, or Magisterium, formerly understood by everybody to have the last word in doctrinal matters.

Many of these same Catholics, including theologians and others in Church leadership positions, came to question openly whether the Church's Magisterium really did enjoy the special assistance of the Holy Spirit, as the Church had always held (and holds). If the Magisterium enjoys the special assistance of the Holy Spirit, it was often asked, rhetorically, then how could the Magisterium have been so wrong in *Humanæ Vitæ*? For many this seemed to settle the question; they failed to ask themselves what the consequences would be if, in fact, the Church were *right* in this encyclical. They failed to ask this question because, henceforth, it was the *world* that was going to provide the new standards by which everything, including faith and morals, was seemingly going to be judged. This was precisely the agenda of Neomodernism, in fact: henceforth the Church's faith and morals were to be subject to the scrutiny of "modern knowledge".

It was to this widespread crisis of faith—unprecedented for the Catholic Church, for, like her divine Founder, she has always taught "with authority" (Lk 4:32)—that Cardinal Ratzinger was evidently alluding when he spoke of "the vicissitudes of theological hypotheses and their often highly questionable diffusion in the mass media". The Church, through her Magisterium, has never failed to be absolutely clear through all these vicissitudes, indeed, through all the manifold confusion of the past several decades, about what she holds and teaches. The Church has been a model of clarity, in fact; the teaching of the Church has not ceased to be there for anyone willing to take the trouble to find out what it was and is.

However, it has been considerably less clear in recent years how wide and deep the acceptance of what the Church holds and teaches has been among all Catholics, especially among those Catholics who belong to what we have called the Church's professional or knowledge class. It has been considerably less clear, in other words, whether and to what extent at least some Catholics even continue to believe and to assent to what the Church, for her part, has never ceased teaching. On the evidence of what they themselves say, it is questionable whether some fairly prominent Catholic theologians and exegetes can any longer even be considered "Catholic" in any traditionally understood sense of that word.

It is in this kind of situation, then, that "many of the faithful", according to Cardinal Ratzinger, "want to inform themselves personally regarding the teaching of the Church." And hence, therefore, the sudden, phenomenal popularity of the *Catechism of the Catholic Church*. This should not really have been so much of a surprise, under the circumstances.

More than that, though, as the Cardinal himself added, "among its intended readership are agnostics, seekers, and inquirers, to whom it is offered as a help to becoming acquainted with what the Church teaches and tries to live."[3] This latter idea, that the *Catechism* just might also be a fit instrument by which the Church might now begin to regain some of the ground lost to the secular world, might now even begin to reevangelize a world desperate for Christ's saving truths, was a persistent theme of the German Cardinal, an eminent theologian in his own right. The Church is obliged to go on proclaiming the saving message of Jesus Christ, even in an era when many of her own children are no longer following the path to which she insistently continues to point.

In presenting the *Catechism* to the international media on December 9, 1992, Cardinal Ratzinger similarly pointed out that:

> After the fall of ideologies, the problem of man—the moral problem—is presented to today's context in a totally new way: What should we do? How does life become just? What can give us and the whole world a future which is

---

[3] Ibid., 18–19.

worth living? Since the *Catechism* treats these questions, it is a book which interests many people, far beyond purely theological or ecclesial circles. It can especially arouse interest because it does not merely present some private opinion invented by somebody or other, but formulates the response that comes from the great communal experience of the Church of all ages.[4]

"The Church of all ages": this is what the *Catechism* represents. The idea that, after all, the Catholic Church just might have some wisdom to offer to a world in serious social and moral disarray surely can be credited as one of the factors that helped push the *Catechism of the Catholic Church* to the top of today's best-seller lists. And even though some Catholics have apparently ceased to look with respect to the teachings of "the Church of all ages", many others have not forgotten what the Church is and what she represents; and, in the midst of today's confusion, many of them were even hungry to obtain an "uninterpreted" version of her teachings, which the *Catechism* was instantly seen to provide. At the very least, there appeared to be much more to the *Catechism*—and to the Church!—than perhaps at first met the eye.

## III

At the same time that the *Catechism of the Catholic Church* was breaking sales records for religious books, another unusual Catholic religious book also came on the market, and *it* promptly climbed to the top of the best-seller lists as well.

---

[4] Cardinal Joseph Ratzinger, "The *Catechism of the Catholic Church* in Context", press conference presenting the *Catechism* to the media, December 9, 1992, in Socias, *Reflections*, 226.

The phenomenon of the *Catechism* was duplicated. This second book was a work personally authored by Pope John Paul II, entitled *Crossing the Threshold of Hope*; it appeared in translation in no fewer than thirty-eight languages.

In this book, among a fascinating variety of personal papal responses to many of the religious questions on people's minds today, John Paul II also offered his own explanation for the unexpected and unprecedented interest in the new *Catechism*: "The world, tired of ideology, is opening itself to the truth", the Pontiff wrote. "As the year 2000 approaches, our world feels an urgent need for the Gospel."[5]

In the Pope's view, the success of the *Catechism* was surely bound to confound the experts, including many within the Church: "Some theologians, at times whole groups," the Pope wrote, "spread the notion that there was no longer a need for a catechism, that it was an obsolete means of handing down the faith, and therefore should be abandoned. They also expressed the opinion that it would be impossible to create a catechism for the universal Church." In reality, however, the *Catechism* could only be considered "indispensable", according to Pope John Paul II's carefully considered opinion.[6]

The Pope's reference to "theologians, at times whole groups," who did not want any catechism was unfortunately true, especially in the United States. The old *Baltimore Catechism*, upon which three or four generations of American Catholics had been brought up, had not only fallen into disuse after Vatican II. It had also, and quite unjustifiably, become something of an object of mirth and scorn as well.

---

[5] Pope John Paul II, *Crossing the Threshold of Hope*, (New York: Alfred A. Knopf, 1994), 164 and 114.

[6] Ibid., 164–65.

It was held to embody everything the modern world considered hidebound and out of date in traditional Catholicism. Unfortunately, too many Catholics hastened to adopt this unfavorable view of what previous generations of Catholics had accepted gratefully and unquestioningly as imparting the saving faith of Jesus Christ.

It was not just the *Baltimore Catechism* that was considered to be the problem, however; the very idea, or genre, of a "catechism" had come to be considered obsolete. This development came about in part because knowledge and acceptance of "Catholic doctrine" itself was no longer universally considered to be an essential and indispensable requirement of being a Catholic. Catholics have always professed, of course, a specific *Creed*, which is to be recited communally and aloud at Masses on Sundays and Holy Days; and the presumption has always been—indeed, could hardly have been anything else—that Catholics necessarily *believe* the things they profess to believe in this Creed. Vatican II's *Lumen Gentium* expressly says that the faithful "must profess before men the faith they have received from God through the Church" (no. 10).

In spite of what should have been a simple and absolutely indisputable point, then, namely, that Catholics are supposed to believe the Church's Creed, and that believing it is essential to being Catholic, a whole school of thought nevertheless strangely grew up after Vatican II that held that believing "doctrine" was not only *not* essential to being a Christian but was in some sense an *obstacle* to being one. "Doctrine", held to be arid and boring, was deliberately downplayed in religion books, and Christian "experience" was substituted for it. The rich and ancient concept of the "pastoral", which went back to the revelation of the saving truths that Jesus had committed to his Church for the sake of those he called his "sheep", was illogically transformed into an antonym of "doctrinal". Doctrine, which was nothing else but a systematic statement and development of the saving truths Jesus had revealed, was nevertheless, somehow, "out". Things like being positive and building a better world were suddenly "in", as though these things were necessarily opposed to "doctrine".

If doctrine was out, the same thing obviously had to apply to any catechism, since a catechism, by definition, is nothing else but an organic and systematic presentation of doctrine—of the saving revelation that Jesus committed to his Church, to be guarded and handed down to all generations. Somehow any catechism at all, however, was now seen to be inessential to the life of the Church and her members. The necessary connection between doctrinal beliefs and pastoral practices became severed in the minds of many.

This whole aberrant trend or attitude, which downplayed or even dropped doctrine (or, at any rate, *some* doctrines), was actually felt by many to have been justified by Vatican II. This claim was made in part because the Council had not called for a new catechism. Unlike its great predecessor, the Council of Trent (1545–63), which both mandated and gave its name to the *Catechism of the Council of Trent* (also called the *Roman Catechism*), Vatican II did not, in fact, mandate any catechism. Instead, the Council called for the preparation of something called a *General Catechetical Directory*.

Many were quick to conclude from this fact that catechisms as such would henceforth have no place in the renewed Catholic Church that was being brought up to date by a myriad of Vatican II-inspired and mandated reforms (and, as we have noted, by a number of other changes *not* really inspired or mandated by the Council). But it was erroneous to conclude that catechisms were therefore obsolete.

A catechism would very soon prove to be necessary, in fact. Doctrinal difficulties had begun to arise in the Church even before the end of Vatican II. In more and more areas, it was becoming increasingly clear that many Catholics no longer necessarily or seriously believed what the Church continued to hold and teach.

The need to commission an authoritative catechism for the Church became especially apparent after the Dutch bishops sponsored their own, questionable, new "Dutch Catechism" shortly after the Council, in 1966. Entitled simply *A New Catechism*, no sooner was this work published—to a nearly universal chorus of praise from liberal theologians and self-selected Vatican II updaters (why did they despise "catechisms" in general but not *this* catechism?)—than Pope Paul VI was obliged to appoint a special commission of cardinals to examine the book's orthodoxy. This commission issued a detailed statement setting forth no fewer than ten different doctrinal problem areas where the Dutch Catechism was seriously deficient and needed to be corrected.

The Dutch Catechism, unfortunately, represented a faithful reflection of a "new theology" and a "new exegesis", which no longer thought that the fact that the Church's Magisterium had decided a question was necessarily decisive.

The corrections Rome ordered to be made in the Dutch Catechism were never made. The report of Pope Paul VI's commission of cardinals was simply printed as an appendix to subsequent editions of the book, and the resulting volume was then presented as "the *Authorized* Edition of the Dutch Catechism" (emphasis added).[7] This was another ominous

---

[7] *A New Catechism: Catholic Faith for Adults with Supplement* (New York: The Seabury Press, 1969).

new sign of the way in which Church authority was coming to be treated.

Especially in view of the difficulties connected with the Dutch Catechism, Cardinal Ratzinger later explained: "At the time, the question arose spontaneously whether the best response to the difficulties connected with this volume might not be to compose a catechism for the entire Church." For his part, though, the Cardinal gave his opinion, an opinion he subsequently held to, that "the time was not yet ripe for such a project." In his view, the full extent of the doctrinal errors, distortions, and omissions that were to mark the three decades that followed Vatican II "had simply not become visible. . . . [A] process of fermentation had just begun which could lead only gradually to the clarifications necessary for a new common word."[8]

Thus, although the prefect of the Congregation for the Doctrine of the Faith granted here that a contemporary, authoritative statement of the faith would no doubt have been desirable in the immediate postconciliar era, in his view it was not really possible to compose one at that juncture. The fact remained that the Council itself had not called for a catechism; no immediate plans to prepare one were therefore made. Instead the Council prescribed the preparation of what it called "a directory for the catechetical instruction of the Christian people".[9]

This was the origin of the *General Catechetical Directory*, a key teaching document issued by the Congregation for the Clergy in Rome in 1971. The GCD aimed to formulate and lay out the basic principles involved in catechesis, or the

---

[8] Ratzinger and Schönborn, *Introduction*, 12.

[9] Vatican Council II, Decree on the Pastoral Office of Bishops in the Church, *Christus Dominus*, no. 44.

teaching of the faith. This Roman document has sometimes been considered to be concerned with methodology, how to teach the faith; actually it is concerned with doctrine as well, what to teach as well as how to teach. The GCD proved to be very conscious of the changed world in which the Church was henceforth obliged to try to impart the faith of Christ. It took for granted that contemporary human society was "a society disturbed by great socio-cultural changes" and that the Church's unchanged mission "to proclaim and promote the faith" could not but be a particularly arduous and difficult one today.[10]

According to the GCD, however, it was not only "society" that was "disturbed" today, thus affecting adversely how effectively the faith could be taught. Rather, this Roman document was one of the first official Church documents to recognize that the faith was endangered also from *within* the Church, in the minds and hearts of many members of the Church, who, increasingly, were beginning to tune out Christ's authentic message as taught by the Church, presumably as they tuned in more sympathetically to the world's often alluring but false message.

The GCD noted that the problem of doctrinal deviancy was especially to be found within the Church's own educational and catechetical structures. This 1971 document frankly spoke of "*errors* which are not infrequently noted in catechetics today" (emphasis added). These errors could be "avoided only if one starts with the correct way to understanding the nature and purpose of catechesis and also the truths which are to be taught by it", according to the

---

[10] Sacred Congregation for the Clergy, *General Catechetical Directory* (Washington, D.C.: United States Catholic Conference, 1971), no. 1.

GCD,[11] thus confirming that "teaching truth" was fundamentally and necessarily what catechesis is indeed all about.
The GCD itself undertook to lay out all the things that
needed to be taught, as well as the best methods of teaching them, for the benefit both of the pastors and teachers
in the Church as well as for the faithful generally.

The GCD succeeded in laying them all out with uncommon skill and lucidity. Had the GCD been heeded and followed to a greater extent than it was in the postconciliar
years, especially in matters concerned with the preparation
of religion textbooks and of catechetical teaching materials
as well as with the development of teaching methods and
strategies, the *Catechism of the Catholic Church* might not
have been thought necessary.

In the event, of course, this was not to be. The GCD was
not generally heeded and followed, particularly by the new
class of professional religious educators who were becoming more prominent and widespread in the Church's educational programs in these same postconciliar years. Nor did
*their* mentors and teachers pay much attention to the GCD.
The mentors and teachers of the new catechists, of course,
were the members of the new class of theologians, scholars,
and exegetes who were busily engaged in establishing their
own claimed scholarly knowledge and expertise as the new
standard for judging Church teachings.

Soon, the judgments of the Catholic bishops teaching in
union with the pope ("the Magisterium"), which had always
been the norm in the Catholic Church—and which Vatican II had quite pointedly reaffirmed in number 25 of its
Dogmatic Constitution on the Church, *Lumen Gentium*—

---

[11] Ibid., foreword.

were no longer considered to be either decisive or definitive. Instead, the decisions of the Church's Magisterium were henceforth to be subject to the critical judgments of a new, self-proclaimed "second magisterium", composed of theologians, scholars, and other experts in various human disciplines.

Among this class, the very existence of the *General Catechetical Directory* was itself often cited as *the reason why catechisms were no longer deemed necessary*: Why do we need a catechism when we already have a directory? So the argument ran. Whether or not one actually used the GCD, or whether or not one used it properly, was a different question entirely. Meanwhile, the line that no catechism was any longer necessary for teaching the faith was nevertheless argued and often adopted, even though the GCD itself plainly said that "the greatest importance must be attached to catechisms published by ecclesiastical authority."[12]

Meanwhile, too, as John Paul II himself was eventually to note, and as we have already quoted him as saying, in certain quarters catechisms as such came to be considered "an obsolete means of handing down the faith".

## IV

The postconciliar history of how Catholic professional religious educators (the "religious-education establishment") have failed to teach the Catholic faith properly, and how they have trained others to do the same, is a long, complicated, and rather depressing history. It need not be retraced

---

[12] Ibid., no. 119.

here, except in briefest outline, especially since it is a story that has already been told.[13]

Highlighting a few major points of this history will suffice here to establish the proper framework for our discussion of one of the basic problems of religious education: namely, how Christ's authentic message can properly be handed on if many of those in the Church with responsibilities for teaching the faithful have themselves come to downgrade and even discard important elements of the Church's teaching that they are supposed to be handing on.

The new *Catechism*, of course, does not fail to teach the integral and authentic faith of Christ. But what about those engaged in teaching the faith at many levels in the Church who, evidently, and on their own testimony, do not agree with the *Catechism*? Unfortunately, they exist. Farther on we shall be looking in some detail at how some of them *are* presenting the *Catechism*. It will become very clear that the problem is a serious one. Few problems, indeed, could be considered more serious than the fact, as we shall show, that the authentic Catholic faith now integrally set forth in the *Catechism* is *not* being properly taught in some of the Church's own educational and catechetical programs.

To be sure, the *Catechism* surely remains every bit the great providential "gift" to the Church that Pope John Paul II, on repeated occasions, has said it is. Nevertheless, by itself it is just a book, and therefore it cannot be entirely self-implementing. It has to be consciously and deliberately made the new basis of the Church's various educational and training programs that are currently located

---

[13] See especially Msgr. Michael J. Wrenn, *Catechisms and Controversies: Religious Education in the Postconciliar Years* (San Francisco: Ignatius Press, 1991).

in Catholic schools, CCD programs, adult-education programs, conferences, workshops, graduate institutes, and the like. It has to be consciously and deliberately made the basis of what parents henceforth teach their children about the faith.

Some basic questions therefore have to be asked and answered: Is this happening? Is the *Catechism* now being made the basis of the Church's religious education? How is the *Catechism* being received, not only by typical religious educators in the Church, but by those who form and train these same religious educators?

These questions are neither hypothetical nor unimportant, especially when we consider the deficient state of religious education that has too often obtained in the postconciliar years. Examples abound, unfortunately, not only of significant errors, omissions, and distortions in many of today's religious-education programs, texts, and teaching materials, but also of an apparent determination on the part of many in the religious-education establishment to continue promoting a "new catechesis" developed over the past half century. Some professional religious educators persist in promoting this new catechesis, in spite of its manifest failures, as evidenced by the *lack* of religious knowledge on the part of those who have been subjected to it.

The new catechesis came into vogue in the years immediately preceding the Second Vatican Council. After the Council, it largely came to dominate the Church's official religious-education enterprise. This was the case even though there never ceased to be considerable dissatisfaction about it, a dissatisfaction that very often translated into complaints from parents, pastors, and teachers. These complaints were sometimes quite vehement, and often those who registered them were dismissed as "right-wingers" for protesting against what the professionals were doing. Test results concerning the knowledge of the faith of those being catechized, however, surely supported the position of the complainers.

Conscious of the general dissatisfaction and itself quite uneasy about the whole catechetical situation, the hierarchy over the years issued a succession of statements and guidance documents intended to remedy a perceived problem within modern religious education. However, there was generally little or no concrete follow-up by the hierarchy to determine whether anybody was really being guided by all the guidance that was issued.

In fact, few ever really grasped *what* the problem with religious education was, and hence, generally, no fundamental challenge was ever made to the positions and assumptions that lay behind the new catechesis, positions and assumptions that the religious-education establishment had by and large adopted. Usually the religious-education establishment went on stubbornly defending the new catechesis, even in the face of massive complaints, as well as in the face of sometimes plainly contrary guidance and direction coming down from Church authorities. The soundness of the new catechesis was considered to be self-evident, and, by and large, the catechetical establishment goes on obstinately defending it to this day.

As one generalization, the new catechesis no longer looks primarily to the Church's Magisterium for its fundamental guidance and inspiration. Rather, it looks to the modern social sciences and to fashionable new secular educational theories. Within the Church it tends to look especially to what we may aptly call the new theologians, the new exegetes, and the new liturgists—those who believe Vatican II transformed them into independent and autonomous experts—

in short, to some of the same revisionists and minimizers responsible for much of the confusion and dissent in the Church.

Throughout the postconciliar period, new catechetical texts based on the new notions of what was entailed in catechesis were published and widely distributed. Religion teachers, not only professionals but volunteer teachers in CCD programs, soon began to be trained, not in the Church's traditional catechesis of the faith, as it had been authentically handed down in the Church, but rather in the new catechesis based on the modern social sciences and on the ideas of dissident theologians, historico-critical exegetes, and liturgical innovators. These very same leaders and theological gurus, often Neomodernists, regularly made the circuit of catechetical conferences and workshops, laying out and reenforcing all the tenets and methods of the new catechesis for a generally eager class of new catechists.

In condemning the original Modernists, Pope St. Pius X had spoken of "the domineering overbearingness of those who teach the errors, and the thoughtless compliance of the more shallow minds who assent to them, create a corrupted atmosphere which penetrates everywhere, and carries infection with it."[14] This sentence could have been written about the relationship of the dissenting new-theological establishment with today's compliant new-catechetical establishment.

The new catechesis caught on both quickly and widely. Typically, it consists of generous elements of an ersatz, Neomodernist *nonfaith*, when it does not actually contain certain elements of what could only be described as an *antifaith*. We

---

[14] Pope St. Pius X, encyclical letter *Pascendi Dominici Gregis*, on the Doctrines of the Modernists, September 8, 1907, no. 3.

shall be citing plenty of examples of it, and the reader can judge. The consequences of the new approach also became evident rather quickly: neither the Catholic children nor the Catholic adults who were subjected to the new catechesis any longer knew or professed their Catholic faith properly.

They no longer knew it because they were no longer learning it properly. They were no longer learning it properly for a very simple and understandable reason: in many, many instances, they were no longer being *taught* it properly. The faith of an entire generation of Catholics—some say two generations—was gravely compromised in this manner within a very few years.

Over the years, of course, there were numerous cases in which parents, pastors, and teachers tried to point out that what was being imparted was no longer the authentic Catholic faith. By and large, however, such protests seem to have had little impact, and the protesters usually earned for their pains nothing but a reputation as troublemakers. The pastors and the hierarchy, meanwhile, have been seemingly little able to deal with, or often, indeed, even to admit, the existence of a situation where some of their own people are evidently the "problem". The degree to which the Church's official religious-education establishment has meanwhile become honeycombed with many dissenters from Catholic teaching has never really been recognized or conceded to this day.

As a result, dissenters from Catholic teaching have too often gone on selecting the books, training the teachers, and managing the programs that are supposed to hand on the official Catholic faith. That this faith has been successfully transmitted is unfortunately shown by few of the results obtained. Too often also, the whole lamentable state of affairs has actually found defenders on the grounds that the issue is not whether or not it is really still the authentic Catholic faith that is being taught; that question has generally been avoided. Rather, the argument of the new catechists has been that the issue is merely one of new and different "theologies" and "methodologies". People raised on the *Baltimore Catechism*, they have contended, can simply not "understand" these new "approaches".

Unfortunately, some of these new approaches seem almost to require the watering down of the faith understood in any doctrinal sense. Even when the new catechists claim successful results, what they think is success is not necessarily related to the authentic Catholic faith. For example, one of the most recent national studies on the "desired outcomes of catechesis," a study on which the catechetical establishment has roundly congratulated itself, actually claims that: "Something is working! It could be that everything is working. . . . The present programs are having their intended effect."[15]

This particular national study, funded by the Lilly Endowment, was conducted by the prestigious Educational Testing Service, which "utilized the expertise of leaders from national Catholic organizations serving catechesis and religious education (the United States Catholic Conference, the National Conference of Catechetical Leadership, the National Catholic Education Association, and the National Association of Parish Coordinators and Directors of Religious Education)".

It sounds impressive. When we look more closely at

---

[15] Quoted by Robert Colbert, "Toward Shaping the Agenda: A Study of Catholic Religious Education/Catechesis", *NPCD News*, the publication of the National Association of Parish Coordinators & Directors of Religious Education, October 1994.

what the desired outcomes of catechesis utilized in the study were supposed to be, however, we soon find that an instilled knowledge and personal transformation in the revealed word of Jesus Christ, issuing in conduct in conformity with that same word, were not the focus of this particular study. Rather, the following "qualities of adult Catholics" represent what catechesis is supposed to be aiming at, according to the designers of this study:

—Having a particular awareness of his or her own value and dignity as a human being.
—Having a clear faith identity.
—Participating in the life of the Church.
—Having a practical spirituality for today's world.
—Participating in a continuing witness in charity.
—Being committed to the proclamation of the gospel.[16]

Now there is nothing wrong with these "qualities of adult Catholics" as far as they go. One would hope they would always be true in some measure of those who are catechized. But in no way can such general and even vague objectives be considered the proper aim of catechesis; nor would possession of all of them at once add up to being properly grounded in the authentic, saving Catholic faith. Not a single one of them refers, even indirectly, to "repenting and believing"—which Jesus specified as the *first* requirements for his followers (cf. Mk 1:15). Not one of them is specifically Catholic; they could be predicated of someone professing only the vaguest and most tenuous kind of Christianity; most of them could be the possession of someone professing no Christianity at all.

"Having a faith identity" or "considering oneself a disciple of Jesus" are not the equivalents of believing and prac-

---

[16] Ibid.

ticing the Creed and tenets of the Church. The important question is not whether one "considers oneself a disciple of Jesus" but whether one *is* a disciple of Jesus. There are objective criteria of authentic discipleship. Do the "adult Catholics" possessing all these qualities believe, or not, that Jesus is the Son of God who died on the Cross for their sins and rose again and ascended to open heaven for them?

It *cannot* be considered sufficient to justify these ill-defined "qualities" by saying something like, "Oh, we take all those beliefs for granted." "Those beliefs" represent precisely what is missing from this sort of catechesis. This is what is meant when it is said that modern catechesis lacks proper "content"; the very heart and core of God's revelation of himself and of his Son become blurred in the midst of these vague "Christian"-sounding sentiments. True doctrine is as absent from such an approach as it has been absent from catechesis generally in the postconciliar era.

Meanwhile, the new catechists congratulate themselves on a successful survey conducted by the Educational Testing Service; the "professionalism" of it all is what impresses them. But it is fluff; it is vain—if the revealed doctrine of Christ is not present. By what authority do these modern religious educators abandon the aims and objectives of catechesis according to such Church documents as the *General Catechetical Directory* in favor of such notions as the "qualities of the adult Catholic" when defining the desired outcomes of catechesis?

## V

For a long time there has been a dim general awareness that something was seriously amiss with religious education and that something had to be done about it. However, the reasons for what ailed religious education have never been very well understood. And there has also been a very great reluctance ever to criticize the architects of it, the new catechists themselves. As a result, the appropriate concrete measures that would have been necessary to deal effectively with what was amiss in religious education have never been strongly applied. Too often they have not been applied at all. The Church's educational machinery has simply ground and clanked noisily on without any of the necessary repairs being made.

Of course the hierarchy never stopped issuing documents and statements aimed at correcting the problems that existed. Unfortunately, however, the entrenched religious-education establishment usually found ways of not really implementing or applying the documents and statements that the hierarchy periodically issued. This tended to remain true even when lip service was prudently paid to such guidance from the hierarchy.

In not a few cases, however, the religious-education establishment has also rather openly undermined and nullified some of the measures taken by the hierarchy to correct a catechetical situation perceived to be deficient. For example, a year after the *General Catechetical Directory* was published by the Congregation for the Clergy, the National Conference of Diocesan Directors of Religious Education in the United States simply declined to "receive" this Roman document. Instead, the NCDDRE published its own interpretation of the GCD in the guise of a "commentary" on it, which deftly softened, and in some cases simply nullified, the GCD's basic directives.[17] This was in 1972.

The next year, the bishops of the United States, respond-

---

[17] See, again, Wrenn, *Catechisms*, 162–69.

ing to complaints about deficiencies in the teaching of religion, published their own directives, entitled *Basic Teachings for Catholic Religious Education*.[18] This bishops' document, too, was downgraded in its importance and effect by the publication of a so-called *Study Aid* purporting to assist religious educators in understanding the bishops' directives, but in reality promoting dissent from the "basic teachings" of the Church. Anyone who read the books recommended in the *Study Aid* got the clear message that the bishops' *Basic Teachings* did not really have to be followed. Yet the *Study Aid* in question was published by none other than the Division of Religious Education-CCD, an arm of the bishops' conference itself.[19]

Essentially the same story was repeated in the course of carrying out, beginning in 1972, a series of elaborate nationwide consultations and then developing and revising successive drafts of what became, six years later, a *National Catechetical Directory for Catholics of the United States*. The U.S. bishops themselves devoted some of their meetings to the development of this NCD, in the end voting hundreds of specific amendments to what became the completed text. This text then underwent an almost year-long examination by several Roman congregations before the final version was approved and promulgated in October 1978.[20] Like the *Gen-*

---

[18] National Conference of Catholic Bishops, *Basic Teachings for Catholic Religious Education* (Publications Office, United States Catholic Conference, January 11, 1973).

[19] See Wrenn, *Catechisms*, 169–76.

[20] National Conference of Catholic Bishops (NCCB), *Sharing the Light of Faith: National Catechetical Directory for Catholics in the United States* (Washington, D.C., 1979). (The text was approved by the NCCB at their general meeting, November 14–17, 1977, and approved by the Sacred Congregation for the Clergy, Second Office, October 30, 1978.)

*eral Catechetical Directory* before it, the *National Catechetical Directory* was quite a good document—if only more people had consented to be "directed" by these Directories! Thus, the already fairly long and melancholy history of rather bold "nonreception" of hierarchical documents by the religious-education establishment was again repeated in the case of the NCD. All this surely has an important bearing on how the *Catechism of the Catholic Church* is being received today as well.

The record of the religious-education establishment in the United States today shows that it has never been unduly impressed by documents from the hierarchy. Even a document as painstakingly reviewed and meticulously revised, both by the U.S. bishops and by several Roman congregations, as the U.S. *National Catechetical Directory* could not, in its view, simply be given to the faithful. No: this time it was the National Conference of Diocesan Directors of Religious Education that expeditiously produced yet another document of their own "explaining" the NCD, this one entitled a "Discussion Guide" (rather than the "Commentary" the NCDDRE had produced on the GCD). Of course, little of substance was left of the original NCD after the "discussion" by this group, an official organization of Catholic diocesan religious-education directors.

Meanwhile, the Department of Education of the United States Catholic Conference published a special issue, devoted to the NCD, of the professional religious-education journal it sponsors, *The Living Light*. In this special issue, again, several "name" religious-education experts, not very subtly, made fairly short work of the NCD, which the au-

---

For a brief account of the preparation of the NCD, see Wrenn, *Catechisms*, 176–86.

thorities of the Church had gone to such great and even inordinate lengths to prepare for the benefit of the Catholic faithful.[21]

It may seem to be a rather remarkable thing that the specialists and experts and leaders in Catholic religious education should themselves have been the ones who most effectively undermined their own enterprise and brought it to the low estate from which it has only now, especially with the publication of the *Catechism of the Catholic Church*, begun to recover; but the facts of the case speak for themselves. One of the more able of these American catechetical specialists, as it happened, fairly early on began to have second thoughts about what was being done to Catholic religious education, putatively in the name of renewing it and bringing it up to date. This was the Rev. Alfred McBride, O.Præm., who had grown increasingly skeptical of some aspects of the new catechesis because it had become progressively more clear to him that its subjects no longer knew their faith. No one has described the general problem of Catholic religious education in the immediate postconciliar years better than Fr. McBride:

> The chaos in religious education today has resulted from an agenda that pretended to implement Vatican II, but in fact subverted it. We are now the heirs of the "bad theory leads to bad practice" syndrome. This bad theory was not taught by the Council or the Magisterium, but by certain theologians and catechetical writers.
>
> Over a period of twenty-five years they gained—in many cases—influence and control of the departments

---

[21] For accounts of the NCDDRE *Discussion Guide to Sharing the Light of Faith* and the special NCD issue of *The Living Light*, see, again, Wrenn, *Catechisms*, 186–93.

of religion and religious education in Catholic colleges and universities, of the publishers of the most widely used religion textbooks, and of the middle management positions in dioceses and archdioceses. They were and are the major speakers at most religious education conventions. Through their books and articles and classroom indoctrination, they shape the minds of the leaders, who in turn pass this on to the classroom and volunteer teachers. They are not teaching Catholicism but rather a mélange of personal opinions that usually resurrect discredited nineteenth century liberal Protestantism and reflect New Age pieties.

Bad theory has led to bad practice. Wrong ideas have led to wrong consequences.

While Fr. McBride's indictment here is certainly a strong one, he himself felt obliged to qualify it in certain respects, and we believe the qualification Fr. McBride added should also be included here in order to serve both justice and balance:

Lest I unfairly paint too bleak a landscape, let me note that many diocesan and parish directors of religious education are exemplary leaders of catechesis today. Thousands of good-hearted and faith-filled lay volunteer and classroom teachers are sharing the authentic faith of the Church. There are numerous professors, authors of articles and writers of textbook series who are implementing the real intentions of Vatican II and the Church's Magisterium. They stand out as encouraging and positive signs in catechetics today. They deserve our support, gratitude, praise, and prayers. God bless them.[22]

---

[22] Rev. Alfred McBride, O.Præm., "Why We Need the New Catechism: Vatican II Promise and Post-Vatican II Reality," in *The Church*

Given the overall situation that had come to prevail, however, it became increasingly clear that additional directives from Church authorities—and even lengthy directories—were not really going to remedy what afflicted Catholic catechesis. Still, the Catholic Church seemed to move with unhurried deliberateness in the matter, in keeping with an institution that is said to "think in centuries". In 1977, around the same time that the U.S. bishops were putting the finishing touches on the NCD, the Synod of Bishops in Rome adopted as the topic of its official deliberations the whole vexed question of "the state of catechesis".

At the conclusion of this session of the Synod, the Synod Fathers transmitted to Pope Paul VI a valuable body of synodal discussions and recommendations on the subject of catechesis, stressing the necessary "Christocentricity" of any Catholic treatment of this subject. Following the death of Pope Paul VI in 1978, these synodal recommendations were fashioned into a first-rate document on catechesis by Pope John Paul II; this was the apostolic exhortation *Catechesi Tradendæ*, on Catechesis in Our Time, published in 1979.[23]

*Catechesi Tradendæ* was one of the first of the long series of outstanding magisterial documents that have been issued during the remarkable pontificate of John Paul II. Moreover, *Catechesi Tradendæ* did correctly diagnose much of what

---

*and the Universal Catechism*, ed. Rev. Anthony Mastroeni (proceedings from the fifteenth convention of the Fellowship of Catholic Scholars, Pittsburgh, Penn.) (Steubenville, Ohio: Franciscan University Press, 1992), 39–40.

[23] Pope John Paul II, *Catechesi Tradendæ*, Catechesis in Our Time, October 16, 1979, in Austin Flannery, O.P., ed., *Vatican Council II: More Postconciliar Documents* (Northport, N.Y.: Costello Publishing Co., 1982), 762–814.

ails religious education today; it also prescribed a number of important remedies. This apostolic exhortation of John Paul II remains, even in the new era inaugurated by the publication of the *Catechism of the Catholic Church*, one of the best sources available for clergy and religion teachers in their study and reflection upon what the handing on of the Catholic faith truly does entail.

In the nature of the case, however, no mere "exhortation", no matter how brilliantly done, could really get at the most fundamental of all the problems connected with religious education today, namely, the fact that too many of those responsible for religious education, whether catechetical experts, catechists, teachers, or even some pastors and parents, evidently no longer wholly agree that *it is what the Church's Magisterium says the faith is that has to be handed on*. We now live in an era of "cafeteria Catholicism", when many individuals believe *they* can decide what the essence or tenets of the faith are that have to be handed on. This same era is one in which the right of dissent from Catholic teaching is often considered to be a more fundamental principle than the Catholic's responsibility to believe with real assent what is professed in the Creed.

In the meantime, the new catechesis expressly aims at passing on a new and truncated, Neomodernist-type version of the faith in which crucial teachings have been importantly modified, if they have not been distorted or omitted outright. At the same time the tenets of other ideologies alien to the faith—radical feminism, extreme environmentalism, liberation theology, and, as Fr. McBride remarked above, so-called "New Age" eclectic religious notions—have often been incorporated into modern catechesis and are now sometimes taught as tenets of the faith every bit as "dogmatically" as ever Original Sin, Transubstantiation, or the

Real Presence were taught by those now scorned as rigid "traditionalists".

Nevertheless, John Paul II's *Catechesi Tradendæ* was able to identify at least one of the basic causes of today's all too typical faithlessness and falling away from the teaching of the Magisterium. The basic cause is the influence of some theologians and other experts who have in our day come to see the Magisterium as just one of the many elements or sources that constitute the whole faith—of which *they*, rather than the pope and the bishops, are henceforth to be the final judges (from whom there can be no appeal). They base their claim to this "authority" on their claimed scholarship and professional expertise.

Speaking of the influence contemporary theology has had on religious education, *Catechesi Tradendæ* points out "that every stirring in the field of theology also has repercussions in that of catechesis. . . . The same must be said of hermeneutics with respect to exegesis." Pope John Paul II, in this document fashioned from the results of the deliberations of the 1977 Synod of Bishops, went on to "insist" that:

> Aware of the influence that their research and their statements have on catechetical instruction, theologians and exegetes have a duty to take great care that people do not take for certainty what on the contrary belongs to the area of questions of opinion or of discussion among experts. Catechists for their part must have the wisdom to pick from the field of theological research those points that can provide light for their own reflection and teaching, drawing, like the theologians, from the true sources, in the light of the magisterium.
>
> They must refuse to trouble the minds of children and young people, at this stage of their catechesis, with out-

landish theories, useless questions, and unproductive discussions, things that St. Paul often condemned in his pastoral letters (cf. 1 Tim 1:3ff.; 4:1ff.; 2 Tim 2:14ff.; 4:1–5; Titus 1:10–12).[24]

The actual catechetical situation that has obtained in the postconciliar era, at least in the United States, has been closer to the opposite of what the Pope insists is called for: many of the truths that have not ceased to be affirmed by the Magisterium are exactly the truths that have become blurred in modern religious education. Meanwhile, the pet ideas of certain modern theologians and exegetes have practically become enshrined as new dogmas—as we shall have abundant opportunities to verify in the pages that follow.

It should be clear from the relatively brief sketch that we have essayed here that by the 1980s, the need for a universal catechism had become pressing, if only in order that, amid all the reigning confusion, people could at least again find out for themselves "what the Church teaches and what she does not", in Cardinal Ratzinger's words. It is to the genesis and development of the *Catechism of the Catholic Church* itself that we must now turn in the next chapter. One of the most striking things about the whole subject is how the *Catechism* came about in spite of, not because of, the reigning majority sentiment of those most visibly involved in theology and religious education.

---

[24] *Catechesi Tradendæ*, no. 61.

# CHAPTER TWO

# How the New Catechism Came About

## I

The history of the genesis and development of the *Catechism of the Catholic Church* has already been told more than once. Among the available accounts explaining it there is even included an especially illuminating one coauthored by the two individuals most directly responsible for producing the *Catechism*, Cardinal Joseph Ratzinger, who headed the Commission for the Catechism for the Universal Church, a twelve-member body of cardinals and bishops appointed to oversee the whole project; and then auxiliary Bishop Christoph Schönborn of Vienna (now archbishop of the same see), who had been a distinguished Dominican theologian at the University of Fribourg before being named a bishop and who served as overall editor of the *Catechism*, while assigned to the Vatican Secretariat created to manage the project.

Together, Cardinal Ratzinger and Archbishop Schönborn have provided a short but most instructive account of how the *Catechism* was put together, what it contains, how it is structured, what the principles underlying it are, what its authority is, and how it can and should be used. This account by Ratzinger and Schönborn has been published in English translation in the United States under the title *Introduction to the Catechism of the Catholic Church*.[1] This slim volume, published in a format uniform with the *Catechism* itself, should be read along with the latter by anybody interested in studying the *Catechism* in depth. How this remarkable work came to be what Pope John Paul II has called a gift to the Church is a truly inspiring story of the faith in our times.

Other accounts of what the *Catechism* represents and how it came to be are also readily available,[2] and hence we shall

---

[1] Joseph Cardinal Ratzinger and Christoph Schönborn, *Introduction to the Catechism of the Catholic Church* (San Francisco: Ignatius Press, 1994).

[2] See Michael J. Wrenn, *Catechisms and Controversies: Religious Education in the Postconciliar Years* (San Francisco: Ignatius Press, 1991), esp. 12–28. Another brief summary of the origins and development of the *Catechism* appears in *DOA: The Ambush of the Universal Catechism* (by an anonymous author, "Catholicus") (Crisis Books, P.O. Box 1006, Notre Dame, IN 46556, 1993), esp. 14–26. Much light on the background and development of the *Catechism* can be found in Rev. Anthony Mastroeni, ed., *The Church and the Universal Catechism* (proceedings from the fifteenth convention of the Fellowship of Catholic Scholars, Pittsburgh, Penn.) (Steubenville, Ohio: Franciscan University Press, 1992). See also Rev. James V. Schall, S.J., "The Church explains Itself in the New Catechism", *Homiletic and Pastoral Review*, June 1993. *Crisis* magazine, in its issue of June 1993, featured an informative symposium on the *Catechism* by five authors. See also Rev. Avery Dulles, S.J., "The Challenge of the *Catechism*", *First Things*, January 1995. For a brief and underenthusiastic account by a pillar of the U.S. catechetical establishment that was so strongly opposed to the preparation of a universal catechism—but who nevertheless ended up being one of the briefers of the U.S. bishops on the finished *Catechism*!—see Rev. Berard L. Marthaler, *"The Catechism of the Catholic Church* in Context", *The Living Light*, fall 1993; and by the same

touch upon its history and background only in briefest outline here, mostly in order to establish a proper context for
the all-important topic with which we shall principally be
dealing in these pages, namely, the *reception* of the *Catechism*,
how this magisterial work is now being received, especially
in the United States, now that the universal Church has
gone to the extraordinary lengths that she manifestly has
gone to in order to produce it.

When Jesus began his public ministry, the double requirement he immediately enjoined upon those who heard his
words was: "Repent and believe in the gospel" (Mk 1:15). In
other words: Change your lives, yes, but in accordance with
certain truths, which I am revealing herewith, and which
you are to *believe*, that is, hold in your mind as *knowledge*.
Jesus elaborated more than once on the necessary connection between living the faith and believing in its truths, for
example, when he said, "If you continue in my word, you
are truly my disciples", whereupon he immediately added,
"You will know the truth, and the truth will make you free"
(Jn 8:31–32). Knowing the truth has an effect on one's life.
This knowledge is essential for conversion to Jesus and his
Way.

The intellectual or cognitive content of the faith referred
to in such scriptural passages is therefore an essential component of the faith. Historically, the Church has seen fit to

---

author, "*The Catechism of the Catholic Church*", *Church*, spring 1993.
Fr. Marthaler also edited the volume *Introducing the Catechism of the
Catholic Church: Traditional Themes and Contemporary Issues* (New York
and Mahwah, N.J.: Paulist Press, 1994), consisting of most of the contributions to a 1993 Catholic University of America catechetical conference ostensibly introducing the *Catechism* but, more fundamentally,
putting the proper "spin" on it for the U.S. catechetical establishment.

formulate this essential component in her creeds; this has been true from the earliest times. Equally early, catechesis became the means of the transmission of this intellectual content of these creeds. It is important to reiterate these points precisely because the misunderstanding, or deemphasis, or even abandonment of them in much contemporary catechesis is exactly what brought about a situation where a catechism became necessary.

The *Catechism of the Catholic Church* makes clear the fundamental cognitive nature of catechesis at the outset, quoting Pope John Paul II's *Catechesi Tradendæ* (no. 18):

> Catechesis is an *education in the faith* of children, young people, and adults which includes especially the teaching of Christian doctrine imparted, generally speaking, in an organic and systematic way, with a view to initiating the hearers into the fullness of Christian life (CCC 5; emphasis in the original).

The imparting of Christian *doctrine* is thus what is involved in catechesis. Nobody denies, of course, that the faith is fuller and broader and deeper than its doctrinal content. The *Catechism* itself, in the passage just quoted, distinguishes the imparting of doctrine from "the fullness of the faith". In yet another article, the *Catechism* makes clear that "we do not believe in formulas but in the realities they express and which faith allows us to grasp. . . . Still we do approach these realities with the help of the formulations of faith. These permit us to express and transmit the faith, to celebrate it in community, to assimilate it, and through it to live ever more fully" (CCC 170).

Again, Pope John Paul II, in *Catechesi Tradendæ*, said about the teaching of the Church that "this teaching is not a body of abstract truths. It is a communication of the living mystery of God."[3] Given the limitations of human beings, however, this living mystery necessarily has to be communicated in human words and human propositions.

The faith is indeed more than doctrine and includes such things as living one's whole life in faith, just as it also includes community celebration of that same faith. Nevertheless, the imparting of doctrine is what catechesis properly speaking is all about. The *General Catechetical Directory* made this clear when it said that the intention of catechesis was "to make men's faith become living, conscious, and active through the light of *instruction*" (emphasis added).[4]

Today, however, we find a common error—an error especially prevalent among contemporary religious educators —that sees "doctrine" as dry and sterile and somehow the antithesis or even the enemy of the "living, conscious, and active" faith that is called for. Many modern religious educators have decided that doctrine is to be downgraded if not actually eliminated, as if the faith somehow contained no necessary truths. We cite an example of this new viewpoint selected virtually at random from a recent journal article. Literally dozens of citations to the same effect could be found in the contemporary catechetical literature, but the following represents an entirely typical one: "Since the Second Vatican Council of the early 1960s," it is said, "the Catholic Church has changed its emphasis in religious education away from catechism—the rote learning of dogma

---

[3] Pope John Paul II, *Catechesi Tradendæ*, Apostolic Exhortation on Catechesis in Our Time, October 16, 1979, no. 7.

[4] Sacred Congregation for the Clergy, *General Catechetical Directory* (Washington, D.C.: United States Catholic Conference, 1971), no. 17, quoting Vatican Council II's Decree on the Pastoral Office of Bishops, *Christus Dominus*, no. 14.

and doctrine—and towards catechesis, the attempt to make Christ present through a variety of experiences: word, worship, community, and service to others."[5]

This may well be what a lot of religious educators sincerely think they have been doing, of course; but the statement is crucially wrong in more than one respect. For one thing, it was not "the Catholic Church" that changed the emphasis in the manner described but rather theologians and professional religious educators who put into practice mistaken catechetical theories in the guise of implementing Vatican II. This particular formulation errs too in what it attempts to include in "catechesis", as we can see if we compare this statement with the quotations from the *Catechism of the Catholic Church* and the *General Catechetical Directory* above. It involves a basic confusion of categories, among other things.

While the total faith in its fullness surely does include "worship, community, service to others", and the like, in addition to just the "word"—and while these things can also be utilized as aids to instruction—catechesis as such continues to be necessarily concerned primarily with imparting the *word*. Catechesis values these other things beyond price; it assumes they have to be present and going on in the life of the Church and of the faithful; it relies on them to reenforce and fecundate its own primary message concerning the truths of the faith.

But these other things are, necessarily, not its own primary concern. Its principal concern is imparting the word, that is, transmitting the truths of the faith, yes, teaching "doctrine". To imagine that doctrine is not fundamental is

---

[5] Michael P. Orsi, "Catechesis in the Third Millennium", *Religious Education* 89, no. 3, (summer 1994), 397.

to contradict Christ's own words in the Gospels. Catechesis, accordingly, provides—formal—"education in the faith", as John Paul II said and as the *Catechism* repeats.

The typical approach downgrading "doctrine", which is found in catechesis today, could thus not be more fundamentally wrong—or more harmful in its results. This has been abundantly shown over the past thirty years. Again we select an example almost at random, in this case from a new book about the *Catechism*, that we shall be looking at in more detail later on. The author of this book, Jane E. Regan, informs us that the modern theologian generally accepted as the father of the new catechesis, Jesuit Fr. Josef Jungmann (1889–1975), "made clear that the core of the Christian message cannot be presented solely through instruction"—the way the *General Catechetical Directory* nevertheless said it *had* to be presented!

Whether Josef Jungmann did in fact make this clear or not is not the important point here. The important thing is that the new catechists believe that he did, and, judging by the typical evidence of their work, they hold and teach this as "dogmatically" as ever any traditionalist ever recited, say, the canons of the Council of Trent. What this means in practice, for them, is that "instruction", precisely, must be deemphasized.

Regan goes farther. Citing a few of the developments in catechetical thinking that took place in the 1950s and the 1960s, she then goes on to conclude that "not even primarily" does catechesis take place "within an instructional setting. . . . It is not primarily instruction, but the very life of the faith community that shapes and forms our faith. . . . Catechesis involves engaging with the ways in which faith comes to expression within our community—communal living, proclamation, teaching, liturgy, and service."

These are conclusions drawn by the modern catechetical movement, and therefore, in Regan's view, they must take precedence over whatever a Catechism or the GCD might say to the contrary.

Also in the view of this particular author, the whole catechetical question has now been

> changed from "How are we to cover all of the topics in our time of instruction?" to "How are we to live within these dimensions of Christian life and learn to reflect on that living?" Once we recognize the community as the agent of catechesis, it becomes clear that the content of catechesis is not something we give or present to the learners, but rather a reality that we attempt to live out and incarnate with the life of the community.[6]

But once we have accepted that "the content of catechesis is not something we give or present to the learners", we are reluctantly obliged to add: then the way has surely been opened up, and the justification handily provided, for henceforth giving little or nothing in the way of formal instruction at all—and for including no substance or truth content at all in catechesis. This, of course, is exactly the unhappy contemporary situation in catechesis, which so many Catholics have noticed and have been complaining about for a long time. This author's formulation of the question, it would seem, is just one more variant of the widely noted tendency in modern religious education simply to provide the students with "experiences" rather than trying to "teach" them anything, that is, the truths of the faith as they have been developed and handed down to us in the Church since apostolic times with the help of the Holy Spirit.

---

[6] Jane E. Regan, *Exploring the Catechism* (Collegeville, Minn.: Liturgical Press, 1995), 16, 18–19.

It is no accident, by the way, that this sort of new catechetical theory, which eschews content, gets itself adopted by professional Catholic religious educators at the very same time as their colleagues in secular education are also engaged in "dumbing down" intellectual content in modern education generally. Thus, in more ways than one, do Catholic religious educators today seem to be looking to the world for their inspiration and models far more than to the Church.

In the true Catholic context, of course, the antidoctrinal viewpoint of the new catechesis fundamentally misunderstands and misrepresents Christian faith. This faith is based first of all on the truths about God and about God's plan for us, revealed first in the Scriptures concerned with the history of God's chosen people and finally revealed in the life and words of Jesus Christ, who intended these things to be perpetuated in his Church. The new catechists make a crucial and fundamental mistake when they try to belittle or drop truth (again, "doctrine") and then perhaps imagine that they can still go on exhorting their students to be "good" and "loving", to serve justice, or to help the poor, and so on.

But what they have abandoned is the possibility of being able to give their students any *reasons* why they should serve justice or help the poor. Why should the students bother, when the whole secular culture urges them so insistently in the direction of self-will and self-satisfaction instead? The results of the attempt of the new catechesis to "catechize", while downgrading or dropping revealed truth were always bound to be disappointing in the nature of the case, and that is exactly the way things have turned out. The *Catechism of the Catholic Church* had to come, and not a moment too soon.

# II

Concrete hopes for a new catechism that would restate the faith of the Church for our modern era began farther back than anyone looking at the current catechetical scene in North America or Western Europe might at first imagine. As far back as the Synod of Bishops in 1974, a Synod session that was devoted to the subject of evangelization, the Polish-language group at the Synod (which included Cardinal Karol Wojtyla, archbishop of Cracow) recommended that a universal catechism be prepared.[7] However, the time was not yet ripe for such a recommendation to be accepted.

At the 1977 Synod of Bishops, which was dedicated to the subject of catechesis, the question of a universal catechism was again raised, but the Synod itself did not officially endorse the idea. However, in *Catechesi Tradendæ*, which was based on the work of this Synod, the Pope did encourage "episcopal conferences of the whole world to undertake . . . in agreement with the Apostolic See . . . to prepare genuine catechisms which will be faithful to the essential content of revelation, up to date in method, and which will be capable of educating the Christian generations of the future to a sturdy faith."[8]

Since he was calling for the preparation of catechisms by the bishops, it is clear that Pope John Paul II did not see catechisms as any kind of obsolete instrument for teaching and learning. On the contrary, the Pontiff steadily saw that the point of catechesis was "educating the faithful . . . in the essential content of revelation".

---

[7] See Dulles, "Challenge of the *Catechism*".

[8] John Paul II, *Catechesi Tradendæ*, no. 50.

In the meantime, though, the anxiety level was clearly rising among many Church leaders as a result of mounting evidence that less and less could Catholics be expected to know their faith on many fundamental points. One study found that only 31 percent of Catholics could name the Books of Matthew, Mark, Luke, and John as the four Gospels of the New Testament; only 38 percent could identify Jesus as the one who delivered the Sermon on the Mount. Another study by the Gallup organization found that only 30 percent of those surveyed about the Eucharist believed that they received the true Body and Blood of Christ at Communion.[9]

No doubt some or even much of the blame for this state of affairs could increasingly be laid to the often overpowering influence of today's morally debased "culture". Few generations since apostolic times have probably deserved more richly than our own such epithets as "crooked and perverse generation" (Phil 2:15), which are so often found in the New Testament, sometimes on the lips of our Lord himself. Today's marked decline in knowledge of the faith—and *practice* of it, for the one follows from the other, whatever modern religious educators may imagine—has certainly only come about because of factors other than just the "culture".

The unpalatable truth, we repeat, is that many Catholics today do not know their faith today for the very simple reason that they have not been—and are not being—*taught* their faith. An *Our Sunday Visitor* survey, for example, found that the lack of knowledge of many Catholics concerning the truths about the Eucharist could be ascribed to "poor religious education and failure to discuss the subject

---

[9] Cited by Rev. Alfred McBride, O.Præm., in "Why We Need the New Catechism: Vatican II Promise and Post-Vatican II Reality", in Mastroeni, *Church and Universal Catechism.*

from the pulpit".[10] Other studies have confirmed the same thing.

As the whole situation deteriorated, important figures in the Church's hierarchy were coming more and more to understand how significant the problem of watered-down and defective teaching had become. During the 1980 Synod of Bishops, dedicated to the subject of the family, so many bishops continued to be concerned about catechesis, and about the lack of an authoritative catechism, that, in Pope John Paul II's 1981 apostolic exhortation *Familiaris Consortio*, on the Christian Family in the Modern World—the teaching document that grew out of this 1980 Synod—the Pontiff was obliged to note that "the Synod Fathers expressed the hope that a suitable *catechism for families* might be prepared, one that would be clear, brief, and easily assimilated by all" (emphasis in the original).[11]

The idea that "catechisms" truly were needed, in spite of what the experts continued to say, was increasingly catching on and finding favor among more and more members of the hierarchy.

In 1983, in an address delivered in both Paris and Lyons, France, as part of a symposium entitled "Handing on the Faith Today", Cardinal Joseph Ratzinger himself returned to the whole subject of the catechism in a way that drew worldwide attention, coming as it did from none other than the prefect of the Congregation for the Doctrine of the Faith. Discussing the sources and transmission of the faith in his address, the Cardinal identified some of the funda-

---

[10] *Our Sunday Visitor*, March 15, 1992.

[11] Pope John Paul II, apostolic exhortation *Familiaris Consortio*, On the Christian Family in the Modern World, November 22, 1981, no. 39.

mental problems in religious education and put his finger on what some of the causes of these problems were. "A fundamental and grave mistake", Cardinal Ratzinger said, "was the suppression of the catechism, together with the claim that the very genre of the catechism had been superseded and 'surpassed'." The implication here was that the teaching of the faith was bound to suffer once the Church dropped, for whatever reason, the use of an instrument that, by definition, provided an ordered and systematic statement of what the faith was. This could only lead, in the Cardinal's view, to a fragmentation of the proclamation of the message, an arbitrariness in explaining it, and, finally, a calling into question of some of its parts—exactly the things that came about in the postconciliar era.

"Certainly, the catechism, as a book, only came into vogue during the time of the Reformation", the Cardinal added. "But the transmission of the faith as a fundamental enterprise, arising from the very logic of the faith, is also as early as the catechumenate, that is, of the Church herself." Cardinal Ratzinger concluded that the use of catechism-type formulations of doctrine in order to teach the faith flowed "from the very nature" of the Church's mission and therefore, he said, "*cannot* be given up or laid aside" (emphasis added).[12]

Not everyone was prepared to applaud Cardinal Ratzinger's conclusions. For example, a well-known figure in the American catechetical establishment, Fr. Berard Marthaler, O.F.M. Conv., of the Department of Religion and Religious Education at the Catholic University of America, said of the Cardinal's 1983 speech that "Cardinal Ratzinger's remarks

---

[12] Cardinal Joseph Ratzinger, "Sources and Transmission of the Faith", *Communio*, spring 1983, 17–34.

were either disingenuous or misunderstood because he knew that the idea of catechisms was neither suppressed nor obsolete."[13]

"He *knew*": whatever else this comment was supposed to signify, it certainly had to be considered a belated admission of some kind, coming as it did from one of the leaders of the modern catechetical movement that had so persistently and so diligently *tried* to suppress catechisms and make them obsolete. Apparently the catechetical movement had not finally succeeded in its aims?

The same Fr. Marthaler had himself once written, in an article that was included in one of the foundational books used in the training of professional religious educators in the United States, about what he called "the chimera of a universal catechism", and in the same paragraph he had called for moving "away from book-centered catechesis".[14] This was the view from the Catholic University of America's religion and religious studies department. Nor should we forget that what the people in the catechetical movement generally follow, as a fairly well-established habit, is not so much what the Cardinal Ratzingers are saying but rather what the Fr. Marthalers are saying.

But Fr. Marthaler and the catechetical movement could not have been more mistaken. With his usual astuteness and penetration, Cardinal Ratzinger had correctly identified in his 1983 speech some of the reasons that had contributed to the dropping by modern religious educators of the cat-

---

[13] Berard L. Marthaler, "The Ecclesial Context of the Catechism", in Marthaler, *Introducing the Catechism*, 13.

[14] Berard L. Marthaler, "The Genesis and Genius of the *General Catechetical Directory*", *Sourcebook for Modern Catechetics*, ed. Michael Warren (Winona, Minn.: St. Mary's Press, 1983), 253.

echism as an indispensable tool of teaching and learning. These reasons, as identified by the German Cardinal, included:

> —A desire "to get in line with general developments in teaching and pedagogy" in the modern world (which Cardinal Ratzinger believed had led to an overemphasis on methodology).
> —A mistaken decision to "limit catechesis to issues for beginners", and another mistaken decision to subordinate truth to practice.
> —An undue concentration on anthropology at the expense of theology (the Cardinal believed that emphasizing method over content made this inevitable).[15]

These were not the only points Cardinal Ratzinger made, or could have made, in his 1983 lecture delivered in Paris and Lyons, concerning the crisis in catechetics that had by then come to be more and more widely recognized. Among other things, he singled out for praise and emulation the four "pillars" of the great *Catechism of the Council of Trent*— Creed, Sacraments, Commandments, and the Our Father. These same four "pillars" would eventually also serve as the pillars of the *Catechism of the Catholic Church* as well.

Nor did the Cardinal fail to link the crisis in catechetics with the larger question of the crisis of the faith itself in the modern world. Though himself a scholar of worldwide reputation—easily the peer and usually the master of any of the dissenting theologians and scholars who regularly attack and belittle him—he nevertheless pointed to the danger of attempting to teach a revealed faith on the basis of the latest discoveries of scholarship or science (as if Christians of earlier generations did not have access to the truths that save).

---

[15] Ratzinger, "Sources".

"When scientific certitude is considered as the only valid, indeed, possible certitude," Cardinal Ratzinger noted in his 1983 speech, "then the certitude of dogma had to appear either as a now by-passed stage of an archaic idea or as the will to power of surviving institutions."[16]

These are results that, sadly, more than a few modern Catholic theologians and exegetes appear to be quite prepared to embrace, followed by many of their disciples in the modern catechetical movement. But they are also results that, it should go without saying, are radically incompatible with "the Catholic faith which comes to us from the apostles". When Catholics embrace them, in whatever degree, they separate themselves from the authentic faith in that same degree.

Coming as it did from the prefect of the Congregation for the Doctrine of the Faith, Cardinal Ratzinger's 1983 lectures attracted wide attention and, apparently, signaled a new determination on the part of the authorities of the Church at the highest level to begin to set a term on the confusion concerning what was to be taught by the Church and how it was to be taught. The stage was thus set for 1985, when the Synod of Bishops held in that year would make the key recommendation that would lead to the *Catechism of the Catholic Church*.

## III

That what became the *Catechism of the Catholic Church* was, in effect, mandated by the Synod of Bishops in 1985 is rather well known. This particular Synod was an extraordinary ses-

---

[16] Ibid.

sion. Pope John Paul II had convoked it to commemorate the twentieth anniversary of the Second Vatican Council.

It was not planned in advance that the universal catechism (not mandated by Vatican II) would be mandated by this extraordinary session of the Synod of Bishops instead. On the very first day of the meeting, however, Cardinal Bernard Law, archbishop of Boston, pointed out to the assembled bishops that today "we have to teach the faith in a world that becomes more and more a global village." In such a world—a world in which "young people in Boston, Leningrad and Santiago de Chile all wear blue jeans and listen and dance to the same music"—in such a world, the Boston Cardinal wondered, why could not a common language be devised in which to express the language of the faith? (It was the part about the "blue jeans" that Archbishop Christoph Schönborn would later remember most vividly about this synodal intervention, especially, perhaps, since Cardinal Law's speech was delivered in Latin: "*Iuvenes Bostoniensis, Leningradiensis et Sancti Jacobi in Chile induti sunt* 'blue jeans' *et audiunt et saltant eandem musicam.*"[17]

Whether or not such considerations really influenced the bishops at the Synod, the fact is that, by then, more and more bishops had come to realize that a modern, authoritative catechism had become quite simply imperative, regardless of what their experts might still be telling them. The idea of a catechism was already found in the preparatory reports for the Synod from the bishops of Korea, Senegal, and Mauritania. Besides Cardinal Law, Archbishop Ruhana of Burundi and the Latin Patriarch of Jerusalem, Archbishop Beltritti, called for a catechism in interventions from the floor. No fewer than six of the nine language working groups at the

---

[17] See Ratzinger and Schönborn, *Introduction*, 39.

1985 Synod ended up favoring the idea of a new catechism proposed by Cardinal Law.[18]

In view of all the interest manifested in a universal catechism at the Synod, it is probably not surprising that the full Synod recommended that such a catechism be prepared. The Final Report of the Synod said:

> Very many have expressed the desire that a catechism or compendium of all Catholic doctrine regarding both faith and morals be composed, that it might be, as it were, a point of reference for the catechisms or compendiums that are prepared in the various regions. The presentation of doctrine must be biblical and liturgical. It must be sound doctrine suited to the present life of Christians.[19]

Pope John Paul II did not conceal his own enthusiasm for the idea, making mention of it more than once. On June 10, 1986, the Pope named a Commission for the Catechism for the Universal Church, with Cardinal Ratzinger as its head. Other members included Roman Curia Cardinals William Baum, Antonio Innocenti, Jozef Tomko, and Simon Lourdusamy, prefects, respectively, for the Congregations for Catholic Education, for the Clergy, for the Evangelization of Peoples, and for the Eastern Churches—a very representative selection of offices within the Catholic Church's "general headquarters", all with a special interest in the teaching of the faith.

Another very logical choice for membership on the com-

---

[18] See Most Reverend William J. Levada, "The Catechism for the Universal Church", in *Collaborators in Catechesis: Bishops, Publishers, Diocesan Directors* (Washington, D.C.: Department of Religious Education, National Catholic Education Association [NCEA], 1990), 52.

[19] "Final Report of the 1985 Extraordinary Synod of Bishops", *Origins*, NC Documentary Service, December 19, 1985.

mission was Archbishop Jan Schotte, general secretary of the Synod of Bishops. Residential bishops from around the world were included on the commission: Cardinal Law of Boston (no doubt especially because of his key role in recommending that a catechism be prepared in the first place); Archbishop Jerzy Stroba of Poznan, Poland; Greek Melkite Archbishop Neophytos Edelby of Aleppo, Syria; Archbishop Henry Sebastian D'Souza of Calcutta, India; Archbishop Isidore de Souza of Cotonou, Benin, Africa; and Bishop Felipe Benitez Avalos of Vallarrica, Paraguay.[20]

It is surely evident from the composition of this commission that its membership was broadly representative of the worldwide Church. Accusations such as those of Hans Küng that the commission represented "the Roman party", in which "everything was decided by a curial commission",[21] are simply groundless.

The commission first met in November 1986 and made a number of key decisions. The commission decided, first of all, that the new universal catechism would be called by that name, rather than, for example, being called a "compendium", that is, a compilation that might perhaps end up on library shelves as a book for reference only. The commission wanted a book accessible to regular readers, "offering not technical knowledge, but proclamation", in Cardinal Ratzinger's words.[22] The book would set forth the faith of the Church rather than mere theological opinions or arguments or products of research.

---

[20] The members of the Commission for the Catechism for the Universal Church were listed in *Origins*, NC Documentary Service, December 19, 1985.

[21] Quoted in Ratzinger and Schönborn, *Introduction*, 19.

[22] Ibid., 17.

It was the commission that also decided that the book would be divided into the same four basic parts as the Church's earlier universal catechism, the *Catechism of the Council of Trent*. These four parts, or "pillars", as found in the table of contents of the completed volume, are: (1) "The Profession of Faith" (Creed); (2) "The Celebration of the Christian Mystery" (Sacraments); (3) "Life in Christ" (Commandments); and (4) "Christian Prayer" (expanded from the Our Father alone).

This arrangement was criticized from the outset (especially by those who did not want any catechism at all); but its usefulness had long since proven itself in the *Roman Catechism* and its offshoots. As was immediately realized and pointed out, the arrangement corresponds to what the Church believes, what the Church celebrates, what she lives, and how she prays. It proved possible to include and explain everything essential to the faith within this overall arrangement, as anyone who has read or worked with the completed book will be aware. For example, treatment of the virtues, as well as Jesus' two great commandments of love, turned out to be easily subsumed under the general heading of the Commandments.

The Commission further decided that the new catechism would not be what in post-Tridentine times came to be called a *catechismus minor*, a "small catechism", that is, what we today would consider a doctrinal textbook for immediate use in catechesis in parishes, schools, and homes. The *Baltimore Catechism*, with its question-and-answer format, is an example of this traditional type of "small catechism".

But the new universal catechism being planned by the commission would be a "great catechism", or *catechismus maior*, like the *Catechism of the Council of Trent* (which was "great", by the way, in its realization as well as in its genre, as the present work also is). And just as the Council of Trent had specified that the catechism it mandated should be addressed primarily to parish priests, *ad parochos*, to aid them in their task of teaching the faithful, so the commission decided that the new universal catechism should be addressed in the first instance to *bishops*, the principal teachers of the faith in each diocese. Bishops are, at the same time, the ones responsible for organizing and overseeing the Church's entire education enterprise in their dioceses, an enterprise commonly extending from a diocesan education superintendent or director, through the pastors, priests, and teachers, down to the newest volunteer CCD teacher in the parish.

The commission hoped that by committing the completed work to the episcopate, greater unity in the faith, as well as in the proclamation and transmission of the faith, would be fostered. The level of the episcopate is the logical level where such unity could most likely be realized.

At the same time, however, the commission in no way intended that use of the *Catechism of the Catholic Church* should be *limited* to bishops or to their professional specialists in religious education. Pope John Paul II himself has made this clear on more than one occasion. For example, in promulgating the *Catechism* on December 7, 1992, the Holy Father made a point of specifying that it is "a gift for all. . . . In regard to this text, no one should feel a stranger, excluded, or distant. In fact, it is addressed to everyone because it concerns the Lord of all, Jesus Christ."[23]

In another address to participants in a workshop on

---

[23] Pope John Paul II, "Catechism Is Truly a Gift to the Church", December 7, 1992, reprinted in *Reflections on the Catechism of the Catholic Church*, comp. Rev. James P. Socias (Chicago: Midwest Theological Forum, 1993), 43.

preparing local catechisms, on April 29, 1993, John Paul II reiterated that the *Catechism* was "addressed to all and must reach everyone. . . . It cannot be considered merely as a stage preceding the drafting of local catechisms, but is destined for all the faithful who have the capacity to read, understand it, and assimilate it in their Christian living."[24]

In September 1993, on one of a number of other occasions when he returned to this subject, the Pope told a group of bishops from Western Canada who were in Rome for their *ad limina* visit that: "It is not just for pastors and specialists—as has been shown by its enthusiastic reception by the laity in many countries—but is destined for all sectors of the Church."[25] It is hard to escape the conclusion that John Paul II believes the *Catechism* is for—everybody.

Cardinal Ratzinger made the same point in his account of the work of the Commission for the Catechism for the Universal Church. "This could not mean", he wrote

that the Catechism would be reserved merely for a "select few", for such an interpretation would not have corresponded to the renewed understanding of the Church and of the common responsibility of all her members taught us by the Second Vatican Council. The laity, too, are responsible co-representatives of the Church's faith. They not only receive the teaching of the Church but also hand it on and develop it through their *sensus fidei*. They guarantee both the continuity and vitality of the faith. In the crisis of the postconciliar period, it was precisely this *sensus fidei* which made a decisive contribution to the discernment of spirits. For that reason it was a matter of principle that

---

[24] In Ibid., 54.

[25] Pope John Paul II, "To the Bishops of Western Canada *ad Limina Apostolorum*", *L'Osservatore Romano* (English Edition), September 22, 1993.

the work also be accessible to interested laymen as a tool of their Christian maturity and of their responsibility for the faith. They are not merely instructed from above but can also say themselves: This is our faith.[26]

The idea expressed by some that with the *Catechism* Rome was trying to "impose" something from above upon an unwilling Church becomes highly implausible in the light of how the Commission for the Catechism for the Universal Church actually operated. The Commission saw itself as, at least in one important sense, acting for and in the name of average Catholics desirous of being able to affirm "this is our faith", in response to contrary modern affirmations based on knowledge or expertise of whatever kind.

Having decided that the new catechism it was commissioned to produce would be addressed to the bishops of the world in the first instance, the commission went on to make another important decision, namely, that the book would be essentially *written* by bishops as well. For this purpose a group of bishops from around the world was selected; it was a group that was almost as broadly representative of the Church as the membership of the commission itself or of the world Synod of Bishops. As things turned out, scarcely a word of the completed book would actually be written *in* Rome!

The bishops selected for drawing up the text included Bishop José Estepa Llaurens, military ordinary for Spain and Bishop Alessandro Maggiolini of Como, Italy, who were made responsible for the first part on the Creed; Bishop Jorge Medina Estevez of Valparaíso, Chile, and Bishop Estanislao E. Karlic of Paraná, Argentina, who were given

---

[26] Ratzinger and Schönborn, *Introduction*, 18.

responsibility for the second part on the Sacraments; and Bishop Jean Honoré of Tours, France, and Bishop David Konstant of Leeds, England, who were assigned to draft the third part on the Commandments, or the Christian moral life.

An American Archbishop, William J. Levada of Portland, Oregon and later of San Francisco, was the seventh bishop-writer commissioned to work on the text; he was given primary responsibility for the index. Finally, a general editor to pull the whole text together and insure uniformity was found to be necessary, and this task was confided to a Dominican priest, later auxiliary bishop, then Archbishop of Vienna, Christoph Schönborn, of the University of Fribourg.[27]

Thus, eight diocesan Catholic bishops were the primary authors (and general editor) of the *Catechism of the Catholic Church*. Henceforth they were referred to as the "editorial committee". They enjoyed expert theological and exegetical advice, of course. In particular, a college of consultors consisting of some forty experts was named to assist the project. Still, we should not lose sight of the fact that the primary authors were working bishops, not one of whom, obviously, was an inhabitant of any ivory tower. Rather, they were pastors with immediate responsibilities for the shepherding of souls.

Choosing actual working bishops to write the *Catechism* was a singularly appropriate decision. When we consider that, as Catholics believe and as the *Catechism* confirms (CCC 880), Jesus Christ himself instituted the episcopacy and intended it as the necessary bulwark of his living Church, we can only consider it a remarkably providential sign that,

---

[27] The names of the writing committee were listed in *Origins*, NC Documentary Service, November 5, 1987.

in the present crisis of faith and of the transmission of the faith that currently obtains in our world and afflicts our Church, it should have been *bishops*, at various levels and from a number of countries, who played such a vital and predominant part in the production of the *Catechism of the Catholic Church*.

The *Catechism* itself, of course, is manifestly one of the providential instruments created to help provide the *remedy* for our double crisis of faith and of the transmission of the faith; and it was no one but the bishops of the Church who produced it: *Nihil sine episcopo*; "nothing without the bishop". St. Ignatius of Antioch had said it before the Church was a hundred years old; it remains just as true today.

It evidently did not prove possible, however, to find a bishop in a timely enough fashion to write the fourth part of the text on the subject of Prayer; and so a French-born priest now living in Lebanon, the Rev. Jean Corbon, a member of the International Theological Commission, was recruited to carry out this indispensable task. He did so in the midst of bombardments in the civil-war-ridden city of Beirut, from which he sometimes had to take refuge in his basement; it is amazing to reflect that his beautiful, serene text on prayer could have been produced under such conditions.[28]

Another interesting aspect concerning the writing of the *Catechism* was how the original text came to be written in French. An early outline of the book was drafted in Latin in 1987 and submitted for comments to the forty consultors around the world. However, this text had apparently been translated *into* Latin from the modern languages in which the writers most naturally worked; and it created as

---

[28] See Ratzinger and Schönborn, *Introduction*, 23.

many problems of understanding and communication as it solved.

It turned out that French proved to be the one language in which all the writers could express themselves with at least some degree of proficiency (and also, no doubt, communicate with the commission and with each other) as successive drafts were produced and revised. So the decision to write the text in French was an essentially practical decision, which had the further advantage, as Cardinal Ratzinger pointed out, that the Church's final, official text in Latin would be able to benefit from having first been produced in French and translated into the other modern languages.[29]

An interesting historical comparison is to be found in the fact that the final version of the *Catechism of the Council of Trent* was also principally written by diocesan bishops—the bishops of the Italian sees of Lanciano, Modena, and Zara —assisted by a Dominican theologian as editorial secretary! Moreover, this Tridentine work was also originally written in the vernacular, in Italian, its definitive Latin text having been produced later by a Renaissance humanist and Latinist. The overall editorial work was supervised by none other than St. Charles Borromeo, nephew of Pope Pius IV.[30]

This original French text of the *Catechism of the Catholic Church* was the one approved by the commission on February 14, 1992; approved by the Holy Father on June 25, 1992; promulgated by him on October 11, 1992, with the apostolic constitution *Fidei Depositum*; and then finally publicly promulgated by him on December 7, 1992. All the other versions in various languages were translated from this text.

---

[29] Ibid., 24.
[30] See Fr. Raúl Lanzetti, "The New Roman Catechism Compared to the 'Roman Catechism' of Trent", in Socias, *Reflections*, 199–205.

It is worth recording that, between 1987 and 1992, this text went through ten separate drafts, which the editorial commission of the Holy See curiously styled "projects".[31]

In particular, what was officially called the "revised project"—the fourth overall draft—was sent out to all the Catholic bishops of the world in November 1989, asking that their comments and suggested amendments be sent in by May 1990 (later extended to October 1990). This was a simply massive "consultation", perhaps unique in the history of the Church. Replies were received from 197 individual bishops, twenty-eight episcopal conferences, twenty-three groups of bishops other than episcopal conferences, twelve theological institutes, sixteen offices of the Holy See, and sixty-two "others". A total of more than twenty-four thousand suggested amendments were sent in, every one of which was individually examined and evaluated.[32]

Anyone who studied or worked on this draft text when it was sent out for consultation—as both the present authors did—can verify how often the suggestions sent in were adopted and the text of what became the final, definitive *Catechism* thereby improved.

Thus, once again, the entire enterprise of producing the *Catechism of the Catholic Church*, far from being something "out of Rome", turned out to be an essentially collegial work carried out by a group of bishop-writers with the active support of the Catholic bishops of the whole world, themselves assisted by theologians and other knowledgeable collaborators. It is imperative not to lose sight of this fact of what

---

[31] Editorial Commission of the *Catechism of the Catholic Church*, *Informative Dossier* (Vatican City: Libreria Editrice Vaticana, June 25, 1992).

[32] Ibid., 17–19; 26.

we may almost term *collective* authorship as we proceed to examine and evaluate how the *Catechism* has been and is being received.

Moreover, in the act of producing this *Catechism*, which they thus collectively produced, the Catholic bishops demonstrated their total and entire understanding of what the Catholic faith *is*, and how it should and must be taught. As the First Vatican Council expressed it: "For the teaching of faith, which God has revealed, has not been proposed as a philosophical discovery to be perfected by human ingenuity, but as a divine deposit handed over to the Spouse of Christ to be guarded faithfully and expounded infallibly."[33]

In *Fidei Depositum*, the apostolic constitution by which he promulgated the *Catechism*, Pope John Paul II solemnly asked that this product of such Herculean efforts and exhaustive consultations be received by the faithful at all levels in the same spirit of faith and hope in which the Church hierarchy had conceived, planned, written, and proclaimed it:

> I ask the Church's Pastors and the Christian faithful to receive this *Catechism* in a spirit of communion and to use it assiduously in fulfilling their mission of proclaiming the faith and calling people to the Gospel life. This *Catechism* is given to them that it may be a sure and authentic reference text for teaching Catholic doctrine and particularly for preparing local catechisms. It is also offered to all the faithful who wish to deepen their knowledge of the unfathomable riches of salvation (cf. Jn 8:32). It is meant to support ecumenical efforts that are moved by the holy desire for the unity of all Christians, showing carefully the

---

[33] Vatican Council I, dogmatic constitution *Dei Filius*, on the Catholic Faith, April 24, 1870, chapter four, in John F. Broderick, S.J., *Documents of Vatican Council I* (Collegeville, Minn.: Liturgical Press, 1971), 48.

content and wondrous harmony of the Catholic faith. The *Catechism of the Catholic Church*, lastly, is offered to every individual who asks us to give an account of the hope that is in us (cf. 1 Pet 3:15) and who wants to know what the Catholic Church believes.[34]

In other words, the *Catechism* is henceforth intended to serve as the authoritative, authentic statement of what the Catholic faith is for as far ahead as we can see into the future.[35]

# IV

Now that we have the *Catechism of the Catholic Church*, what is it that we have? The Holy Father has stated it very plainly: the book is nothing else but a statement of "what the Catholic Church believes". In the very same apostolic constitution *Fidei Depositum* in which he promulgated it, the Pope further described it as "a statement of the Church's faith and of Catholic doctrine, attested to or illumined by Sacred Scripture, Apostolic Tradition and the Church's Magisterium. I declare it to be a valid and legitimate instrument for ecclesial communion and sure norm for teaching the faith."[36]

What could be plainer—or stronger? We must continue to bear in mind both the force and the solemnity of the Holy Father's words about the *Catechism* here as we go on to review, in the chapters that follow, the ways in which some

---

[34] Pope John Paul II, apostolic constitution *Fidei Depositum*, October 11, 1992, in Socias, *Reflections*, 27–34.

[35] The remainder of this chapter appeared in somewhat modified form as an article in *Crisis* magazine, June 1995.

[36] John Paul II, *Fidei Depositum*.

in the Church have nevertheless found themselves able "to receive" this document, in spite of the force of the Pope's solemn words.

It is beyond dispute, however, that what we have in this *Catechism* is an entirely faithful, as well as remarkably clear and intelligible, modern compendium of "the faith once delivered to the saints" (Jude 3), as it has developed over the centuries and has been faithfully guarded and handed down by "our mother the Church" (CCC 171):

> Through the centuries in so many languages, cultures, peoples, and nations, the Church has constantly confessed this one faith, received from the one Lord, transmitted by one Baptism, and grounded in the conviction that all people have only one God and Father (CCC 172).

It sets forth the tenets of the faith as contained in Scripture, tradition, and the Magisterium, along with the essentials of what follows from these tenets, in its short and lucid 2865 numbered paragraphs. Included in these numbered paragraphs is a veritable treasure trove of quotations from the Fathers, doctors, and saints of the Church; true gems are to be found on page after page. For example:

—St. Augustine (the most frequently quoted individual author): "I would not believe in the Gospel had not the authority of the Catholic Church moved me" (CCC 119).

—St. Thérèse of Lisieux: "If the Church was a body composed of different members, it couldn't lack the noblest of all: it must have a heart, and a heart burning with love." (CCC 826).

—St. John Chrysostom: "Priests have received from God a power that he has given neither to angels nor archangels" (CCC 983).

—St. Gregory Nazianzen: "We must remember God more often than we draw breath" (CCC 2697).

But the *Catechism* is much more than a collection of sayings, however true and inspiring; it is an orderly and systematic presentation of the whole Catholic faith. Archbishop Schönborn points out that, like the *Catechism of the Council of Trent* before it, its four parts really represent a magnificent "diptych", in which around 60 percent of the book (Creed and sacraments) is devoted to the works of God on behalf of man, while around 40 percent (Commandments and prayer) cover man's necessary response to God. "God is first; grace is first", Archbishop Schönborn concludes. "This is the true hierarchy of truth."[37]

One very interesting difference between this contemporary *Catechism* and the Tridentine one, however, is that while both books do devote around 60 percent of their total space to the *magnalia Dei*, the marvelous things God has done for us, the *Catechism of the Council of Trent* allots 37 percent of its total space to the Sacraments and only 22 percent to the Creed. This proportion is approximately reversed in the new *Catechism*, which devotes only 23 percent to the Sacraments and 39 percent to the Creed, or beliefs.

This difference is entirely explicable when we reflect that, while Trent was reacting to the challenge the Protestant Reformation posed to the Sacraments and the sacramental system, today what we have is, precisely, a fundamental crisis of faith or belief. The new *Catechism* has accordingly not only not failed to address the fundamental problem we do, in fact, face today, the question of the truth of the faith; it has done so in an admirably sensitive manner that indicates a lively awareness of the difficulties faith encounters today.

Even a quick reading will confirm that the *Catechism* has squarely and creditably addressed and responded to the

---

[37] Ratzinger and Schönborn, *Introduction*, 49.

problems of disbelief and dissent that we face in the Church today. The text does not normally say that this is what it is doing. It is not argumentative; it simply does it. The *Catechism* explicitly upholds and reaffirms virtually every single point of faith and morals that has been disputed by the theological dissenters in the Church over the past generation and more.

The following represent only some of today's "disputed questions", on which the *Catechism* invariably upholds the Church's traditional teaching: Original Sin (CCC 388–89); the existence and power of Satan (CCC 391, 635); the existence of angels (CCC 327); the fact that Satan is an angel (CCC 2864); Purgatory (CCC 958, 1030–31), not to speak of the four last things ever to be remembered, which we once learned about in childhood, namely, death, judgment, heaven, and hell (CCC 633, 1022); the perpetual virginity of Mary (CCC 499–501); the teaching authority of the Church (CCC 953); the strict obligation to profess the faith and accept the teaching authority of the Church (CCC 3, 14, 892, 1270, 1466, 1816), which, not incidentally, simply excludes modern-style "theological dissent"; the truth that the end can never justify the means (CCC 1753); Transubstantiation (CCC 1376); the institution of the seven Sacraments by Christ (CCC 1114); the limitation of sacred ordination to baptized males (CCC 1577); the truth that priests are not "delegates" of the people (CCC 1533); the indissolubility of the marriage bond (CCC 1614–16); the prohibition of remarriage after divorce (CCC 1649–50), of the use of contraception (CCC 2370), and of homosexual acts (CCC 2357), and so on.

These represent only a few of the traditional Church teachings that the *Catechism* unhesitatingly reaffirms, even though certain supposedly up-to-date theologians and others—often apparently remaining "in good standing" in the Church all the while—have tried to convince the faithful that these same points have been "changed" since Vatican II.

Of course there never was any confusion at the top about any of these teachings. The supreme pontiffs of our day, John XXIII, Paul VI, and even John Paul I, every bit as much as John Paul II, have never failed to teach the authentic doctrine of the faith, usually in a clear and exemplary way. The bishops, too, have quite consistently issued excellent statements concerning what the Catholic Church continues to teach and stand for.

But there has nevertheless been more than one persistent problem: How much of the official teachings of the popes and the bishops ever really filtered down to the average Catholic? Or how much got hopelessly distorted by the media in the telling, often with the help of dissenting "Catholic" commentators? Or how much of what Catholics always knew perfectly well was Church teaching nevertheless came to be imagined or represented as having been "changed" at or after Vatican II? Or how much simply got lost amid the general cacophony of dissident modern voices?

Whatever the confusion about all these things over virtually an entire generation, the publication of the *Catechism of the Catholic Church* now does inaugurate the possibility of a wholly new era. There no longer need be, nor should there be, any question or dispute about what the Catholic Church in fact does hold and teach, for the *Catechism* now provides the indispensable "point of reference" about this: anybody can look it up! The *Catechism* is accessible to everyone, and hence no one need be any longer in doubt.

This is as true of questions of faith as it is of questions of morals; it is as true in the public forum as it is of what is being taught in Catholic schools and CCD courses: again, anybody can look it up. (Concerning religious instruction, there no longer need be any dispute about, for example, memorization; the *Catechism* strongly recommends it (CCC 24), the only "teaching method" it does endorse, as a matter of fact.)

In adverting to all the confusion and dissent about Catholic teaching in our time, we are not principally concerned with accusing or pointing fingers at those who have helped bring the teaching and public affirmation of the Catholic faith in our day to such a generally low estate. It is the *Catechism of the Catholic Church* itself, in effect, that "accuses" and "points fingers" at them. The *Catechism* does this by reaffirming, unequivocally, the very things that not a few of the new theologians, new exegetes, and new religious-education gurus have been so diligently trying to downgrade or deny throughout the postconciliar period.

But now the new catechesis has been proven to be *wrong*; its failure has been *shown*—dramatically—by the issuance of a new fundamental teaching instrument that reaffirms and reenforces all the doctrinal truths of the Catholic faith that so many parents, pastors, and teachers had been trying in vain to get restored to catechesis for so long, only to be put off or put down, most of the time, with some such sibylline pronouncement from one of the new religious educators as, "Oh, we don't teach like that any more."

But the *Catechism of the Catholic Church does* teach "like that." Precisely. The *Catechism* has declined to buy into the brave new Church. Instead, it has reaffirmed the real Church, the permanent Church, the Church of all time—which is also the Church of the future.

Among its unequivocal reaffirmations, the *Catechism* reminds us that the Catholic faithful have a *right* to be instructed in the true faith (CCC 2037). The promulgation and diffusion of the *Catechism* itself thus constitutes a giant step forward in making possible for the faithful around the world the authentic instruction that is called for. The great importance of this document, therefore, resides not only in the fact that it so clearly and so comprehensively states the faith; it also lies in the fact that it is basically accessible to anybody who can read. It might often profit from, but it in no way strictly requires, the mediation of "experts". Again, anybody can look it up.

## V

A final word concerning the importance of the *Catechism of the Catholic Church* will complete this chapter, and it is this: just as the *Catechism* makes the traditional Catholic faith itself accessible again, so it also makes accessible, finally, the Second Vatican Council! In a very important sense, this book is the Catechism of Vatican II, just as the *Catechism of the Council of Trent* of 1566 was the book of the sixteenth-century Tridentine council.

Pope John Paul II himself has described the *Catechism* as "the most mature and complete fruit of the Council's teaching; [it] presents it in the rich framework of the whole of ecclesial Tradition."[38] The book, although drawing upon "the whole of the Church's Tradition", nevertheless also expressly describes itself (CCC 11) as aiming to present "an organic synthesis of the essential contents of the Catholic doctrine as regards both faith and morals, *in the light of the Second Vatican Council*" (emphasis added). The *Cate-*

---

[38] John Paul II, Homily at St. Mary Major, December 8, 1992; quoted by Archbishop Jan P. Schotte, "*Catechism's* Origin and Content Reflect Episcopal Collegiality", in Socias, *Reflections*, 67.

*chism* singles out the Council, in other words, as one of its own principal sources. After sacred Scripture itself, in fact, Vatican II is the single most frequently quoted source for the *Catechism*'s teachings. John Paul II concludes *Fidei Depositum*, the official document promulgating the *Catechism*, significantly, with the words: "Given October 11, 1992, the thirtieth anniversary of the opening of the Second Vatican Ecumenical Council."

All this is important. Vatican Council II, the twenty-first general council of the Catholic Church, even though it was itself one of the most significant Church events of the entire twentieth century—General Charles de Gaulle, while president of France, once remarked that it was the most important event of any kind in the twentieth century!—has nevertheless also been one of the most misunderstood. In the experience of the average Catholic it has also been, too often, a clumsily misapplied event, and hence it still remains widely misunderstood.

Students of the history of the Church can make an excellent case that Vatican Council II was not only necessary, it was long overdue. The work of the First Vatican Council, after all, had never been formally completed, having been interrupted by the entry of an Italian occupying army into Rome in September 1870. Vatican I was never either reconvened or officially closed. Several subsequent popes thought of reconvening it, but what finally happened, as everybody knows, is that Pope John XXIII decided, in 1959, to convene an entirely new council, which became Vatican II.

Vatican II, as it actually took place, had two kinds of results. It had "official" results, embodied in the sixteen documents issued by the Council, and in the further legitimate and "official" reforms that issued from *them*, enacted by the authority of the Church. Unfortunately, it also had some other, rather dramatic, "unofficial" results as well, results that arose at least partly out of the fact that certain liberal elements in the Church desirous of "change" seized upon what they called "the spirit of Vatican II" in order to import into the Church's life many things the Council had neither mandated nor called for.

Meanwhile, many traditionally minded "good Catholics", especially in North America, had never really seen the point of the Council anyway. For them the Church seemed to be "just fine" as she was, and no "changes" were considered necessary. When, however, what appeared to be almost a mania for change for the sake of change then came to seem to be the principal result of the Council, it is perhaps not surprising that some of these Catholics reacted against what they understood "the Council" to be.

Indeed, some traditionally minded Catholics, even today, continue to hearken back nostalgically to the preconciliar days when the Church had indeed seemed "just fine"— when there were more reverent and better attended Masses, sounder teaching, stricter moral practice, more respect for authority, conversions up, priestly and religious vocations up, fewer divorces, and so on. It is not terribly hard to understand, in fact, a preference for the Church as she was in those days, before she was beset with all the problems that have obviously plagued her since.

It does not matter that many of these problems stem as much as anything from the intrusion of the modern culture of the world into the Church. The fact remains that in certain important respects the Church no longer appears to be what she appeared to be before the Council; *post hoc, ergo propter hoc!*

Moreover, it remains true that all of the changes in Church practices legitimately voted by the bishops at Vatican II *did*—and necessarily so—mean the inauguration of an official "era of change" in the Church. In the course of this particular era of change, however, a number of other agendas besides Vatican II's official agenda were also unfortunately introduced into the life of the Church. Too often these alien agendas were successfully promoted by various interested parties working in such areas as theology, liturgy, catechetics, and the like. Some of these same alien agendas are still present in today's Church.

Much of the confusion in the Church over the past quarter century, in other words, including especially that brought about by the new catechesis itself, came in under the guise of changes supposedly mandated by Vatican II, whether or not that was actually the case. Vatican II, again, *did* mandate many changes. It did not, however, mandate all of those that have actually occurred, nor, certainly, was it responsible for the *way* in which some of them occurred. The new catechesis, though it is demonstrably incompatible with the doctrines of Vatican II, was nevertheless successfully represented and widely implemented as something that had indeed been mandated by the Council.

The average Catholic, of course, could not, and, generally speaking, cannot, distinguish between changes legitimately mandated by proper authority and changes introduced on their own by zealots and innovators working within the Church's own structural "system". Indeed, it has sometimes even seemed that many pastors and bishops have sometimes had trouble distinguishing between changes that are legitimate and those that are not, according to the authentic mind of Vatican II as set forth in its official enactments.

Doctrinally speaking, of course, Vatican II changed nothing, even while it clarified much and signaled important and legitimate doctrinal developments. Few of the faithful, however, have ever directly studied the sixteen documents of Vatican II in depth. Instead, Catholics, out of long-standing habit, have naturally tended to rely on their priests and theologians to interpret and implement all the changes for them. Consequently, depending upon whether the Church's official Vatican II agenda or a dissenting variant of it was being implemented in any particular case, Catholics generally have gotten widely varying versions of just what it was the Council actually taught and mandated and entailed. In fact, some of this confusion continues to reign. Discerning what is authentic according to the true mind of the Church is not always easy.

In such a confused situation, it is perhaps not surprising that some sincere Catholics could even come to question the legitimacy of Vatican II itself. At the very least, it is understandable that they might have reacted quite negatively to certain things reputed to result from "Vatican II". A few traditionalist Catholics even imagine, apparently, that the whole conciliar and postconciliar experience has been nothing but a bad dream and that somehow, some day, in their view, the Church will just wake up and restore the Latin Mass and the other practices of what is remembered as the Church of Pope Pius XII (or imagined to be such by those who never experienced it) back before all the unpleasantness began.

This "traditionalist" view, of course, is quite untenable: there is no way that Vatican II can be considered anything but an entirely legitimate ecumenical council of the Catholic Church. Its doctrinal teachings are guaranteed by the assistance of the Holy Spirit promised to the extraordinary Magisterium of the Church, and its legitimate practical mandates are incumbent upon all loyal Catholics. All the supreme pontiffs of our day, from John XXIII through John Paul II, have understood and accepted the Council in precisely these terms.

And with the publication of the *Catechism of the Catholic Church*, it is now possible for the most traditionally minded of Catholics to be able to *see* how Vatican II really fits into the long and inspired history of the Catholic Church. Up to now the sixteen documents of Vatican II have been largely *terra incognita* for too many Catholics, who have generally reacted to the Council more or less according to how it happened to impinge upon their lives in their parishes. Now, however, these sixteen documents of Vatican II have been marvelously integrated into the *Catechism*'s systematic presentation of the Church's whole faith and life.

Dozens, indeed hundreds, of individual *Catechism* entries consist mostly, if not entirely, of direct quotations from the documents of Vatican II (for example, CCC 51, 781, 898, 909, 913, 954, 1163, 1422, 1555, 1667, 1776, 2371, 2527, and so on). Over and over again, the reader is struck by how aptly and pertinently a reference to or even a direct quotation from the Council does enshrine the Church's perennial teaching on this or that point of faith and morals.

Not the least important thing about the *Catechism of the Catholic Church*, then, is that it has finally and at long last made the Second Vatican Council accessible to the average Catholic. The late Pope Paul VI liked to refer to Vatican II as "the catechism of our times", but too many Catholics did not understand what he meant, and a few of them still do not.

Now, however, the means exist to enable us to begin to see how it all fits together. The true renewal of the Church originally envisaged by Pope John XXIII and enacted by the Council, so often sidetracked and even derailed by dissident agendas within the Church, can now finally be carried out in reality. With this *Catechism*, Catholics can now turn confidently toward a future that must necessarily include a program for the evangelization (including, in many places, the reevangelization) of the world. This, after all, is fundamentally what Vatican Council II was supposed to be all about, as Pope John XXIII originally conceived it. The *Catechism*, marvelous gift to the Church that it represents, cannot but be one of the providential instruments that we now possess in order to aid us in this task of evangelization to which we are all called.

# CHAPTER THREE

# The Initial Reception of the Catechism

## I

The amazing popular reception accorded to the *Catechism of the Catholic Church* in the United States, as shown by the huge volume of sales that the book quickly racked up, was in some ways duplicated by the *official* reception given to the *Catechism* here, notably, but not exclusively, by the hierarchy. Even before the English translation of it was available, the new *Catechism* had become the subject of numerous articles, lectures, and conferences; many Catholic organizations devoted special meetings and conventions to it; it was the topic of the hour.

There was even more than a flurry of press and media interest in this new compendium of Catholic doctrine, although some of it went no deeper than commenting on the new "list of sins" the book was said to contain.

By and large, the position and tone adopted toward the *Catechism* by most Catholic organizations and publications were respectful. Once it became clear that the *Catechism* was definitely coming out, even many of those who had earlier opposed it did not continue their public opposition. This was true even of some who had criticized both the idea of any catechism at all and the draft of the work in progress that had been sent out to the bishops of the world for comment in late 1989. With the promulgation of the *Catechism*, many early critics were suddenly to be found back in the mainstream again, "loyal sons and daughters of the Church".

In subsequent chapters, we shall be looking closely, and more than a little critically, at just how sincere some of the apparent public "conversions" to the cause of the *Catechism* really were. In any case, much of the newly minted favorable comment on the book rather quickly gave way to criticism again, as soon as it became clear that the Holy See was not going to release the original English translation of the *Catechism*.

This original translation was made using the so-called "inclusive language" favored by radical feminists, that is, language that avoids the use of "he" or "him" in a generic sense referring to all human beings rather than just to adult males. This explosive—as it turned out—issue of "inclusive language" was the primary thing that delayed the appearance of the *Catechism* in English for more than a year. This issue will be examined in more detail in the next chapter.

Regarding the general reception of the *Catechism*, the attitude of the U.S. bishops was almost wholly positive. In 1992, the bishops established a special subcommittee of the Committee on Education of the United States Catholic Conference (USCC) in order to handle the implementation of the *Catechism* in this country. It was this USCC subcommittee that made the arrangements for the publication and marketing of the book in the United States. The same subcommittee also prepared information packets about it, both for the media and for interested Church organizations and institutions around the country; it commissioned the preparation of articles and other material about the book and encouraged various organizations to devote their conferences and conventions to it as well; and, finally, in keeping with the key role played by bishops in the *Catechism* project from the beginning, the subcommittee organized an all-day symposium on it for all the American bishops which was held in conjunction with their regular June 1993 meeting in New Orleans.

On the episcopal level, then, there was manifestly no visible neglect or downplaying of the importance of the *Catechism*. On the contrary, its appearance was treated as an ecclesial event of the first and greatest importance, and the bishops were clearly recognized and identified as the foremost interested parties in all that pertained to it. Most bishops appeared to take their role quite seriously in this regard.

"This emphasis on the bishops as principal recipients of the *Catechism*", implementation subcommittee chairman Bishop Edward T. Hughes of Metuchen, New Jersey, explained, "affirms our own responsibility as chief teachers in the Church and reenforces some of the concerns most of us have had about our somewhat limited role in the catechetical procedure. At times we may have felt that the content and methodology of our catechetical approaches were not really responsive to our leadership and teaching." Bishop Hughes further emphasized very clearly that his subcommittee's charge was "to plan for the implementation of the *Catechism*, not to debate its contents".[1]

The New Orleans symposium on the *Catechism* organized by the implementation subcommittee for all the American

---

[1] Bishop Edward T. Hughes, Chairman, Subcommittee for the Implementation of the *Catechism*, USCC, "Report to the Spring General Meeting of Bishops, June 22, 1992", *The Living Light*, summer 1993, 78.

bishops in the summer of 1993 was addressed in person by then Bishop Christoph Schönborn, secretary of the editorial committee of the *Catechism*. This same address was later reprinted in *The Living Light* and later still appeared as a chapter in the *Introduction to the Catechism of the Catholic Church*.[2] In it the Dominican theologian and Austrian prelate explained among other things how the *Catechism* was based on "the hierarchy of truths" in a true and exact sense. The issue of the "hierarchy of truths" had been a big issue with some American theologians who had opposed the universal catechism project; it was alleged that the draft *Catechism* had failed to respect this principle.

Bishop Schönborn explained the issue admirably to the U.S. bishops at the New Orleans symposium on the *Catechism*: that there is such a "hierarchy of truths" does not mean in any sense that some truths are "less true" than supposed "essentials" of the faith (and might possibly, therefore, be downplayed or even laid aside). This latter idea, as a matter of fact, had been a *very* common misconception in certain theological and catechetical circles in the United States.

Bishop Schönborn explained, however, that the hierarchy of truths "simply means that the different truths of the faith are 'organized' around a center"; it involves the organic structure of the multiple and complex truths—all true!—that make up the whole of the Christian faith. The Austrian bishop explained that the *Catechism of the Catholic*

---

[2] Christoph Schönborn, "Major Themes and Underlying Principles of the *Catechism of the Catholic Church*", *The Living Light*, fall 1993; and in Joseph Cardinal Ratzinger and Christoph Schönborn, *Introduction to the Catechism of the Catholic Church* (San Francisco: Ignatius Press, 1994), 37–57.

*Church* was consciously organized around the central truths concerning the mysteries of the Blessed Trinity and of Jesus Christ, true God and true man, and also around the fourfold truths of the Creed, the Sacraments, the Commandments, and Prayer.

In the conclusion to his address, Bishop Schönborn quoted the *Catechism* itself to the effect that it "emphasizes the exposition of doctrine. It seeks to help deepen the understanding of faith. . . . It is oriented toward the maturing of that faith, its putting down roots in personal life, and its shining forth in personal conduct" (CCC 23). The challenge of catechesis, he told the American bishops, is to combine "the objective truth of the Church's doctrines and the intensely personal character of the believer's possession of them".

No more pertinent point could have been made to an American gathering, even a gathering of bishops. In the United States, for more than a quarter of a century, the catechetical establishment in place had been vainly trying to produce a "maturing of . . . faith", and a rooting of it in personal life, *without* adequate reference to doctrine and, hence, to truth. Bishop Schönborn properly concluded, however, that "doctrine is not opposed to life. How can we live without understanding?"

Ironically, Bishop Schönborn shared a platform in New Orleans with one of the pillars of the U.S. catechetical establishment: the Warren Blanding Professor of Religion at the Catholic University of America, Fr. Berard L. Marthaler, O.F.M. Conv., a noted American catechetical theoretician, opponent of "book-centered catechesis", and public dissenter from the papal encyclical *Humanæ Vitæ*. In the mysterious way in which organizations sometimes go on blindly doing what they are accustomed to do regardless of new circumstances, Fr. Marthaler was one of those chosen to brief the U.S. bishops on the new *Catechism*, even though he had been among those most visible in his public opposition to it.[3]

Fr. Marthaler was no doubt chosen for this role despite his opposition to the document—and his record of public dissent from Catholic teaching—simply because he was one of the most prominent and visible catechetical "experts in the field". Reliance on, if not actual subservience to, presumed professional expertise has practically become a superstition in the United States today and seems to take precedence over nearly every other consideration. What other explanation is there for inviting an opponent of the *Catechism* and an open dissenter from Catholic teaching to address the official teachers of the faith?

In his remarks to the bishops, Fr. Marthaler did not fail to inform their excellencies that he and his colleagues would certainly take a look at the *Catechism*: "The catechetical community will *study* the pages of the *Catechism* to *see* the light that it will throw on a whole series of questions that affect programs and methods" (emphasis added).[4] No doubt the day had already passed when catechetical professionals might ever feel obliged to accept anything on the authority of the Church, even though their very mission derives from this Church. Thus, they would have to "study" the *Catechism* and "see", according to Fr. Marthaler. The new catechists themselves would be the ones to decide what is

---

[3] See the chapter Fr. Marthaler contributed to the *Universal Catechism Reader*, an open and savage assault on the draft *Catechism* by a number of the prominent members of the U.S. theological and catechetical establishments; the book was edited by Fr. Thomas J. Reese, S.J., and published by HarperCollins in San Francisco in 1990.

[4] Berard L. Marthaler, O.F.M. Conv., "The *Catechism of the Catholic Church* in the U.S. Context", *The Living Light*, fall 1993, 70.

suitable, and what can be accepted, out of all that Catholic bishops had labored so hard to produce for the whole Church.

Fr. Marthaler was nothing if not consistent here in reflecting the typical basic attitude of the new theologians and the new catechists. The question is whether anybody in his audience of bishops ever took notice of this basic attitude or caught on to what he really represented.

The other speakers at this symposium organized by the USCC's Subcommittee for the Implementation of the *Catechism* were considerably more positive about the merits of the document. Bishop Donald W. Wuerl of Pittsburgh, who had been one of the forty expert consultors during the drafting phase,[5] saw the completed work as "an instrument that facilitates the supervisory role of the bishop", both as teacher and overseer of the catechesis in his diocese. Bishop Wuerl urged his brother bishops to take a personal and active part in implementing the *Catechism* in each diocese, both in the establishment of catechetical criteria based on the *Catechism* and in the training of teachers and catechists to use it.

The Pittsburgh Bishop further provided a number of practical suggestions as to how bishops could go about doing this. His suggestions included developing a diocesan team of core personnel, including both educational and administrative people, to coordinate and develop all aspects of the implementation process. He thought the bishop should be personally involved in the training at this level, so that the members of the diocesan team could then go on to provide the proper grounding in the *Catechism* directly to teachers, catechists, CCD and other parish volunteers, as well as to youth and campus ministry people. Bishop Wuerl also

---

[5] Mentioned in *Origins*, CNS Documentary Service, March 8, 1990.

thought that the sessions in which the bishop himself was involved might well be videotaped for re-presentation to other groups down the line.[6]

Bishop Wuerl's contribution to making the *Catechism* better known, by the way, was not restricted to his efforts in his own Pittsburgh diocese or at conferences such as this New Orleans one. Bishop Wuerl writes a monthly column on the faith in the Catholic publication with the largest circulation in the United States, the Knights of Columbus magazine *Columbia*. Since the publication of the *Catechism*, he has been regularly and rather systematically expounding it in these columns, thus familiarizing a very wide audience with its basic content.

The New Orleans symposium on the *Catechism* also included other positive presentations, one by the director of an archdiocesan catechetical office (in the archdiocese of New York) and another by an archdiocesan director of religious education (in the archdiocese of Boston). All in all, the USCC Subcommittee for the Implementation of the *Catechism* demonstrated both imagination and zeal in seeing that this new doctrinal sourcebook of the universal Church was properly launched in the United States. And the U.S. bishops generally responded both positively and seriously to its advent.

Once the book was actually launched, though, this particular subcommittee gave way to another committee, the Ad Hoc Committee to Oversee the Use of the *Catechism*, a body that continues in being at the present time. The archbishop of Indianapolis, the Most Reverend Daniel Buechlein, was

---

[6] The Most Reverend Donald W. Wuerl, "The Diocesan Bishop's Perspective on Implementing the *Catechism*", *The Living Light*, fall 1993, 73–78.

made chairman of this latter committee, which immediately became involved in such questions as providing guidance for the use of the *Catechism* in secondary texts, evaluating catechetical materials in the light of the *Catechism*, serving as a clearinghouse for any textual errors discovered, developing plans for the electronic and mass-market editions of the work, distributing video and other materials related to it, as well as considering, along with the bishops' regular Education Committee, the idea of a possible U.S. national catechism, based upon the *Catechism of the Catholic Church*.

Once again, this Ad Hoc Committee to Oversee the Use of the *Catechism* evidenced great concern that its implementation be properly and expeditiously carried out.[7] "Whenever the *Catechism* is used," Archbishop Buechlein declared, "we want to be sure that it is done with integrity and wholeness."[8] This attitude seemed to be an accurate reflection of U.S. episcopal sentiment generally.

Thus, at the level of the bishops, the reception accorded to the *Catechism of the Catholic Church* was every bit as positive as the popular reception accorded to it. Both the bishops and the public saw the appearance of the *Catechism* as a major and very welcome event in the life of the Church, and they treated it as such.

## II

From the moment the *Catechism* was promulgated, the U.S. bishops were urged to get personally and actively involved in

---

[7] See "Agenda Report: Documentation for General Meeting", National Conference of Catholic Bishops/United States Catholic Conference, Washington, D.C., November 14–17, 1994, 94–95.

[8] Quoted in *Indianapolis News*, June 15, 1994.

implementing and promoting it. Some bishops seized upon the opportunity with alacrity.

Cardinal John O'Connor, the archbishop of New York, for example, in the course of the year 1994, preached a year-long series of homilies on the *Catechism* from the pulpit of St. Patrick's Cathedral. Collected and printed, this series of homilies constitutes one of the best existing commentaries on the *Catechism* produced in the United States.[9]

Cardinal O'Connor was evidently much taken with the *Catechism* from the outset; he obviously studied it with great care and was profoundly influenced by it. Both his own talent and, no doubt, a lifetime of pastoral practice gave the Cardinal a special knack for selecting and quoting basic "doctrine" from the *Catechism*, which he then immediately applied to the faith and life of the Christians in his congregation, illustrating his exposition with lively and pertinent remarks and examples, often anecdotal. One imagines he rarely lost the attention of his cathedral congregation while preaching these homilies on what so many religious educators continue to claim is "dry", namely, Catholic doctrine.

In order to provide an illustration of how effective this pastoral method was for expounding and applying the doctrine of the *Catechism*, we shall look at only one of Cardinal O'Connor's series of homilies, the thirty-ninth, preached on November 27, 1994.[10] In this homily, dealing with the subject of prayer as that important subject is treated in the fourth part of the *Catechism*, Cardinal O'Connor substan-

---

[9] Cardinal John O'Connor, *A Moment of Grace* (San Francisco: Ignatius Press, 1995).

[10] Cardinal John O'Connor, "Ways to Pray", thirty-ninth homily on the new *Catechism of the Catholic Church*, reprinted in *Catholic New York*, December 1, 1994.

tially covered paragraphs 2623–724. He first related prayer
to the liturgical season, which happened to be Advent:

> During Advent we are doing the final section of the *Cat-
> echism*, which is on prayer. This is so appropriate because
> this is the period of expectancy, of prayer, of getting ready.
> It is the period during which we are reminded of the long-
> ing of the entire human race for the potential of salva-
> tion after Original Sin. It is the period during which we
> are reminded of the longing of the Israelites when they
> were on pilgrimage in the desert after having escaped from
> slavery to the Egyptians, wandering, weary, lost, confused
> just as are we so often, praying that they would get to the
> Promised Land, which is the symbol of heaven. Advent
> is a reminder of those nine months of prayer, in which
> surely Mary was engaged, praying to the Father, praying
> to the Son within her, awaiting His advent, awaiting His
> birth on Christmas Day.

Having established the close correspondence of sustained
prayer with the season, the Cardinal did not fail also to relate the scriptural readings for the day to his general theme
of prayer. As it happened—as so often happens where the
Holy Scriptures are concerned—the readings for the day
were particularly appropriate to his subject. They included
1 Thessalonians 5:16–18: "Be joyful always, pray at all times,
be thankful in all circumstances"; and, marvelously, these
readings also included Luke 21:36: "Pray constantly for the
strength to escape whatever is in prospect, and to stand secure before the Son of Man."

These readings provided a wholly natural and unforced
entrance into a discussion of the types of prayer set forth by
the *Catechism*: the prayer of blessing and adoration (CCC
2628); of petition (CCC 2629); of intercession (CCC 2634);
of thanksgiving (CCC 2637); and of praise (CCC 2639).

Cardinal O'Connor discussed each of these types of prayer in his homily, sometimes reading what the *Catechism* says about them, other times explaining it in his own words, and yet other times illustrating it by quoting, for example, the beautiful Canticle of Daniel from the same morning's Divine Office in order to illustrate the nature of the prayer of blessing ("Bless the Lord, all you works of the Lord / Praise and exalt him above all forever").

In some cases, the Cardinal included an often simple example of how people today relate to or are affected by the various types of prayer. In the case of the prayer of blessing, he noted:

> Yesterday I was in an airplane and one of the flight attendants came and sat beside me for a moment and asked me, "Will you give me a blessing?" I said a little prayer over her. This is a very beautiful, common Hispanic custom. Many times when I meet Hispanics in New York, even on the street, they will ask me for a blessing.

Turning to the prayer of adoration, Cardinal O'Connor first quoted the essence of what the *Catechism* says about it and then added his own comments relating this to the immediate experience of his congregation:

> "*Adoration* is the first attitude of human beings acknowledging that we are creatures before our Creator. It exalts the greatness of the Lord who made us and the almighty power of the Savior who set us free from evil" (CCC 2628).
>
> The prayer of adoration must include a sense of reverence. We must have a sense of reverence for the Christ that we will receive in Holy Communion today. If we are really going to pray, we must try to concentrate when we come up here despite all of the distractions, despite the

number of people in this packed cathedral. We must try to achieve this one-to-one union with Christ. I always ask the ushers to be very gentle in directing people toward a particular priest when the lines get heavy so that there is no pushing or sharpness. This should be a moment of great reverence, as when Almighty God called to Moses from the burning bush. When Moses was arriving he said, "Take the shoes from off your feet because the ground on which you stand is holy ground."

Similarly, in explaining the prayer of intercession, the Cardinal illustrated it by an immediate and concrete example:

This moves us then to the prayer of intercession. Yesterday, as I walked along the street someone said to me, "Say one for me." I hear that so often. People will stop me, not because I am anybody, but because I am a priest. They see the collar and they will stop me and say, "Father, my wife is sick. She just learned she has cancer. Will you say a prayer for her?" Or "I have just lost my job. Will you say a prayer for me?" This is what is called prayer of intercession. It goes all the way back, as far as we know, at least to the days of Abraham. It is a very unselfish form of prayer.

Again, explaining the prayer of thanksgiving, the Cardinal linked it, as the *Catechism* itself does (CCC 2637), to the Eucharist:

The very word "Eucharist" means a thanksgiving. The Eucharistic prayer is a prayer of thanksgiving. We have just celebrated the civil feast of Thanksgiving. So often we forget that that feast was established in the early days of our Republic as a thanksgiving to Almighty God for delivery from religious persecution in Europe, a delivery from the elements here. It was a feast in thanksgiving for survival in this new world. Did we celebrate it in that fashion?

And so on. It is evident from the few examples taken from Cardinal O'Connor's thirty-ninth homily on the *Catechism of the Catholic Church* that expounding the essential doctrines of the faith is in no way alien to the preaching and practice of the faith; nor is it in any way tedious or unrelated to people's lives. Cardinal O'Connor instantly found one example after another to illustrate the "doctrine" he was expounding. Why is this so difficult for some modern religious educators? Why do they find doctrine "boring"? What is *less* boring than the "good news" of our sanctification and salvation in Jesus Christ?

Having expounded and explained the types of prayer, Cardinal O'Connor then went on in this homily to treat, briefly, "the tradition of prayer" (CCC 2650–62), including, especially, how prayer relates to the three theological virtues of faith, hope, and love; "the way of prayer" (CCC 2663–82); and, finally, "the expressions of prayer" (CCC 2700–724), including vocal prayer, meditation, and contemplative prayer—all in all, a rather remarkable series of subjects to be treated in a homily from the pulpit before an average Sunday Mass congregation.

Obviously, neither Cardinal O'Connor nor any other homilist could treat comprehensively in one homily a topic as large as what the *Catechism of the Catholic Church* has to say about prayer. But it is surprising how much he could and did cover in an interesting way in one single homily. And surely no congregation can be unimpressed when the Cardinal Archbishop himself pays such close attention over many weeks to a single enterprise, expounding the Church's doctrinal heritage from the new *Catechism*. It is a pretty safe bet that anyone who sat through all, or even most, of the homilies that the Cardinal Archbishop of New York devoted to the *Catechism* emerged with a pretty solid regrounding in exactly what the Catholic faith says and is.

This is precisely where a whole generation of new catechists fell down. They ceased to see the faith as interesting because they ceased to focus on the fact that the faith is, first of all, *true*. It possesses the truths that pertain to our sanctification and salvation. The *Catechism of the Catholic Church* can thus help us to restore the priority and primacy of truth, as Cardinal O'Connor has clearly grasped.

## III

Cardinal John O'Connor of New York was not the only U.S. bishop to greet the advent of the new *Catechism* as an event important enough to justify such efforts as devoting a year-long series of homilies to commenting upon it. Other bishops greeted the work with equal seriousness. For example, the archbishop of Washington, Cardinal James Hickey, was one of a number of bishops to issue a pastoral letter on the *Catechism*. His pastoral letter proved to be especially timely and pertinent to the real significance of the document. It is worth more than a superficial glance here, as it is indicative of what can be done with the *Catechism* now that we have it.

Entitled *Looking to Christ in Faith*,[11] this pastoral letter had as its announced aim the implementation of the *Cate-*

---

[11] Cardinal James Hickey, *Looking to Christ in Faith*, A Pastoral Letter on the Implementation of the *Catechism of the Catholic Church* in the Archdiocese of Washington, September 14, 1994.

*chism.* Cardinal Hickey unambiguously declared on the first page of it:

> This is not a pastoral letter about family heirlooms. It concerns the living faith of the Church, which is expressed in a complete and trustworthy manner in the *Catechism of the Catholic Church*. . . . I am calling for a fundamental change in attitude about the important work of sharing the faith of the Church with others.

"A fundamental change in attitude" on this subject, of course, is exactly what the Church has needed for a good while now. Cardinal Hickey recognized that the *Catechism* did not arrive on the scene a moment too soon:

> The need for the *Catechism* is great. To discover that need we do not have to look far. A recent poll published in the *New York Times* indicated that only 33% of Catholics of all ages believe in the Real Presence of the Lord in the Eucharist. Some 17% do not believe that the Lord Jesus is really divine. Either many people were not instructed properly or else they have difficulty accepting what they were taught. Some, I am sure, are simply confused, because the Church's faith is often misrepresented in the media and popular literature, including religious literature.

In his pastoral letter, Cardinal Hickey candidly admitted the reality of the catechetical situation in the archdiocese. Virtually the same thing could be said about practically every other diocese in the United States. His pastoral letter is thus worth quoting at some length on this point, for it rather accurately describes where we are in this country, catechetically speaking:

> But this letter is not just about a national problem; it is primarily about a *local* problem, which I invite you to ad-

dress with me. We need to do a better job of guarding and transmitting the deposit of faith within this Archdiocese. Yet improving the way in which the faith is taught is not just a matter of working harder or employing new strategies. It means changing our attitudes and priorities; it entails a conversion process in ourselves and in our homes, parishes and schools.

Cardinal Hickey correctly identified some of the tendencies in modern catechesis that have contributed to the current low state of knowledge of the faith and education in the faith. Some of the points he made are pertinent enough to be spelled out here. He identified the following "tendencies":

—"*A tendency to filter all Church teaching through vague and tired categories like 'liberal' and 'conservative' or 'pre-Vatican-II' and 'post-Vatican-II.'* " On this point, the pastoral letter quotes Pope John Paul II's apostolic constitution *Fidei Depositum* to the effect that "the faith is always the same yet the source of ever new light."

—"*A tendency to place Scripture in opposition to doctrine.*" Here the pastoral letter points to the necessary and inseparable interconnection between Scripture, Tradition, and the Magisterium of the Church.

—"*A tendency to think that only the principal doctrinal teachings of the faith require our assent.*" Here the pastoral letter repeats Archbishop Christoph Schönborn's point about the central truths around which the faith as a whole is organized, pointing out how the *Catechism* itself "helps us see how all the truths of the faith are related to one another and how they all demand our assent".

—"*A tendency to undervalue the role of precise doctrinal statements in religious instruction and formation.*" Here the pastoral letter quotes the *Catechism* itself (CCC 89) to the effect that "dogmas are lights along the path of faith" and are a necessary means for "interpreting the meaning of what we experience and the purpose of life itself".

—"*A tendency to doubt that doctrinal statements refer to something real.*" Here the pastoral letter points out how "the *Catechism* insists on the *reality* of the faith we celebrate, profess, and live. The Son of God really did assume our human nature; Christ really did rise from the dead; at Mass the bread and wine truly are transformed into the Body, Blood, Soul, and Divinity of Christ." And so on.

Since Cardinal Hickey's admirable pastoral letter sees so clearly the reality of much present-day catechesis, it is not surprising that it goes on to prescribe a definite series of concrete steps to be taken in the archdiocese of Washington in order to implement the *Catechism* properly. This list of remedial steps is both realistic and sensible and would serve equally well in almost any diocese.

In a preamble to these "Archdiocesan Efforts", the Cardinal also points to the most essential of all requirements for the proper use of the *Catechism* when he says: "The first step in implementing the *Catechism* is for each of us to welcome it as believers." In addition to this indispensable step, Cardinal Hickey then lays out what is to be done throughout the archdiocese. We quote verbatim from his pastoral letter:

—The *Catechism* is already being used to gauge the adequacy of religious education textbooks. Only those texts which faithfully reflect and effectively communicate the Church's teaching in its completeness will be approved for classroom use.

—On the basis of the new *Catechism* the entire Catechist Formation and Certification Program will be revised. Master Catechists will be expected to have a thorough knowledge of the content of the *Catechism*. Lesson plans for both the basic and the intermediate levels will be amended and expanded to reflect clearly the content of the *Catechism*.

—Seminarians from the Archdiocese of Washington are expected to be thoroughly familiar not only with the contents of the *Catechism* but also with its practical, pastoral application.

—The *Catechism* will become a basic textbook for the formation of permanent deacons. Each course will be based on the appropriate section of the *Catechism*. Candidates for the permanent diaconate will be examined on their knowledge of its contents.

—Training for all non-ordained parish ministries such as extraordinary ministers of the Eucharist and parish evangelists will be based on the *Catechism*.

—During the coming year [the archdiocesan newspaper] will feature weekly articles that will systematically cover the content of the *Catechism*.

—All programs of evangelization will be carefully evaluated and revised in light of the new *Catechism*.

—Family life and marriage preparation programs will be reviewed and enriched with reference to the teaching of the *Catechism*.

—Workshops and other programs in the area of social justice sponsored by the Archdiocese will be based on the *Catechism*.

There can be no doubt that the implementation of only some of the above items in any diocese would quickly result not only in a tangible and verifiable improvement in education in the faith—but in the knowledge and practice of the faith as well.

## IV

On the record, it seems quite evident that the bishops of the United States have greeted the *Catechism of the Catholic Church* with appropriate and even quite admirable seriousness and application. The efforts and initiatives on the episcopal level—we have cited only a few of the concrete instances by way of example—cannot be anything but very encouraging to anyone concerned about the Catholic faith and its future in the United States. These efforts and initiatives complement and reenforce those taken by the Holy See and the episcopate worldwide to inaugurate the new era of evangelization and catechesis signaled by the publication and dissemination of this *Catechism*. Christ's plan of grounding the Church on the apostles and their successors can thus again in our day be definitely shown not to have failed.

It cannot be said, however, that the *Catechism* has been greeted with equal acceptance, seriousness, and enthusiasm at all levels within the Church. In particular, the current theological and catechetical establishments in the United States, as is rather well known—and as Cardinal Hickey's treatment of the subject in his pastoral letter on the implementation of the *Catechism* rather candidly and dramatically confirms—have long been opposed to doctrinal catechesis and the use of catechisms. At various stages in the process of the *Catechism*'s preparation, some of the prominent people in both of these two establishments did not scruple to attack it.

It is true, as we have noted, that public opposition to the *Catechism* became more muted once it was clear beyond any doubt that the Church was indeed going to proceed to the issuance of a universal catechism. At that point discretion became the better part of valor, and at the very least lip service became more commonly paid to the proposition that, of course, all those involved in religious education would without question now sincerely commit themselves to implementing what could no longer be prevented.

Nevertheless, it cannot be assumed that all the earlier opposition to the project of a catechism has now been dissipated or rendered harmless. Some of it may just have gone underground. Certainly many of the people who opposed the project of a catechism are still around; many of them still occupy crucial positions in the catechetical establishment. While their opposition was more open, vocal, and even vehement in the past, it may now seem to some of them more prudent to wait out the current period of the *Catechism*'s remarkable initial popularity. The wind may shift again, after all, some of them may be thinking.

As catechetical expert Fr. Berard L. Marthaler told the U.S. bishops themselves, "a peculiar trait of American culture is the enthusiasm with which we greet the new. At times it seems like sheer faddism that causes us to latch onto the latest book, buzz word, or technique as if it were a panacea, only to discard it when something newer comes along. There is danger that even the *Catechism of the Catholic Church*, a best-seller at Christmas, will be collecting dust on the shelves by Easter."[12]

Certainly that could happen if some of those with formal responsibilities for implementing it are, in reality, desirous of *putting* it on the shelf. The "danger" of this is surely much greater if the religious educators themselves view the whole thing with anything less than enthusiasm. Certainly,

---

[12] Marthaler, "*Catechism* in U.S. Context".

too, the high level to date of episcopal attention to questions related to the implementation of the *Catechism* is almost bound to diminish with time and with the inevitability of episcopal diversion to new priorities. The initial phase of admirable, hands-on oversight by the bishops could thus rather quickly give way to a new period of benign neglect of what is happening on the catechetical front. That would mean that more responsibility for actual implementation measures would fall back into the hands of the professionals in religious education, who are, after all, still in place—and some of whom have a far from unblemished record of enthusiasm for the new *Catechism*.

Meanwhile, the question remains of how well all the positive episcopal directions and exhortations concerning the *Catechism* have been filtering down into the structures of the Church's educational system. Opposition to catechism-based teaching and learning has been strong in professional religious-education circles virtually since the end of Vatican II. In an earlier chapter we noted instances where the catechetical experts have not scrupled to undermine express measures taken by the hierarchy to remedy the doctrinal crisis in catechetics. Opposition to the project of a universal catechism was likewise strong from the time the idea was first seriously broached at the Extraordinary Synod of Bishops in 1985. Nor was this open opposition notably long-suffering—or even always temperate—in expressing itself.

One example of this was especially notorious. When the draft provisional text of what became the *Catechism* was circulated to all the bishops of the world at the end of 1989, it was sent *sub secreto*. This invoked the same kind of confidentiality that would normally be respected in the secular world of today for an organizational "policy statement" still in the process of being prepared. Organizations have a right to keep their own documents under wraps until the definitive version of what the organization itself has to say is ready to be presented in the form preferred by the organization. Published exposés of such uncompleted drafts are rightly considered to be both unethical and unprofessional, just as failure to respect time "embargos" on press releases and similar documents is generally so considered.

Respect, however, was hardly the predominant attitude adopted by an aggressive group of self-appointed theologians and other experts who promptly organized a "scholarly symposium" highly critical of the draft under the auspices of the Woodstock Theological Center located on the campus of Georgetown University in Washington, D.C. The scholars assailed the draft from almost every quarter, publishing some of their papers against it in *America* and *Commonweal* as well as later in book form.[13] They even called a press conference to draw maximum public attention to their open efforts to discredit the draft *Catechism* and undermine the authority of the Church.

The conclusion reached at this Woodstock symposium was that the draft was "fatally flawed" and that it failed to "reflect contemporary developments in Scripture, history, liturgy, catechetics, and moral theology, as if the last thirty years [had] never happened."[14]

We need not dwell here on the unedifying spectacle of such Catholic theologians, exegetes, canonists, liturgists, and catechetical experts (including, alas, one bishop). In a previous work, one of the present authors provided a brief

---

[13] See Reese, ed., *Universal Catechism Reader.*
[14] Ibid., introduction, 11.

chronicle of their efforts.[15] An anonymous author, "Catholicus", also subjected the views of some of the participants
in this same Woodstock symposium to critical analysis in a
book called *DOA* ("Dead on Arrival").[16]

On the whole, the attack launched by this pretentious
Woodstock group proved to be more ideological and polem-
ical than scholarly. All they really succeeded in doing was to
demonstrate their fundamental disloyalty to both the process and the product that the Church had instituted. The
quality of the completed *Catechism* wholly gives the lie to
their—as seen in retrospect—frantic and even desperate efforts to discredit it.

In any case, once it was clear that the *Catechism* could
no longer be stopped, the focus shifted from attacking it
outright to somewhat more subtle efforts to belittle its significance and usefulness for the Church of today. This was
the line adopted by yet another symposium of experts, this
one held in the spring of 1993 under the sponsorship of the
School of Religious Studies of the Catholic University of
America. This symposium signaled the advent of what was
evidently a new tactic on the part of the theological and
catechetical establishments: namely, go through all the motions of accepting and receiving the *Catechism*, meanwhile
stressing all the ways in which it was still inadequate and
therefore still in need of adaptation, "inculturation", and,

---

[15] See Msgr. Michael J. Wrenn, *Catechisms and Controversies: Religious
Education in the Postconciliar Years*, (San Francisco: Ignatius Press, 1991).
For commentary on the Woodstock Center's 1990 Georgetown sym-
posium against the *Catechism*, see, esp., 5–12, 38–64, and 68–73.

[16] See *DOA: the Ambush of the Universal Catechism* (by "Catholicus")
(Notre Dame, Ind.: Crisis Books, 1993), esp. 53–66 on the Woodstock
symposium.

in general, mediation and interpretation by—who else but the experts of the religious-education establishment themselves?

This new tactic of smothering the *Catechism* in a farrago of professional expertise included, if the 1993 Catholic University symposium was any gauge, pointing out all the ways in which the *Catechism*, as approved by the Church, was much too complex and difficult for the average Catholic, even while it also failed to include all the desired insights of modern scholarship. At the same time, the new tactic meant constantly reminding everybody how the mind-set of the *Catechism* simply did not "fit" with modern American culture (as if today's grossly decadent and anti-Christian culture could possible serve as a model for anything Catholic!).

By the time all these points, and yet others, had been made about the *Catechism*, little was left of the original *Catechism* itself. What the Synod had recommended, what the bishops had labored so hard to produce, and what the Pope had promulgated with such confident high hopes for the universal Church was effectively reduced to something marginal and secondary in the minds of anyone listening to this kind of treatment by members of the catechetical establishment.

The anonymous author of the book called *DOA*, mentioned above, devoted the major part of his analysis to this conference held in May 1993 at the Catholic University of America. This author found, and documented, an all-pervasive and fundamental anti-*Catechism* bias on the part of the theological and catechetical professionals assembled at this conference—which was supposedly organized to expound and explain the *Catechism*. We do not have to cover this same ground here but can simply refer readers to the *DOA* study.

It is of no little interest and significance, by the way, that the very volume that the Paulist Press published of the official transcripts of most of the speeches delivered at this 1993 conference at the Catholic University of America on the *Catechism* substantially confirms the testimony of *DOA*. Although the speakers at this conference tended to be prudent in manner and very concerned to appear "moderate"—as the author of *DOA* in fact described them—nevertheless, even a hasty reading of the proceedings yields such strictures against the *Catechism* as former CUA Professor Gerard Sloyan's harsh judgment that the *Catechism* "cannot be promoted as a dependable book for use as it stands because of the uneven quality of its treatments. . . . It requires a second, revised edition very soon." According to Fr. Sloyan, the *Catechism* "cries out for nuance, supplementation, and correction".[17]

Then there is the erroneous judgment of current CUA Professor of Theology Dr. Peter Phan, who alleged, in reference to the *Catechism*, that "while Vatican II is copiously cited, its spirit, as many commentators have lamented, is conspicuously absent." Dr. Phan's contribution evidences further fears about the *Catechism*: "To affirm *tout court* that 'the old law is a preparation for the Gospel' (CCC 1982) runs the risk of anti-Semitism"; worse than that, "these formulas can be turned into shibboleths by conservatives to gauge the orthodoxy of current and future catechisms."[18] In other

---

[17] Gerard S. Sloyan, "The Role of the Bible in Catechesis according to the *Catechism*", in *Introducing the Catechism of the Catholic Church: Traditional Themes and Contemporary Issues*, ed. Berard L. Marthaler (New York and Mahwah, N.J.: Paulist Press, 1994), 34.

[18] Peter C. Phan, Ph.D., "What Is Old and What Is New in the *Catechism*", in ibid., 61.

words, we must object to the *Catechism*'s presentation of Catholic doctrine because it might give aid and comfort to "conservatives".

Surely this is nothing but modern political correctness: a professor at the Catholic University of America is more concerned *not* to appear a "conservative" or an "anti-Semite" than he is to appear a professing Christian. At least he has not lost the concept of sin (being "conservative" or "anti-Semite"). But this is scarcely Catholicism. Ideology now apparently counts more than faith in CUA's School of Religious Studies.

We could cite more examples of the same type from the official speeches given at this CUA conference reprinted in a book that purports to be an "introduction" to the *Catechism*. But the two examples we have cited already indicate clearly enough the mind-set of these modern religious educators supposedly introducing the book. Can such remarks by a Fr. Sloyan or a Dr. Phan really be considered in any sense an "introduction" to it?

Our Holy Father, Pope John Paul II, has styled the *Catechism* "a precious, splendid, profound, and timely gift for all".[19] Fr. Gerard Sloyan, however, judges it "uneven" and in need of "correction". Dr. Peter Phan, for his part, sees conservative "shibboleths" in it. Whom should we believe about this? In whom should we place our confidence here? How does the new magisterium of theologians stack up against the real Magisterium?

More disturbingly, how did the likes of Fr. Sloyan and Dr. Phan ever get into the business of "introducing" a document

---

[19] Pope John Paul II, "Discourse on the Occasion of the Promulgation of the *Catechism of the Catholic Church*", quoted in *The Living Light*, summer 1993.

of which they apparently think so little in the first place? And at the Catholic University of America no less! It would seem to be a pretty serious business when the "national" Catholic university to which the faithful are asked to contribute through their parish envelopes is found sponsoring and subsidizing the subversion of the Church's *Catechism*.

But we should not make any mistake about the influence of such academics as these; they are not isolated cases. This was not just any conference. Those who were the presenters as well as the several hundred people who were in attendance virtually all hold positions somewhere in the Church's official religious-education system. The conference addresses were not only published in book form by the Paulist Press —which billed the volume as *the* "introduction" to the *Catechism* in this country—the talks were also videotaped for wide distribution in training programs on the *Catechism*. And no doubt they are being widely used for that very purpose now, owing especially to the name and prestige of the School of Religious Studies of the Catholic University of America.

The question has to be asked: How could such important aspects of the implementation of the *Catechism* in the United States be allowed to fall into the hands of people like Fr. Sloyan and Dr. Phan?

# CHAPTER FOUR

# *The English Translation of the* Catechism

## I

Questionable interpretations of its intent and content were not the only problems the *Catechism of the Catholic Church* was to encounter in the United States. For there was also the whole controversial saga of the *translation* of the work into English.

When Pope John Paul II promulgated the approved French text of the *Catechism* in early December 1992, it was initially expected that an approved English version of it would not be very long in coming. What could possibly go wrong? It was a simple matter of translation. Primary responsibility for supervising the translation of the text into English was assigned to Boston's Cardinal Bernard Law, along with Bishop David Konstant of Leeds, England.

Cardinal Law, of course, had been highly instrumental at the 1985 Synod of Bishops in getting the whole project of a universal catechism launched in the first place; he had also served as a member of the Commission on the Catechism for the Universal Church. In addition, he was one of five bishops, symbolically representing the five inhabited continents, to whom the Holy Father formally presented copies of the *Catechism* when it was finally completed; he it was who formally responded to the Holy Father on that occasion on behalf of all the bishops of the world.[1] Few deserved greater personal credit for the whole vast enterprise of the *Catechism* than Cardinal Bernard Law of Boston.

Bishop David Konstant, for his part, had served as one of the seven key bishop-authors (and one priest) of the *Catechism*, and hence his own personal contribution to the project was also of the highest order. Few could match or even come close to the contribution that both of these prelates had already made to the whole enterprise. The choice of them to supervise the English translation thus seemed to be an especially auspicious one.

In the event, however, the translation of the *Catechism* into English turned out to be one of the most difficult and contentious things encountered in the entire course of the almost seven-year writing and editing project. The biblical Jacob labored for seven years for the comely Rachel, only to discover at the end of the seven years that he had the uncomely Leah on his hands instead. This is pretty much how the initial project to translate the *Catechism* into English fared as well.

It had early been decided that the task of rendering the text into English should be primarily done by a single translator, both to ensure a consistent narrative style and to produce a relatively rapid translation. In principle, this was a very good decision. On the basis of a sample translation submitted, a pastor in Richmond Hill, Georgia, Fr. Douglas Kent Clark, was chosen to be the translator. He was a former North American College classmate of the rector of

---

[1] See Fr. John E. Pollard, "Planning the Implementation of the *Catechism of the Catholic Church*" *The Living Light*, summer 1993, 75.

Boston's St. John's Seminary; earlier, he had been one of a small number who had provided Cardinal Law, at the latter's request, with critiques of early drafts of the *Catechism.*

Two editorial committees were established to assist Fr. Clark in preparing the English translation: one in Britain, headed by Bishop Konstant; and one in the United States, headed by Boston's seminary rector, Msgr. Timothy J. Moran. According to his own account, Fr. Clark worked at the seminary, taking a leave of absence from his parish for that purpose. He began work on the translation in January 1992 and completed a draft in October of that same year. Having circulated this draft for comments and criticisms, he completed his final version in time for submission to the Holy See by February 1993.[2]

That was when the trouble started. The public record as to what actually happened is sparse. Rumors of course abounded—and naturally multiplied over the period of more than one year before an English translation of the *Catechism* was finally approved by Rome. In the course of that same protracted year, and more, during which no official English version of the text was available and there was no public explanation of the fact nor any certainty as to when an English text would be available, statements were made at different times by various interested parties, not all of which served to clarify the real cause of the delay.

The brief account that follows of what lay behind Rome's difficulties with Fr. Clark's translation and of what Rome then proceeded to do in order to get an acceptable translation is quite deliberately limited, except where explicitly noted, to facts already in the public domain.

---

[2] See Douglas Kent Clark, "On 'Englishing' the *Catechism*", *The Living Light*, summer 1993, esp. 14–15.

Both the present authors have worked as professional translators from the French. The question of the translation of the *Catechism* was naturally a matter of intense interest to both of us. As it happened, one of us, Msgr. Wrenn, came into possession of a copy of the Clark translation. After reading and studying this translation, and consulting with others about it, he became greatly disturbed since he found serious—and he thought obvious—deficiencies. He soon sought the assistance of another New York archdiocesan priest, also fluent in French, Fr. Gerald E. Murray, and the two of them spent many hours laboriously comparing the Clark translation with the original French text.[3] It soon became abundantly clear that this English translation that had been submitted to Rome for approval fell far short of the standard required for the *Catechism of the Catholic Church.* The deficiencies both priests found were carefully documented so that they could be given to those in a position to call them to the attention of Roman authorities.

Further, from late 1992 through 1993, Msgr. Wrenn worked with Fr. Joseph Fessio, S.J., head of Ignatius Press in San Francisco, and with Erasmo Leiva-Merikakis of the University of San Francisco, to document the pervasive errors in translation and, as part of this process, to provide examples of an accurate, literary translation. This documentation was submitted to interested ecclesiastical authorities.

It became clear enough later that these were not the only reservations about the translation prepared by Fr. Clark that had been submitted to Church authorities or that Roman analysts themselves discovered and developed. Very early, apparently, the Roman authorities already had a soberly ob-

---

[3] Kathleen Nowacki Correia gave valuable assistance in serving as secretary for this effort.

jective appreciation of the deficiencies of the translation that had been submitted to them.

In the course of the year 1993, the Holy See came under increasing pressure, from more than one bishops' conference in the English-speaking world for neither producing an approved English-language version of the *Catechism* nor explaining what the delay was all about. At this time, Msgr. Wrenn approached Mr. Whitehead for further assistance on the whole question of the translation of the *Catechism*.

Because the chorus of disapproval against Rome was swelling by then to new heights, we decided to prepare our own article-length critique of the Clark translation so that Catholics in English-speaking countries would be enabled to understand that the translation *had* to be delayed. This article, entitled "The Translation of the *Catechism*", was published simultaneously in late 1993 and early 1994 in periodicals in Australia, Britain, Canada, Ireland, and the United States (as well as, in an adapted French version, in France).

Our article attracted a fair amount of attention at the time, and we hope and trust that it served to convince many that there were very good reasons for the delay in Rome in releasing an approved English translation of the *Catechism*. In our view, we provided ample documentation and analysis to justify delaying the translation. The reader may reach his own conclusions about this particular question, though, since we have included in Appendix One of this volume the complete text of this article, "The Translation of the *Catechism*", as it was originally written and published.

What the general public record indicates concerning Rome's unwillingness to accept the English translation originally submitted is that Cardinal Bernard Law and Bishop David Konstant met in Rome on February 3–4, 1993, with Cardinal Ratzinger and others connected with what came to be called the Interdicasterial Commission for the *Catechism of the Catholic Church*. We know of no published record of what actually occurred at that meeting. In a later public lecture, Archbishop Schönborn remarked in passing that the proper principles of translation were discussed and decided upon at this meeting.

About a week after the meeting, however, Bishop David Konstant issued a statement that simply stated that "the principal matter under discussion was the inclusive use of language. It was agreed that great sensitivity must be paid to this matter. In translation the meaning must be clear and accurate. This will require great attention to how the word *man* is used."[4]

By the end of March 1993, however, further press accounts had surfaced that indicated that the meeting had in fact been highly critical of the translation, mostly, it seemed —but not entirely—because of the inclusive-language issue. One press account related that "Cardinal Joseph Ratzinger told Cardinal Bernard Law of Boston that there was *too much* inclusive language",[5] while another press account reported that "the Vatican has delayed publication of the English translation of the Roman Catholic Church's Universal Catechism, concerned that language used to assuage feminists could alter the text's theological meaning."[6]

However that may be, it would appear that, whatever was said at the meeting in Rome in early February, the criticisms

---

[4] Quoted by Peter Hebblethwaite, "Rome Mishandled *Catechism*'s Language", *National Catholic Reporter*, March 26, 1993.

[5] Quoted by Dawn Gibeau, "Changes Delay English-Language *Catechism*", *National Catholic Reporter*, March 26, 1993.

[6] Larry Witham, "Gender-Neutral *Catechism* on Hold", *Washington Times*, March 26, 1993.

cannot have been either unduly harsh or entirely definitive, since the immediate public reaction of Cardinal Law was to publish in the issue of February 12, 1993, of his archdiocesan newspaper, *The Pilot*, a defense of the translation that had been made, indicating that the translator, Fr. Douglas Kent Clark, had "rendered a magnificent service to the whole Church in putting into English the *Catechism of the Catholic Church*". The Boston Cardinal wrote that "there was a time when *man* would generally be understood in the light of a context as meaning all human beings. This is not always true today," he declared, "given the cultural shifts concerning inclusivity." Cardinal Law indicated at the same time that the criticisms made in Rome could easily be remedied and that Fr. Clark should be able to do so "in several weeks".[7]

Nearly a year and a half later, after the *Catechism* had finally appeared in English, British Vaticanologist-journalist Peter Hebblethwaite, looking back, reported that "Law and Konstant thought Clark would be well able to respond to the objections. . . . There was no sense of danger. . . . Immediately after the February 1993 meeting, Clark set to work to respond to the ninety-three pages of criticism to which his work had been subjected."[8] This same report would seem to indicate, by the way, that Cardinal Law, Bishop Konstant, and Fr. Clark were themselves given every opportunity, without any public disclosure or possible embarrassment, to provide the necessary corrections to the translation that Rome had found to be unacceptable as it was.

Apparently their decision (judging from Cardinal Law's laudatory article in *The Pilot*) was to try to defend the trans-

---

[7] Quoted by Hebblethwaite, "Rome Mishandled".
[8] Ibid.

lation as made. Fr. Clark produced an eighty-one-page reply to the objections that had been registered. Peter Hebblethwaite later judged Fr. Clark's response to be simply superb —but then he saw nothing wrong with the original translation or with the use of inclusive language.

At the May 1993 conference on the *Catechism* at the Catholic University of America already mentioned above, Fr. Clark denied, contrary to what Bishop Konstant had plainly said, that inclusive language was the major issue. He claimed that the problems with his translation "largely revolved around æsthetics"; his critics, he said, preferred "a Latinate style". (He also claimed that "two priests" had "leaked", presumably deviously and secretly, criticisms of his translation to Rome. Since Rome was reviewing the translation at that time, it is hard to see how privately transmitting criticisms to competent authority can be described as a "leak".)[9]

Fr. Clark turned out to be, at the Catholic University conference and also in print, an almost belligerent defender of radical feminist language, claiming that "so-called inclusive language reflects a concern that is almost overwhelming in the United States"[10]—a proposition that could be classified as true only if the phrase "among radical feminists and those influenced by them" were added to it. One has to wonder what sort of people a priest such as this meets and talks to; it is hard to picture parishioners in Richmond Hill, Georgia, being "overwhelmingly concerned" with the issue of inclusive language.

Even while defending the decision to use inclusive lan-

---

[9] See *DOA: the Ambush of the Universal Catechism* (by "Catholicus") (Notre Dame, Ind.: Crisis Books, 1993), 113–14.
[10] See Clark, "On 'Englishing' the *Catechism*".

guage, however, Fr. Clark asserted that the decision was not his alone but was made by the editorial committees he worked under. He concluded the *apologia* he published about it by citing testimonials to the supposed excellence of his translation from former skeptics converted to the cause of inclusive language by reading his translation.[11] In point of fact, Cardinal Law, in his Boston *Pilot* article mentioned above, seemed to be stating his belief that inclusive language was here to stay. Bishop Konstant, too, has been publicly quoted as saying that inclusive language is "basically a matter of ordinary development of language", which, the English prelate added, "pressure groups who try to associate the use of inclusive language with the feminist movement . . . should not be allowed to politicize."[12]

On this subject, the present writers must strenuously beg to differ. First of all, we refer the reader to Appendix One, where Fr. Clark's *Catechism* translation is examined at some length; and also to Appendix Two, where the principles of translation on which Fr. Clark claimed to be working are similarly subjected to scrutiny in a paper that one of the authors delivered at a conference in late 1993. Appendix Three further includes a few examples comparing the Clark translation both with the original French text and with the final English text approved by Rome.

What is very clear in retrospect is that the Roman authorities did not fail to notice the manifold defects in the Clark translation, regardless of who it might have been who first called their attention to these defects (or who, in the colorful language of Fr. Andrew Greeley in his syndicated

---

[11] Ibid.

[12] Quoted by Linda Piwowarski, "I'm Not a Man of God", *U.S. Catholic*, October 1994.

newspaper column, first "snitched" on the American bishops about the whole thing).[13]

In our view, it would have been hard to miss these defects. Evidently the eighty-one-page rebuttal of criticisms that Fr. Clark submitted was also considered insufficient, in spite of the confidence Cardinal Law and Bishop Konstant apparently reposed in it. Their own views in favor of inclusive language would appear to have badly misled them here.

However that may be, some time around April 1993, the final decision was made in Rome to undertake a thorough revision, if not an outright rewrite, of the English translation of the *Catechism* that had been submitted. This decision inevitably meant that there would be a rather considerable delay in the publication of the *Catechism* in English.

Peter Hebblethwaite later reported that "the battle for inclusive language was lost in a special subcommittee of the Congregation for the Doctrine of the Faith set up after the February meeting. While Clark toiled away at his answer to the objections, the decision was being made to entrust the revision to Joseph Eric D'Arcy, archbishop of Hobart, Tasmania, the island off the southern coast of Australia."[14]

It should be further emphasized that the defects of the Clark translation were not limited to the question of inclusive language. The same Peter Hebblethwaite whom we have been quoting—mostly because he was the principal journalist who continued to write about the issue—had reported, following the February 1993 Rome meeting with Cardinal Law and Bishop Konstant, that only "some of the objections" to the translation went back to the inclusive-

---

[13] Andrew M. Greeley, "Father Fessio's Power", *Daily Southtown* (Chicago area), November 27, 1994.
[14] Hebblethwaite, "Rome Mishandled".

language issue. Other objections were ascribed to what Hebblethwaite coyly styled "an ideology that dare not speak its name", but which we may probably understand in normal English to be *theological* objections: in other words, the translation was not doctrinally sound in certain respects, quite apart from the inclusive-language issue.

All along, then, it was the responsibility and, indeed, the *duty*, of the Congregation for the Doctrine of the Faith not to allow such a translation to go forward. In particular, it is worth noting, again according to Peter Hebblethwaite, that "the latest delay is due to a sixty-five-page catalog of objections from Dominican Bishop Christoph Schönborn, auxiliary of Vienna, and secretary of the committee that composed the *Catechism*."[15]

In short, by all indications, there were serious, very serious reasons why Rome had to decline to accept the initial English version of the *Catechism*. Anyone interested in seeing the *Catechism* done right in English—and that should mean *everyone*—should surely have applauded the vigilance and perception of the Holy See in this matter. Any authority responsible for the basic integrity of any organization, or for its basic "policy documents", would have been strictly obliged to take the same kind of action that Rome took on this translation. This would have been standard "management" practice in the secular world.

In the event, a drumfire of constant, carping criticism was heard in many English-speaking countries throughout the entire course of the year and more that no *Catechism* in English was available. The U.S. bishops even passed a resolution at their June 1993 meeting in New Orleans express-

---

[15] Peter Hebblethwaite, "Holy See Compiles Tome of Objections to British Edition", *National Catholic Reporter*, March 26, 1993.

ing their "serious concern about the pastoral implications of the continued delay of the *Catechism*'s publication".[16] In September 1993, a group of U.S. bishops on their *ad limina* visit to Rome raised the issue again with the Pope himself, and so did a group of Canadian bishops the same month.[17] Similar criticisms were still being made as late as December 1993, when the Pope reportedly "shrugged his shoulders as if to say, 'it's coming.' "[18]

Frustration was understandable. Many programs, conferences, workshops, and the like had been organized on the assumption that an English-language *Catechism* would soon be available. The original timetables of the publishers had to be scrapped. Hundreds of thousands of buyers of the book, who had ordered advance copies, were left empty handed *sine die*. What could possibly have gone wrong with what should have been a relatively simple translation from the French? "Everyone is aware that it is an embarrassment to have it still not out", Bishop John C. Reiss of Trenton, New Jersey, was quoted in the press as saying.[19]

It was an embarrassment, all right. But where did the fault for it lie? Was it the fault of the Congregation for the Doctrine of the Faith, or of the Interdicasterial Commission for the *Catechism of the Catholic Church*? This was what the average person was more or less led to believe, based on the publicly available information and news stories: "The Vatican" had been presented with a perfectly good Eng-

---

[16] "Resolution on *Catechism* translation", *Origins*, CNS Documentary Service, July 1, 1993.

[17] CNS news story, "English *Catechism* Not Ready before End of Year", *Arlington Catholic Herald*, September 30, 1993.

[18] CNS news story, "English-Language *Catechism* Still under Review", *Arlington Catholic Herald*, December 16, 1993.

[19] Ibid.

lish translation, but for tortuous, capricious, and otherwise incomprehensible reasons, it was continuing to hold it up. And, as usual, nobody in Rome ever offered any explanation (perhaps so as *not* to have to state publicly—and embarrassingly—the fact that the translation submitted was, in fact, *not* "a perfectly good English translation").

It is unfortunate that this Roman decision was not everywhere accepted. Like a dedicated military officer concerned for the morale of his men, Cardinal Law, in particular, seemed to consider it his special duty to defend the translator and the original "team" that had been engaged to do the work. In a way, this is admirable, of course, but not when carried to Richard Nixon-style lengths of defending *whatever* one's men end up doing. Surely the conscientious decision of the Roman authorities who reviewed and decided to reject the translation deserved some respect as well. Yet as late as September 1993, Cardinal Law was still being quoted in the press as saying that questioning the motives of the team that did the original translation was "manifestly unjust and not in the spirit of the Gospel. . . . [They had] one agenda, and one agenda only, and that was to render an accurate, effective, useful English translation."[20]

That may very well be. But on the basis of the public record that is available, it is not clear that questioning the motives of anybody has ever been an issue. In the nature of the case, it is impossible to know what the motives of the translator and his collaborators were, beyond their own publicly stated reasons for doing what they did.

The objections made to the translation, however, were

---

[20] CNS news story, "English *Catechism* Not Ready".

patently based, not upon motives, but upon an examination of the end product that was submitted. Whatever the motives of the translator and his team, their product was carefully and responsibly "weighed in the balance and found wanting" (Dan 5:27). Any objective judgment of the case would have to conclude on the evidence that it was, first of all, Cardinal Law and Bishop Konstant themselves who were not well served by the "team" that was initially engaged by them to do the English translation.

This has long been a not uncommon phenomenon in the postconciliar Church: the principal shepherds and teachers "sent out" by Christ, the bishops, have not always been well served by the secondary and tertiary "apostles" whom they have "sent out" in their turn. Indeed, it is no exaggeration to say that the successors of the original apostles have sometimes been let down rather badly in recent years, and we certainly have another instance of that here.

## II

In early 1993, when Roman authorities evidently realized that a thorough revision of the English translation of the *Catechism of the Catholic Church* submitted to them was going to be necessary, these same Roman authorities turned, characteristically, to another residential bishop in order to get the job done properly. We have repeatedly stressed in this narrative the extent to which the *Catechism* has been, quite simply, the work of bishops. This has been consistently true from the outset of the project, and it proved to be true again when it came to producing an acceptable English translation of the work.

The superintending Providence that has evidently overseen the conception, development, completion, and publication of this new *Catechism* has hovered over a process of absolutely first-class execution of the work at nearly every stage. This has only been possible, humanly speaking, because of the ability—and the availability—of specific ordained successors of the apostles for each important phase of the work. Christ's plan providing for the episcopacy to guide his Church on the human level most certainly did not go awry as far as this *Catechism* is concerned.

In the matter of the English translation, the bishop to whom Rome was able to turn at the critical juncture was the Most Reverend Eric D'Arcy, archbishop of Hobart, Tasmania, Australia. Archbishop D'Arcy is probably best known in the United States for his book *Conscience and Its Right to Freedom*, published by the original Sheed and Ward firm back in 1960. At that time, the young Fr. D'Arcy was a lecturer in philosophy at the University of Melbourne, and, in this book, he undertook to show from a primarily Thomistic standpoint that, properly understood, Catholic doctrine not only allows but positively demands full freedom of conscience for all, even those who unfortunately happen to be in error.[21]

When we consider that the book was written five years before Vatican II enacted its Declaration on Religious Freedom, *Dignitatis Humanæ*, it has to be considered an even more remarkable and seminal achievement. Some Catholic traditionalists have long darkly suspected that the American Jesuit Fr. John Courtney Murray somehow put the Fathers of the Council up to something outside the Catholic tradition when they came out in favor of religious free-

---

[21] Eric D'Arcy, *Conscience and Its Right to Freedom* (New York: Sheed and Ward, 1960).

dom. These traditionalists have failed to reckon with the fact that an independent investigator, the young Fr. Eric D'Arcy, derived the same conclusion from the same Catholic, Thomistic tradition independently of, and before, the Council.

That the same man, since become an archbishop, should have been called upon more than thirty years later to correct the English translation of the *Catechism of the Catholic Church* no doubt constitutes a major irony. In point of fact, though, Archbishop D'Arcy had long been seriously interested in the problems of catechesis. He had also perceptively written of the need to *combine* the doctrinal approach of conveying truth to the mind with a more experiential approach effecting a more solid assimilation into one's life of the truths taught. His model here was Cardinal John Henry Newman, who, Archbishop D'Arcy has noted, "insists passionately on the objective truths of Christian doctrine, but he insists with equal passion on the intensely personal character of the believer's possession of them". "For Newman," the Archbishop has emphasized, "authentic Christian faith involves both intellect and heart."

"Experience is indispensable for making the truths of the faith one's own", Archbishop D'Arcy has further written. Nevertheless, the truths of the faith themselves still remain, as too many of today's new catechists have evidently forgotten and have therefore tried to form and motivate the pupil instead on the basis of "experience" alone. The truths of the faith are what the Church proclaims, of course, most recently and comprehensively in the *Catechism of the Catholic Church*. The Archbishop considers the latter "a providential initiative of the universal Church". And "to catechetical writers and publishers," he believes, "it holds out the most glorious opportunity in four hundred years." "An active knowledge of the catechism is a *motivum credibilitatis*", he further quotes Newman as saying.[22]

In brief, the bishop called upon to rescue the English translation of the *Catechism* was fluent in French and thoroughly knowledgeable about modern catechesis and its problems, including especially its overemphasis on experience at the expense of truth and knowledge. He was also thoroughly knowledgeable about how the *Catechism* can and must fit into the larger picture of the Church's life today.

By May 1994, after the approved official text in English had finally been unveiled—this text was first formally presented by Cardinal Ratzinger to the ongoing Special Assembly for Africa of the Synod of Bishops on May 4, 1994[23]—it had generally become publicly known that Archbishop D'Arcy had been the one primarily responsible for making the corrections and revisions in the English translation of the *Catechism* and for producing what we now possess in the published English text.

On May 21, 1994, the London *Tablet* interviewed Archbishop D'Arcy about how the revision was done. The published article based on this interview probably represents the most unvarnished public account we have about how the *Catechism* was finally able to make its entry into English-language discourse.[24] According to this article, Archbishop D'Arcy received the text of the Clark translation in April

---

[22] Eric D'Arcy, "The New *Catechism* and Cardinal Newman", *Communio*, fall 1993; see also Eric D'Arcy, "The Universal Catechism and Anglo-American Philosophy", *The Living Light*, winter 1991.

[23] Cardinal Joseph Ratzinger, "A Single English Translation: Cardinal Ratzinger Presents *Catechism* Text to African Synod", *L'Osservatore Romano* (English Edition), May 11, 1994, 15.

[24] See "Doctoring the *Catechism*: Chris McGillion Interviews Eric D'Arcy", *The Tablet*, May 21, 1994.

1993 and worked on it intensively for more than three and a half months, after which the revision he had made was sent out by Rome to various consultants for comments and criticisms. Presumably further work was then done on the basis of the responses received. The Archbishop was assisted in his task by another Australian priest and lecturer at the University of Tasmania, Fr. John Wall.

Archbishop D'Arcy made no claim to be the sole crafter of the final revised and rewritten English translation. He remarked in his *Tablet* interview that he had no sure way of knowing what the final version would look like, although he had no reason to think it would depart significantly from the revision he had made. The "final" final version was evidently completed in Rome and was communicated to the heads of the episcopal conferences in English-speaking countries by the Interdicasterial Commission for the *Catechism of the Catholic Church* in February 1994.[25]

Although Archbishop D'Arcy bore the burden of making all the tedious textual corrections and revisions, he was exceedingly generous in his appreciation of the Clark translation. "Eighty percent of Clark is still there", he said at one point in his *Tablet* interview. "Our contribution is maybe one percent." Or again: "To my mind, Clark reads better stylistically than what we gave. My hope is that we conveyed less elegantly, but a little more closely, the substantial content of the French original." (In the view of the present writers, this is a gracious understatement of rather considerable magnitude.)

Even though he was thus very modest about his own contribution and treated the version he was commissioned to correct more than fairly, Archbishop D'Arcy still did not

---

[25] Ratzinger, "Single English Translation".

fail to bring out certain abiding key issues with regard to the whole translation question. On the basis of the quoted comments of the Archbishop in this interview, we formulate several generalizations on this subject; each of these generalizations is followed by some of his own remarks:

—*It is the responsibility of a translator to render what an original text says, not what someone thinks it should have said.* Archbishop D'Arcy's interview: "I think that for the first translation a lot of language was taboo, and I think that if you are translating an original you mustn't treat anything as taboo. You've got to put it in, whether you furiously disagree with it yourself or not, whether or not you would express it that way. I think you've got to find the most faithful counterpart you can to the original."

—*The use of so-called "inclusive language" inescapably distorts the meaning of many texts.* Archbishop D'Arcy's interview: " 'Mankind' and 'humankind' . . . I don't think that there's much difference in the connotation or the denotation. Those who propose inclusive language are often anxious to avoid the word 'man', so they often put in 'mortal' or 'mortals'. Well, I don't think that has the same connotation as 'man'. But feminism and inclusivism, I suppose, they're both subspecies, are they, of politically correct speech?"

—*The distortions that arise from using inclusive language can cause doctrinal distortions in theological texts.* Archbishop D'Arcy's interview (in answer to the question of whether inclusive language carries doctrinal implications): "On occasion, yes. The second divine person became man—that would be the clearest example. But in a way, even more sinuously throughout the whole thought, it seems to me, one of the many teachings being developed throughout the whole *Catechism* is the relationship between God and man. If you use different words you dilute the richness of that relationship. . . . The relationship between the two is one of the main teachings of the *Catechism*, and it is more perspicuous if you keep the same words."

—*Those who claim to be offended by the traditional generic language that is a natural feature of English are denying to others the right to know what the original text says.* Archbishop D'Arcy's interview: "I do hope they're not offended at us trying to give a faithful rendering. It would be wrong for us to be bowdlerizing and avoiding words that give offense— well, that's what Bowdler did, didn't he: he went through Shakespeare and anything that would bring a blush of shame to a maiden cheek went out. We think that you're entitled to know what Shakespeare said and that you're entitled to know what this *Catechism* says. Our revision isn't meant to be at all insensitive. It's trying to convey faithfully what's there in the French original."

Even if there were no other objections to the use of inclusive language—and there are, of course—all these points made by Archbishop D'Arcy in his London *Tablet* interview by themselves add up to a rather decisive indictment against the attempt to render the Catholic Church's own modern statement of her faith and life in such artificial language. The combination of both blindness and arrogance inherent in such an attempt is really breathtaking, in fact. Although we should not lose sight of the fact that there were other things wrong with the Clark translation besides the inclusive language, this issue nevertheless did surely constitute the greatest single obstacle to the acceptance of any such translation for the *Catechism of the Catholic Church*.

The rather dramatic failure in this instance of the radical feminist version of what novelist George Orwell aptly called totalitarian "newspeak"—ideologically driven artificial language employed to serve politicized ends—is significant not only as far as catechesis is concerned. Hopefully, it will have further implications in the life of the Church at large, most especially in the liturgy, since there appear to be not a few liturgists in official positions in the Church today who evidently believe that radical feminist imperatives must override nearly every other consideration of meaning, tradition, taste, or practice.[26]

One such influential liturgical expert recently wrote, rather in wonderment, with regard to the very idea that anyone might ever want to question the use of inclusive language: "Most people supposed [it] had been largely resolved in the liturgical and biblical fields during the 1970s and 1980s."[27] What he appears to mean by "largely resolved" is that he and his like-minded colleagues have been steadily introducing inclusive language into both liturgical texts and scriptural translations, and, for a long time, nobody in authority objected.

Not only had the bishops of the United States not objected up to then, for example, but in 1990 they actually issued their own set of "criteria" for "evaluating" the use of inclusive language in ecclesiastical texts. Fr. Douglas Kent Clark did not fail to seize upon precisely these bishops' criteria as at least partial justification for his own use of this artificial, feminist-inspired type of language in his translation of the *Catechism*.[28] In the light of Rome's decision on the Clark translation, however, it is no longer clear whether these criteria can continue to stand.

---

[26] See especially Helen Hull Hitchcock, ed., *The Politics of Prayer: Feminist Language and the Worship of God* (San Francisco: Ignatius Press, 1992).

[27] Frederick R. McManus,"Texts and Translations: The ICEL Story", *The Living Light*, spring 1995.

[28] See Clark, "On 'Englishing' the *Catechism*".

It is amazing how so many people today seem to take it for granted that inclusive language simply has to be used, that somehow it truly does constitute the wave of the future, without these questions ever having been seriously discussed or debated. This, of course, is one of the dangers of simply leaving important questions to those in "fields" such as Scripture, liturgy, or catechetics; as part of an educational elite, they are as likely as not to be so out of touch with the average person, and even with the society or culture as a whole, as simply not to know any longer what is appropriate and what is not. Such people are the natural prey of ideologues of the modern radical feminist type, who somehow successfully persuade them that the feminist cause— while it is actually fading in society at large as its deleterious consequences become more and more evident—is still of "overwhelming concern" to everybody.

Surely Christ "sent out" average men as his apostles —fishermen, tax collectors, tent makers—in part *to guard against* the potential tyranny of "experts" and "establishments" of every kind. But not even the system Christ established is going to work if those "sent out" elect to put themselves instead back into the hands of the ideological elites who are our modern experts and the mainstays of our various scriptural, theological, liturgical, and catechetical establishments.

When Rome was faced in the cold light of dawn with the full-blown text of an entire *Catechism* attempting to set forth Catholic doctrine in inclusive language, however, it must have rather quickly become evident that the whole thing was simply not going to work. Even those who perhaps had no antecedent objection to the attempt to use inclusive language could no longer fail to grasp the reality of the situation. Confronted with the actual result, there really was no choice except to reject it, whatever the other difficulties and embarrassments that might then ensue. One senses the realization of this even behind the unfailing courtesy and generosity of Archbishop D'Arcy's remarks: whatever praise he might have seen fit to bestow on the Clark translation, and however sincerely in the particular situation, there could surely not have been, at the same time, any doubt whatsoever in his mind that this translation would simply never do.

Faced with the ineluctable fact of the actual inclusive-language translation, others have independently reached the same conclusion. One of the most sober and sensible of all the evaluations of the question came from another one of the bishops who had already played a vitally significant role in bringing the *Catechism* into being. This was Archbishop William J. Levada, then ordinary of Portland, Oregon and later of San Francisco, one of the seven bishop-writers (and one priest) who served on the international editorial committee for the *Catechism*.

Ever since he became a member of the hierarchy, Archbishop Levada has apparently been cognizant of a large, twofold fact about the Church in our day, a fact of which many, many people are equally conscious and knowledgeable but which, for whatever reason, has never been officially admitted by the hierarchy as a whole to be the case. This large, twofold fact consists of the following: namely, that (1) there is widespread public dissent from authentic Catholic teaching in the Church today, especially on the part of some theologians and other Church professionals; and that (2) this dissent from Church teachings, far from being a theoretical, academic, ivory-tower-type (and therefore relatively harmless) phenomenon, sometimes ends up being *taught* as normative in Catholic classrooms at all levels in the Church.

In the 1980s, Archbishop Levada discovered in a publication issued by the National Catholic Education Association (NCEA) that Catholic educators were henceforth supposed "to *teach . . . students* the importance of dialogue and respectful *dissent*" (emphasis added). Many American Catholics had already made the same or a similar discovery, to their dismay; but as a member of the hierarchy, the then Archbishop of Portland was in a position to do something about it. And he did.

He went before the NCEA's 1986 national convention as a featured speaker and told the assembled Catholic educators in no uncertain terms that:

> Catholic theology does not recognize the right to dissent, if by that we mean adopting conclusions which are contrary to the clear teachings of the authoritative, noninfallible magisterium and which are presented to the public in such a way as to constitute equivalently an alternative personal magisterium.[29]

This is a careful, measured statement—but an exact one. To our knowledge it constitutes the first time that a member of the American hierarchy ever spoke out before a national forum and excluded the type of theological dissent that has unfortunately been only too common in the United States in the postconciliar era. No doubt it took both courage and persistence on the part of the Archbishop to do this. Moreover, the statement was actually made prior to the definitive decision of the Congregation for the Doctrine of the Faith that pioneer dissenter Fr. Charles E. Curran of the Catholic University of America was no longer eligible to teach Catholic theology because of his public espousal of such dissent.

---

[29] Archbishop William Levada, "Dissent and the Catholic Religion Teacher", *Origins*, NC Documentary Service, August 14, 1986.

And Archbishop Levada's statement also came four years before the CDF finally issued a definitive ruling on the question. The CDF "Instruction on the Ecclesial Vocation of the Theologian" (May 1990) said, in effect, what Archbishop Levada had already said to the NCEA convention, namely, that theological dissent was not legitimate.

On the subject of the Clark translation of the *Catechism*, the Archbishop again forthrightly came forward to explain why this translation simply could not in the nature of the case be suitable, however sincere and dedicated the translator and the members of his team may have been. His analysis was not a critique of the translation as such. Rather, it was an examination of Fr. Clark's own exposition of the principles upon which his translation was based. Archbishop Levada, in an article that proved to be a model of both clarity and charity, showed how these principles were necessarily defective and inadequate for the kind of translation the *Catechism* represented.[30]

In his article, the Archbishop spoke favorably of Fr. Clark as a "knowledgeable and dedicated craftsman", who had undertaken the "daunting task" of producing "an English text which is contemporary". Nevertheless, in Archbishop Levada's judgment, and on the basis of the same principles Fr. Clark had enunciated in his article in *The Living Light* which we have already drawn upon above,[31] "a thorough revision of this translation was necessary." Indeed, the Archbishop thought that "the process of producing the English translation should probably have had a wider consultation."

---

[30] Most Reverend William J. Levada, "The Problem with 'Englishing' the *Catechism*", *The Living Light*, spring 1994.
[31] See note 2 *supra*.

"One can imagine", he wrote, "projects for which a freer translation, even a paraphrase, might be desirable. The *Catechism* is not one of them"—not if it is going to be a "compendium of all Catholic doctrine concerning both faith and morals", which is what the 1985 Synod of Bishops had called for.

In order for the *Catechism* to be the "sure norm" for teaching the faith that Pope John Paul II had said it was, Archbishop Levada believed it had to be "the same in every language, and it must be exactly what has been approved as an exercise of the ordinary magisterium of the pope." In this connection, it was surely a mistake to adopt, he thought, as Fr. Clark had adopted, principles of translation developed for liturgical texts. Since these texts must be proclaimed aloud, words and phrases may sometimes have to be added, or omitted, or sometimes moved around, in order to produce a smooth-flowing oral text. Applying similar principles to the translation of the *Catechism* "frequently produced an English text which substantially alters the original", in Archbishop Levada's view.

On the specific question of inclusive language, Archbishop Levada recalled that "the earliest discussions of the translation project did not object to such an attempt." Viewing the result, however, he concluded that "the translation of a doctrinal text such as the *Catechism* into an 'inclusive' English translation is always difficult and may not even be possible." In his view, "the decision to produce a (horizontal) inclusive-language translation took on a priority to which even the principle of fidelity to the original was sacrificed." He thought the same thing to be true of the New Revised Standard Version of the Bible, which was used by the Clark translation: textual accuracy was "sacrificed . . . to the principle of inclusivity".

Archbishop Levada adduced and discussed several examples from this NRSV Bible that tended to prove his point. For example, the NRSV begins Psalm 1 with: "Happy are those who do not follow the advice of the wicked"—instead of the Revised Standard Version's "Blessed is the man who walks not in the counsel of the wicked." According to Archbishop Levada, the NRSV version does not allow the "traditional liturgical sense of the Church praying the psalms with Christ, when it changes the singular person of the Hebrew original to the plural". Just so.

## III

In many ways, producing an acceptable English translation of the *Catechism of the Catholic Church* proved to be as difficult as writing it in the first place. Moreover, the fact that this English text—necessarily—came out written in the traditional generic English that has characterized the language for more than a thousand years proved to be as big an obstacle to the proper reception of it, at least in certain quarters, as did the fact that it continued to insist on teaching Catholic "doctrine".

We have seen how the Roman authorities realized that the translation produced for them by what we may surely characterize as "typical" modern Church "professionals" simply could not be used. This has been true of the *Catechism* project generally. If it had been left to today's typical experts and professionals, it is a pretty sure bet that there never would have been any *Catechism* at all. The sad fact is that too many of today's professionals and experts in the Church are simply attuned too closely to the *Weltanschauung* of the contemporary secular world. They are convinced that what Vatican Council II meant is that Catholics should henceforth adopt many of the standards of the modern world.

What the Council really meant, of course, is that Catholics should go out into the modern world with the standards *of the Church*! It is the decadent modern standards of what Pope John Paul II has aptly styled our contemporary "culture of death" that must yield to the tenets of the ancient faith that once, for a period of time, did provide the foundations and standards for the Western world.

The tenets of this ancient faith are now embodied in a wholly contemporary form in the *Catechism of the Catholic Church*. The *Catechism* project was able to be realized when the successors of the apostles of Christ, the Catholic bishops, took Christ's commission seriously and determined to do what was necessary to fulfill the teaching aspect of that commission by providing an authoritative and usable compendium of Catholic truths and practice for modern man. There is an important lesson residing in the fact that all this was carried out on the episcopal level.

The same thing turned out to be true of the translation of the *Catechism* into English: only when the bishops themselves took the task in hand did an acceptable product materialize. As we have just been recounting, one archbishop had to take in hand the task of correcting the defective translation produced, as it were, by the "experts"; and another archbishop had to undertake personally the public defense of the need to revise that translation in the pages of a journal too often given over to the conventionally liberal revisionist views of the today's catechetical establishment.

In the climate that currently prevails in the Church, however, especially among these same Church professionals and experts, it is by no means assured that these sterling efforts personally exerted by members of the hierarchy will themselves be accepted.

On the contrary, the long delay in bringing out an official English translation of the *Catechism* came in for sharp public criticism. The delay was caused, in the view of two of the current pillars of the catechetical establishment in the United States, by "an organized effort led by a group of dissidents who had their own agenda".[32]

The irrepressible Fr. Andrew Greeley blamed Fr. Joseph Fessio, S.J., for persuading Rome to reject the inclusive-language translation. Fr. Greeley called Fr. Fessio "the most powerful person in American Catholicism", a priest who supposedly "won a one-on-one with Cardinal Law" in getting the Clark translation suppressed.[33] It was implied that Archbishop D'Arcy, who made the revisions, was no doubt the subservient tool of all these same "dissidents"; perhaps Cardinal Ratzinger or even Pope John Paul II have now fallen under their sway as well! We can guess what these American Catholic establishmentarians must think of the cardinals and bishops who produced the *Catechism* itself.

If anything, though, this kind of criticism from people whose salaries are paid by the bishops, and, ultimately, by the faithful, turned out to be even sharper *after* the responsible Church authorities had fully and carefully explained why they had been strictly obliged to act as they did. Archbishops D'Arcy and Levada, for example, certainly provided reasonable and persuasive justifications for the actions taken by

---

[32] Mary Collins and Berard L. Marthaler, preface to *Introducing the Catechism of the Catholic Church: Traditional Themes and Contemporary Issues*, ed. Berard L. Marthaler (New York and Mahwah, N.J.: Paulist Press, 1994).

[33] See Greeley, "Father Fessio's Power".

Church authorities, as we have seen. Nevertheless, the periodical *Church*, for example, published by the quasi-official National Pastoral Life Center and widely distributed within the Church's own organizations and among Church professionals, quite intemperately denounced, in its fall 1994 number, the whole process by which U.S. Catholics obtained their *Catechism* in English.

"The Vatican displayed a dramatic lack of collegiality in the way it heard but did not heed the U.S. bishops, who had endorsed an inclusive language translation", an editorial in *Church* thundered. "Nor did the Vatican let them play any part in producing or approving the final text", it charged.

And again: "The Vatican walked the extra mile, albeit a mile out of its way, to offend many English-speaking women and men by replacing the inclusive-language text with a masculine-language one." "The *Catechism*, or substantial parts of it, will have to be retranslated in inclusive terms before it can be used effectively in many quarters", this editorial in *Church* concluded.[34]

The shallowness, as well as the inaccuracy, of this type of snap judgment is striking. This editorial evinces no concern whatsoever for the integrity of Church doctrine, for the idea that the Church is strictly obliged to "guard what has been entrusted" to her (1 Tim 6:20). It is devoid of any appreciation for the obviously arduous and extraordinary efforts of the prelates involved to do the right and necessary thing with the least possible offense to anyone. Instead, it is wholly and uncritically caught up in the coils of a modern ideology of radical feminism fundamentally alien to the Catholic faith.

Unhappily, even some American bishops appear unwisely

---

[34] "Translating the Faith", *Church*, fall 1994.

to have become caught up in the same cause. In a 1995 document submitted to the U.S. bishops' Ad Hoc Committee on Mission and Structure concerned with restructuring the bishops' conference, these particular bishops included the following complaint:

> On vital issues of a pastoral nature, the bishops sometimes feel ignored. A recent example was the English translation of the *Catechism*. This was taken completely out of our hands and the hands of other English-speaking conferences. The English draft that we saw earlier appears to have been "intercepted" by a small group who succeeded in reintroducing sexist language at considerable delay, all this without consultation with us. We patiently waited, almost like children. This is cause for some wonder and suggests the need to develop a more mature, adult, collegial relationship with Rome.[35]

Unfortunately, this type of judgment is not untypical of those who particularly like to think they are "modern Catholics" today. We could cite other views against the generic English translation in the same vein. But let us again quote the late Vaticanologist-journalist Peter Hebblethwaite and his cry of indignation over the "offense" now given by the Catholic Church to "women" by issuing the *Catechism* in standard English: "Man, man, man booms like a cannon. It would be offensive even if we did not know the Clark ver-

---

[35] "Issues in Restructuring the Bishops' Conference", *Origins*, CNS Documentary Service, July 13, 1995. This document was signed by Archbishop Rembert Weakland of Milwaukee; Bishops Raymond Lucker of New Ulm, Kenneth Untener of Saginaw, Walter Sullivan of Richmond, and William Hughes of Covington; Auxiliary Bishops P. Francis Murphy of Baltimore, Thomas Gumbleton of Detroit, Peter Rosazza of Hartford, and Thomas Costello of Syracuse; and retired Bishops Charles Buswell of Pueblo and John Fitzpatrick of Brownsville.

sion. Knowing the Clark version, it becomes gratuitously offensive and almost incomprehensible. It involves a certain paranoia."[36]

According to Peter Hebblethwaite in the same article, "ordinary courtesy and late 20th century usage demands that inclusive language be used whenever possible."

Why is this thought to be so? Nowhere has it been demonstrated by anybody that inclusive language is what "women" either need or want, or that "women" have simply been excluded from English discourse for the last thousand years. There has, of course, been a sustained ideological push for inclusive language over the past twenty or thirty years by the radical feminists, and many people have inescapably been influenced by this. There are even people who go on *trying* to use inclusive language. Perhaps there are even many who are convinced that it ought to be used. Perhaps there are even some women who really are "offended" when it is not used; they have certainly been told often enough they *should* be offended.

Nevertheless, inclusive language still naturally strikes most native speakers of English as artificial, stilted, inelegant, and clumsy. Few people ever *do* resort to it unless they are specifically thinking about it, and even then the results they come up with are rarely happy, as some of them almost ruefully realize themselves. Inclusive language is *unnatural*, in short, and native speakers of English *know* it.

Some people who pay close attention to questions of style in writing or speaking have the growing impression that the fad or fashion for this highly contrived type of speech is in any case beginning to fade in the secular world at large. Even some convinced feminists are increasingly lapsing into nor-

---

[36] Hebblethwaite, "Rome Mishandled".

mal speech. It is true that some recently published dictionaries, in response to feminist pressure, now list the definition "an adult male human being" as the *first* definition of "man"; but these very same dictionaries have also retained the meaning "human being" or "member of the human species" in their definition of the word. They have retained this definition for the simple reason that these meanings also continue to be basic English usage. It is almost impossible to speak the language without resorting to these meanings, at least sometimes. If the *Catechism* translation exercise proved anything, it certainly proved this: inclusive language does not work.

In other words, the word "man" still *does* "include" women when used in a generic sense—a sense always recognizable and understandable by any native speaker of English, feminist sympathizer or not. The notion that standard English usage is inherently offensive to women, however, is still imagined to be the case by some Church professionals, including, sad to say, some clerics and even bishops, as we have seen. Catholic priests (and bishops) may even be particularly vulnerable to feminist-style propaganda in this regard, since there was a time, not very long ago, when the typical clerical culture in the United States did sometimes tend toward neglect of certain women's concerns. There was even at times a deliberate clerical avoidance of contact with women—prudently keeping one's distance, as it were. Today's feminists have not been slow to exploit possible feelings of uneasiness, or even of guilt, about this former clerical culture on the part of some of those in Holy Orders.

But decisions concerning the Church's new *Catechism* for the twenty-first century and beyond should never be made on the basis of such superficial and even transient considerations. The Holy See's action in the matter of the English translation of the *Catechism* was exactly right. Where, indeed, would we be without the oversight of the Holy See on this as on a number of other issues? Over and over again its judgments on some controversial matters have been resoundingly vindicated.

We may fittingly conclude this chapter by looking briefly at Cardinal Joseph Ratzinger's own serene account of the whole English-translation process. In view of all the rumors, charges, and countercharges that swirled around this whole affair at its height, the Cardinal's own sober and careful summary of what took place deserves to be noted. First of all, the Cardinal spoke of the need for an accurate *single* English translation for use in various countries where perhaps the "demand" for inclusive language may not be quite as visible as it is in the United States and the United Kingdom. Secondly, Cardinal Ratzinger stressed that the translation had to be *accurate*—faithfully reflecting what the original *says*. It also had to be in a style "in keeping with the magisterial nature of the text".

Cardinal Ratzinger did not fail to thank publicly the episcopal conferences for their contributions and to thank Cardinal Law and Bishop Konstant warmly by name as well. It cannot be said that Rome failed to give them every opportunity to extricate themselves from the inclusive-language morass without any embarrassment to them personally or to their bishops' conferences. Indeed, it is no exaggeration to say that Rome simply took the heat, without complaint or evasion, on the whole *Catechism*-translation business.

Thus, Cardinal Ratzinger, on behalf of the Holy See, can certainly not be said to have failed to accord both maximum respect to the concerned bishops and maximum credit where credit was due. Furthermore, his own description of what subsequently took place could hardly have been more delicately or judiciously stated. One keeps hoping and wishing that Rome would sometimes at least get credit for the respect and sensitivity with which it *does* typically proceed in these matters, as the following paragraph of Cardinal Ratzinger's account evidences:

> The [translation] was subsequently revised by the Congregation for the Doctrine of the Faith. The revision, which by the same token was necessary for every translation of the *Catechism*, was carried out in accordance with the procedure specified by the Interdicasterial Commission established by the Holy See on 28 February, 1993, to deal with all questions relating to the *Catechism* after its promulgation. In examining the various translations of the *Catechism* (to date, about 60), the Congregation is particularly concerned to ensure that the content of the translation faithfully corresponds to the originally promulgated text. . . . For the revision of the English translation, the Congregation also made use of the collaboration of several diocesan ordinaries and various experts with competence in the different theological disciplines, who belonged to English-speaking countries.[37]

This last sentence would certainly seem to be a remarkably tactful way of mentioning the central role of Archbishop Eric D'Arcy in the revision of the English translation.

What is there to be added? When the official English version of the *Catechism* was presented to the Holy Father on May 27, 1994, there were present at the ceremony not only Cardinal Law and Bishop Konstant, as was entirely fitting and proper; there was also present Archbishop Joseph Eric D'Arcy of Hobart, Tasmania, Australia![38]

---

[37] Ratzinger, "Single English Translation".

[38] See *"Catechism* Is Instrument of Church's Unity", *L'Osservatore Romano* (English Edition), June 1, 1994.

# CHAPTER FIVE

# *A Catechetical Establishment Response to the* Catechism

I

From the time the idea for a universal catechism was first broached, there were those within the Church who were critical of the whole project. Many of these critics were to be found in the ranks of academics, theologians, and religious educators, and, in general, among people involved in Church affairs—seemingly, the very kind of people who should have been interested in a clear, consistent post-Vatican-II statement of what the Catholic Church holds and teaches.

But the fact is, in the postconciliar era, Catholic doctrine has not been the principal interest of many of the people most heavily involved in Church affairs. Nor has the appearance of the *Catechism* so far seemed to have changed many minds on this score. Nor do many of those seem to have been converted who never wanted any catechism in the first place.

Those familiar with the religious-education scene in the United States in the postconciliar era will already have some

---

An abridged version of this chapter appeared as an article in *The Catholic World Report*, October 1995.

inkling of the reasons why today's typical new catechists, and the theological gurus who stand behind them, do not like the new *Catechism*. They do not like it because it asserts definite truths, whereas they tend to prefer indefinite, interminable "searching"; because it is cognitive and doctrinal, whereas they would prefer something more social and "experiential"; because it is traditional, whereas they almost always prefer something new; because it is authoritative, whereas they invariably prefer "consultation" and "democracy", regardless of whether these things even apply to the case; because it is concerned with redemption from sin by Christ and looks to our sanctification in this life and salvation in the world to come, whereas they almost compulsively prefer self-help, self-expression, "community", and vague uplift, combined with a this-worldly social activism.

These and similar preferences are widely shared today within what we may call the catechetical and theological establishments in the United States. If pressed, of course, most members of these establishments would probably hasten to deny that they object to Catholic doctrine as such. For one thing that would surely give the game away, once and for all, and they badly need to maintain their positions within the Catholic education structure.

As likely as not, they will say that they prefer the diversity and particularity of many different national and regional expressions of Catholicism to any single "Vatican-mandated" compendium of Church teachings. Of course, in expressing such a preference, they normally do not address the question of whether their preferred "national and regional expressions" are compatible with the Church's teachings (in today's era of dissent, this can no longer be assumed).

Since, however, in spite of all the antecedent objections that were raised against the whole idea of a catechism, the

Pope has nevertheless mandated a single, central modern expression of the Church's faith and morals, theological and catechetical establishmentarians accustomed to today's ways of thinking are now faced with a problem: What to do about the *Catechism of the Catholic Church*? The reactions to the *Catechism*, especially from within the catechetical establishment, have accordingly been quite interesting. One theology professor has recently summarized the principal reactions among modern catechetical professionals probably as well as anybody ever could summarize it:

> Some have suggested that the *Catechism* not be distributed widely to the faithful, that it is not designed for classroom use, that it is only a set of guidelines and certainly not a text to be read at home, that it is only a framework for adaptation, that it represents merely one ecclesiology among many rather than the fruit of the Council. We are told far more about what the *Catechism* is *not*, than what it is, what we are *not* to do, than what we might do. . . .[1]

To this perceptive recital of the ways the current catechetical establishment is tending to look at the new *Catechism*, we can add the comment of a former diocesan director of religious education, who has announced to the world that, if we are to read the *Catechism* in an "adult way", the "sure teaching" that the Pope has assured us the *Catechism* contains "must be *in dialogue* with the *actual practice* of the Christian" (emphasis added).[2]

In other words, if there are Catholics out there who do not believe and follow what the Church teaches, as certain

---

[1] Rev. Stephen F. Brett, S.S.J., "Reception and the *Catechism*", *Homiletic & Pastoral Review*, October 1994, 21.

[2] Fr. Jeffrey Godecker, "How to Read the *Catechism* in an Adult Way", *The Criterion* (Indiana), June 19, 1994.

recent polls and studies certainly do seem to indicate, then the task of the religious educator is no longer to reaffirm what the Church nevertheless still does teach, as the *Catechism* attests; the task of the religious educator is rather to enter into "dialogue" with this disbeliever about what his "actual practice" might be.

Suddenly, "actual practice" seems to have been placed on the same level as what the Church teaches. Some of us might strain to recall where in the Gospels Jesus Christ ever dealt in this manner with the sinners he encountered (or where he mentioned that we must receive his message in an "adult way" for that matter). But then that was presumably back in a period before the potential of "dialogue", as we understand it today, had been brought out in all its fullness.

This same diocesan director of religious education also believes that the *Catechism* "will contribute to the continuing tension of *balancing the weight of the tradition with the insights of theology*" (emphasis added)[3]—as if "the tradition" needed to be "balanced" with anything, or as if "the insights of theology", even valid ones, were even remotely on the same level as what has been guarded, interpreted, developed, and handed down in the Church with the help of the Holy Spirit for the sake of our sanctification and salvation ("the weight of tradition").

Actually, the idea of "balancing" what the Church teaches with "the insights of theology"—presumably theology at variance with what the Church teaches; otherwise what is being "balanced"?—is unfortunately consistent with the idea that we should simply "dialogue" with Catholics who reject in their "actual practice" what the Church teaches. No doubt we should remain in touch with such Catholics, if pos-

---

[3] Ibid.

sible. But this continued contact should be primarily in order to attempt to *bring them back*; any "dialogue" with them that does not include a reiteration of what the Church does in fact teach would be dishonest. We *owe* them our witness to the authentic message of Christ, as the Church bears witness to it and as it is now systematically and authoritatively laid out for us in the *Catechism*.

Unfortunately, however, this is not always very clearly seen today. We keep encountering these same ideas about dialogue and balancing with alarming frequency, in fact, as we look at what some of our religious educators are doing today. We are therefore obliged to point out that these ideas are fundamentally *mistaken*. Indeed, they are actually ruinous to the idea of the faith as *true*.

A religious educator "sent out" by the Church cannot legitimately take any other position but that what the *Catechism* teaches *is* true, just as it is also incumbent upon all who wish to follow Christ to believe these truths. Christ most emphatically did *not* say: "Go, therefore, and *dialogue* —and *balance* what I say with what others say!"

The *Catechism* itself quotes Vatican II's Declaration on Religious Freedom, *Dignitatis Humanæ* (no. 14), to the effect that we are "to treat with love, prudence, and patience those who are in error or ignorance with regard to the faith" (CCC 2104). But the *Catechism* nowhere suggests that the faith itself can be downplayed or diluted in any way when approaching those in ignorance or error, even if they are "modern Catholics". It is a characteristic idea of our own decadent modern culture, not of the Catholic faith, that we may simply "split the difference", where matters of fundamental truth or principle are concerned.

The *Catechism*, quoting both the Gospel of Matthew and Vatican II's Dogmatic Constitution on the Church, *Lumen*

*Gentium*, insists that it is one of the primary duties of all Christians to uphold the faith in its integrity at all times:

> The disciple of Christ must not only keep the faith and live on it, but also profess it, confidently bear witness to it, and spread it: "All, however, must be prepared to confess Christ before men and to follow him along the way of the Cross, amidst the persecutions which the Church never lacks." Service and witness to the faith are necessary for salvation: "So every one who acknowledges me before men, I also will acknowledge before my Father who is in heaven; but whoever denies me before men, I also will deny before my Father who is in heaven" (CCC 1816).

One important gauge or measure of how religious educators are carrying out their responsibilities in this regard is: How are they receiving the *Catechism of the Catholic Church?* Do they accept it as coming to them with the authority with which Christ endowed the Church? Do they intend henceforth to make it the basis—the "point of reference" —for what they are teaching? Or are some of them perhaps anxious to resist or evade the implications for the teaching of the faith that the *Catechism* now brings? One of the best ways to find the answers to these questions is to take a closer look at how some of the leading religious educators in the field are treating the *Catechism*, how typical members of the catechetical establishment are responding to it. Let us look, then, at a typical example.

## II

One of the first commentaries on the *Catechism of the Catholic Church* to appear in English was authored by two members of the theology department at Xavier University in Cincinnati, Ohio: Dr. Brennan Hill and Dr. William Madges. Their book is entitled *The Catechism: Highlights & Commentary*. For convenience we shall henceforth refer to it as *H & C*.[4]

It is an important book, and not only because it appeared so quickly after the *Catechism* itself, was fairly widely publicized in religious education circles, and was almost immediately favorably reviewed in religious-education journals.[5] It is important because it is more than just a book. For one thing, an only slightly abridged version of the book appeared in seven successive issues of *The Religion Teacher's Journal* between September 1994 and April/May 1995, and thus it represents a commentary that has undoubtedly reached a sizable number of the people in religious education. For another thing, its publisher also simultaneously issued a series of six heavily promoted catechist-training videos based upon it. Also, an Australian edition of the book came out at the same time as the American edition.

In short, *H & C* represents what thousands of religious-education directors, teachers, and catechists are hearing and learning about the *Catechism of the Catholic Church*. It is surely no exaggeration to describe the book, along with its serialized version and the videos that go along with it, as one of the more significant responses to the *Catechism* from the catechetical establishment.

Why, indeed, have a *Highlights & Commentary* on the *Catechism* at all? Why not just use the *Catechism* itself, which is what would occur to the average person? One of the favor-

---

[4] Brennan Hill and William Madges, *The Catechism: Highlights & Commentary* (Mystic, Conn.: Twenty-Third Publications, 1994).

[5] See reviews in, e.g., *The Catechist*, September 1994, 19; also *Church*, spring 1995, 47.

able reviews of the book provides one clue when it speaks of the "somewhat complex and tedious structure of the *Catechism* itself" and finds this book of Hill and Madges "invaluable for parish DREs, clergy, pastoral ministers and other Church professionals who aren't likely to wade through the *Catechism* itself".[6]

Professors Hill and Madges also provide their own answer to the question. Unlike many other readers, they too found the text of the *Catechism* "quite long and rather difficult to read and understand". So they developed this book out of a desire to answer the following questions:

> What is the person to do who wants to know the basic content of the *Catechism*, yet is unable to sit down and read the 600-page text? What is the person to do who can read the entire text, but who does not know how it relates to the church's long history of catechesis? Where can a person turn if he or she wishes to know how contemporary theological developments relate to the content of the *Catechism*?

We note immediately from this explanation, incidentally, that, unlike the *Catechism* itself, *H & C* employs so-called "inclusive language" ("person . . . he or she"). This is pretty consistent throughout the text, in fact, even when the authors are supposedly summarizing articles in standard English from the *Catechism*, without adding any comment of their own. The following is an example of this:

> Through revelation God makes it possible for individuals to respond to God and to know and love God in a way that is far beyond the response that is possible solely from natural reason [Note: "God . . . God . . . God": the writers cannot bring themselves to use the pronoun "him"].

---

[6] In *The Catechist*, September 1994.

God's self-communication is addressed to all human-kind and culminates in the person and mission of Jesus Christ. God's covenant reaches all people [cf. CCC 52–53].

In short, *H & C* restores exactly what the Holy See thought it had eliminated when it rejected the original English translation of the *Catechism* done in inclusive language and insisted on a translation in standard English. *H & C*'s decision to resort to an artificial form of speech that the supreme authority of the Church had specifically seen fit to exclude is, unfortunately, only too symptomatic of many other things in this book. This particular abuse is carried to the point where paragraphs 2566–69 of the *Catechism*, for example, are summarized as: "God has always called people to relationships with God's self. All religions give evidence of humanity's search for God and their [*sic*] response to God's initiative."

From the kind of language in this "summary", we can surely catch something of a glimpse of how the whole *Catechism* in English would have read if Rome had not intervened.

The basic method of the volume is to summarize the content of the *Catechism* in a series of very brief articles and then to provide a short "commentary" by the authors on the content that has thus been summarized. The authors openly state that one of their primary intentions is "to place the teachings of the *Catechism* into *dialogue with other trends in contemporary theology*" (emphasis added).

So here is that code word "dialogue" again! What it appears to signify in this context is that the *Catechism* just cannot be taken by itself. No: it has to be taken in "dialogue with other trends in contemporary theology", and otherwise interpreted for the catechist by experts such as Professors Hill and Madges. For them, "contemporary theology" evidently enjoys a position and prestige that puts it on the same level, if not above, the level of the *Catechism* itself. Presumably what the *Catechism* says represents merely one "theology", and hence the "other trends", implied to be of equal validity, must be used to supplement the *Catechism*.

In addition to providing their own interpretation and comparison with other theological trends along with their summary, Professors Hill and Madges also list "suggested readings" for each chapter, some of which would scarcely reenforce the authority of the *Catechism* as normative for Catholic belief and practice, since not a few of these "suggested readings" are by open, and, in some cases, notorious, dissenters from Catholic teaching.

We shall cite only a few examples that indicate that this is indeed the way Professors Hill and Madges understand the meaning of the "commentary" they provide in *H & C* on the summarized text of the *Catechism*. Typically, they blandly note how this or that contemporary theology or theologian "goes beyond" what the *Catechism* says. Or else they remark that this or that theological view represents a "broader perspective" than the one adopted by the *Catechism*—as if such a "perspective", merely because it is "broader", would automatically take precedence over God's word mediated for us today in the *Catechism* guaranteed by the authority of the Church.

Knowledgeable and perceptive readers of *H & C*, however, will not fail to note that the kinds of instances mentioned by the authors, as often as not, modify, undermine, and even nullify what the *Catechism* itself says. The whole point of the exercise seems to be not to "comment" on the text so much as to let religious educators know what they should *really* think about what the *Catechism* says.

Those with reasonably long memories will recall that this is exactly the way the catechetical establishment has typically dealt with official Church documents and directives in the postconciliar era. Faced with unwelcome documents from the hierarchy, the catechetical establishment has regularly prepared its own "commentaries" on them and provided its own "suggested readings" about them. This is how the catechetical establishment dealt with Rome's 1971 *General Catechetical Directory*, with the U.S. bishops 1973 *Basic Teachings for Catholic Religious Education*, and with the 1978 U.S. *National Catechetical Directory*.[7]

The method adopted in *H & C* is ideal for this kind of exercise. The book first "highlights" what the *Catechism* says in its short summaries; and then, in effect, it takes as much back as the authors wish by explaining what the "broader perspective" is or how some modern theologians have "gone beyond" the *Catechism*'s position. We need to look at a few examples of exactly how this method is carried out.

The *Catechism* reaffirms, for example, as the firm teaching of the Church, that the existence of God can be known with certainty by the natural light of reason but that because of human sin and other natural human limitations revelation and grace are necessary (CCC 35–38). *H & C* summarizes this adequately enough in this instance (although this cannot be said of all its summaries); but then, in the commentary, the book goes on to say:

> Karl Rahner, the twentieth-century Jesuit theologian, moved beyond this view by proposing that people have been created in "openness to God." He explained that

---

[7] See Msgr. Michael J. Wrenn, *Catechisms and Controversies: Religious Education in the Postconciliar Years* (San Francisco: Ignatius Press, 1991), esp. 160–76 and 186–93; and also Chapter One *supra*.

human nature bears a "supernatural existential" which enables people to find God as the answer to their questions and the ground of human experience. Bernard Lonergan, another twentieth-century Jesuit theologian, proposed that there is indeed a level of human consciousness whereby people can reach out to God. Other theologians have offered similar methods for more closely co-relating humans and their culture with God as their accepted horizon. They point out that all creation, and uniquely human beings, has been "graced" with God's presence and power.

In other words, the revelation and grace given through the Church, which the *Catechism* is at such pains to emphasize, turns out to be not so necessary after all, since human beings have all been "graced" in any case. We are not, by the way, taking any position here on the theological opinions of Rahner or Lonergan as they are described in *H & C*; we are simply showing how Professors Hill and Madges insist on viewing the *Catechism* in a modern theological perspective that the document's bishop-authors consciously and expressly avoided, confining their exposition to the faith of the Church.

*H & C* thus insists on including what the Church decided should be left out. Not incidentally, in this case, what is thus reinstated on the sole authority of the two commentators happens to be a favorite theme of the catechetical establishment: revelation and grace and the whole great and magnificent drama of salvation history all tend to boil down in the end to "human experience" anyway!

It is no accident, in this regard, that the *H & C* summary simply passes over in silence paragraphs 57–65 of the *Catechism* concerning the role of Abraham, Israel, and the prophets in divine revelation. This kind of simple omission of what is not thought important is unfortunately typical of the book's summaries of the articles of the *Catechism* generally.

And in this same perspective, it is no longer any surprise that the commentary goes on to emphasize that "revelation is understood to be given to all . . . [promoting] a deeper respect for truth claims of other churches and religions. [This] alerts people to be attentive to revelation as it emerges through personal and communal experience."

Far be it from us to belittle "respect for . . . other churches and religions". The *Catechism* does inculcate this within the proper perspective. The way *H & C* represents it, however, distorts and exaggerates almost beyond recognition the *Catechism*'s position. The way *H & C* represents it, we as well as many catechists reading this book might get the idea that the *Catechism* need not be considered so important after all: for all we really need to do is start getting in touch with our own feelings!

So much for grace and revelation, then. Let us look at another doctrine of the *Catechism* as *H & C* summarizes and then comments on it. In the section dealing with God the Father, *H & C*, in its summary, while granting that God has revealed himself as a "Father", scarcely goes beyond mentioning that word. In its commentary, however, it emphasizes that:

> The *Catechism* points out that God is not an anonymous force for Catholics, but a living, loving, and saving presence. It acknowledges at the same time that this God is Mystery, and beyond our temporal and spatial considerations. It deems both feminine and masculine images as acceptable ways to describe God's love. Interfaith dialogue, liberation theology, process thought, and feminist theology have suggested many alternative possibilities for

imaging God beyond those mentioned in the *Catechism*. Whereas in the past there was a stress on the transcendence of God, the emphasis today seems to have shifted to the immanence of God. This shift is most evident in the effort to link Christian theology with ecological concerns—a concern duly noted in the pages of the *Catechism*.

Yes, but the *Catechism*'s ecological dicta cannot even remotely be considered in the same perspective as is given in this very strange paragraph, which so indiscriminately legitimates things as foreign to the *Catechism*'s perspective as process thought and liberation theology at the same time that it ascribes to the *Catechism* an immanentist tendency that really belongs to the "modern theology" the authors are trying to add to the picture.

Moreover, an important dimension of the truth content of the *Catechism* is lost when God's primary revelation of himself as "Father" is minimized the way it is here and when it is implied that a "Mother" image might do just as well. As a modern theologian who will undoubtedly never be quoted by Professors Hill and Madges explains: " 'Fatherhood' is eloquent of God's transcendent origination of the world." Fatherhood stands for transcendence, while motherhood implies immanence. Even while it recognizes God's immanence, the main thrust of Scripture is to emphasize his transcendence. The meaning of the primary male-gender imagery for God in Scripture accordingly signifies "the discontinuity between God and the world". The masculine gender is "the gender farther from the process of 'birthing. . . .' In himself, as the *Catechism* points out, God is neither male nor female: that fact does not, however, justify *our* transgression of the (theologically crucial) rules of biblical discourse"—namely, understanding God's revelation of himself as primarily a "Father".[8]

Professors Hill and Madges, however, are evidently unconcerned about "the rules of biblical discourse". Rather, they are concerned to equate "motherhood" with "fatherhood" where God is concerned precisely because they are interested in promoting God's immanence ahead of his transcendence, contrary to the usage in Scripture—and in the *Catechism*.

In any case, explanations of this muddled type hopelessly distort the basic meaning and thrust of the *Catechism*. What the latter actually says that may have prompted the assertion that "both feminine and masculine images" of God's love are equally "acceptable" is that God's "love for his people is *stronger* than a mother's for her children" (CCC 49); and that God's "parental tenderness can also be *expressed* by the image of motherhood" (CCC 239) (emphasis added). This latter article, in fact, is precisely the one where the *Catechism* points out that God transcends the human distinction between the sexes. In any case, this purely descriptive language can in no way justify the implied idea that "motherhood" is used as frequently or as effectively as "fatherhood" in God's basic revelation to us of his own nature.

It would seem to be evident here that *H & C* is using the *Catechism* merely as a peg on which to hang some of the authors' own favorite ideas and ideologies. And it is these same ideas and ideologies, not what the Church herself has issued, that the religious educator seeking to understand the *Catechism* through a book such as this is going to get.

---

[8] See Aidan Nichols, O.P., *The Splendour of Doctrine: The Catechism of the Catholic Church on Christian Believing* (Edinburgh, Scotland: T & T Clark, 1995), 35.

## III

In order to grasp the misleading method used by Hill and Madges in *The Catechism: Highlights & Commentary*, it is worth tracing a particular doctrine or theme through the book to see how it is consistently treated. Let us, therefore, look at how *H & C* deals with the question of sin, particularly Original Sin, both in the parts of the book dealing with the *Catechism*'s part one, on doctrine, and in those treating part two, on the Sacraments.

As has been fairly widely noted, the *Catechism* unambiguously reaffirms the Church's doctrines of the Fall of man and Original Sin. According to the *Catechism*, the Fall involved a real deed "that took place at the beginning of history" (CCC 390), as the Second Vatican Council also plainly taught: "Although set by God in a state of rectitude, man, enticed by the evil one, abused his freedom at the very start of history."[9]

This is the traditional teaching of the Church; and the *Catechism* does not fail to reiterate it (cf. CCC 397). There is no way to evade or avoid this doctrine, however "hard" a saying it might seem to the Neomodernist mentality. If you want to be a Catholic in the true sense, you are obliged to believe in Original Sin.

Typically, though, *H & C* tries to blur the whole thing:

Twentieth-century biblical exegesis has offered valuable insights on the sources and original meaning of the creation stories in the Book of Genesis. From this perspective, the ancient myths symbolized in Adam and Eve and

---

[9] Vatican Council II, Pastoral Constitution on the Church in the Modern World, *Gaudium et Spes*, no. 13.

the story of the Fall show how sin has been part of humankind from the beginning. Original sin is seen as a universal tendency to sin, a tendency that is influenced by the sinful structures into which all people are born. Some theologians hold that this view seems to be more compatible with the findings of contemporary anthropology and the social sciences than the view found in the *Catechism* that speaks of a historical fall from a state of original justice.

We should note here how quietly and imperceptibly what is actually a firm teaching of the Catholic Church simply becomes "the view found in the *Catechism*". This characterization is slipped in so naturally and unobtrusively that it almost inevitably *seems* to be all right; the reader tends not to balk at it but simply to read on. If the authors had emphasized the point, saying, in effect, "we are defying the authority of the Church and asserting contrary to it that the notion of a historical fall from a state of original justice is nothing more than a 'view' which the *Catechism* happens to espouse, although 'other theologies' today have different ideas", the reader's suspicions might have been aroused.

As it is, *H & C*'s soothing method tends to raise minimum misgivings of any kind, and the religious educator is thereby more easily brought to have a different view of the Fall and Original Sin than the Church clearly states in the *Catechism*.

What *H & C* lamely describes in this paragraph as a "universal tendency that is influenced by sinful structures", the *Catechism* unequivocally describes as "the tragic consequences of the first disobedience" (CCC 399). According to the Church's teaching, the tendency to sin had a concrete, specific cause, namely, the actual sin of our first parents. *H & C*'s "sinful structures" did not just happen to be there.

As the *Catechism* relates, much more truly and capably than
*H & C*:

> The harmony in which [Adam and Eve] had found them-
> selves, thanks to original justice, is now destroyed; the
> control of the soul's spiritual faculties over the body is
> shattered; the union of man and woman becomes sub-
> ject to tensions, their relations henceforth marked by lust
> and domination. Harmony with creation is broken; visible
> creation has become alien and hostile to man. Because of
> man, creation is now subject to its "bondage to decay"
> (Rom 8:21). Finally, the consequence explicitly foretold
> for this disobedience will come true; man will "return to
> the ground" (Gen 3:19), for out of it he was taken. *Death
> makes its entrance into human history* (CCC 400).

The very next article of the *Catechism* remarks that "after that first sin, the world is virtually inundated by sin"
(CCC 401). For their part, however, Professors Hill and
Madges think "pollution and exploitation" are what need
"to be stressed at this time. . . . Likewise today there is a
profound awakening to the truth of the equality of genders",
they say.

*H & C*'s treatment of sin generally recalls nothing so
much as the sort of Pelagianism to which most modern religious liberals today still tend to subscribe. In this connection, it is salutary to recall what Pope John Paul II wrote
on this same subject in his too often neglected 1984 apostolic exhortation *Reconciliatio et Pænitentia*. In this document,
the Pope spoke *inter alia* of the typical modern usage that
"contrasts social sin and personal sin . . . in a way that leads
. . . to the watering down and almost the abolition of personal sin." This approach to the problem of evil and sin,
according to the Pope, derives "from non-Christian ideologies and systems". "Blame for sin is to be placed not so

much on the moral conscience of the individual, but rather on some vague entity or anonymous collectivity such as the system, society, structures, or institutions."

This, of course, is exactly how Hill and Madges approach the question in their reference to "sinful structures". This may be a common fashionable "out" for modern theologians unwilling or unable to affirm the faith of the Church in the matter. Pope John Paul II nevertheless makes it abundantly clear that "whenever the Church speaks of situations of sins, or condemns as social sins, she knows and she proclaims that such cases of social sin are the result and the concentration of many personal sins."[10]

In dealing with the sacraments instituted by Christ as, among other things, specific remedies for sin, *H & C* again evidences serious problems. On the subject of Original Sin, the book actually asserts that in the *Catechism*'s treatment of baptism "there is not the former emphasis on removal of Original Sin." In another place, the *H & C* commentary informs us that "Original Sin is a later notion that is not constitutive of baptism."

On the contrary, however, the *Catechism*'s paragraph 1250 plainly affirms that "born with a fallen human nature and tainted by Original Sin, children also have need of a new birth in Baptism to be freed from the power of darkness and brought into the realm of the children of God, to which all men are called." Similarly, paragraph 1263 says that Original Sin and all personal sins are forgiven by baptism, while the very next numbered paragraph, 1264, restates the Church's traditional belief concerning the temporal consequences of sin.

---

[10] Pope John Paul II, apostolic exhortation *Reconciliatio et Pænitentia*, December 2, 1984, no. 16.

But it is in its treatment of the sacrament of Penance, or Reconciliation (including personal confession of sins), that the basic approach of *H & C* can be most clearly seen. We have pointed out that the book's basic method is first to summarize (more or less) what the *Catechism* states and then, in effect, to modify or take back whatever is deemed necessary by the way the commentary is worded.

Thus, the *Catechism* says that confession of sins to a priest "is an essential part of the sacrament of Penance" (CCC 1456). *H & C*, however, informs the reader, who in all likelihood is a religious educator trying to become properly grounded in the *Catechism*, that "some scholars continue to maintain that the actual confession of sins is not integral to the sacrament."

The *Catechism* further specifies that "children must go to the sacrament of Penance before receiving Holy Communion for the first time" (CCC 1457). This firm requirement of the Church is actually enshrined in the new 1983 Code of Canon Law.[11] *H & C* nevertheless assures the unsuspecting religion teacher that "there seems to be a consensus that young children do not have sufficient moral awareness or responsibility to commit serious sins, and are thus *not* obliged to confess their sins before receiving communion" (emphasis added). We might ask: "Consensus" among whom? Theologians? Religious educators?

This statement directly contradicts both the *Catechism* and the Code of Canon Law, but this is evidently not sufficient to secure the book's removal from catechist-training programs.

But there is more. The *Catechism* further teaches that mortal sin, if "not redeemed by repentance and God's for-

---

[11] Canon 914.

giveness . . . causes exclusion from Christ's kingdom and the eternal death of hell" (CCC 1861). This is very serious. *H & C*, however, trivializes the very notion of mortal sin—like many Neomodernist theologians, they prefer the term "serious sin"—and instead informs the reader, perhaps someone teaching people whose souls could be lost as a result of unrepented sin, that "the term 'fundamental option,' although it is not used in the *Catechism*, has gained acceptance among many moral theologians and religious educators as a way of describing the direction of one's moral life."

What they fail to mention here is that the Church not only does not mention this "fundamental option" idea; the Church has specifically considered it and rejected it. The disingenuous comment that the idea is "not mentioned" in the *Catechism* provides no hint whatsoever of this firm Church position; indeed, it is probably intended to be misleading.

No one professionally involved in theology and religious education at the university level, as Professors Hill and Madges are, can possibly be ignorant of the fact that the Catholic Church has fairly recently, and amid no little publicity and controversy, decisively and definitively rejected the fundamental-option theory. In 1975, the Congregation for the Doctrine of the Faith, in its Declaration on Certain Questions concerning Sexual Ethics, *Personæ Humanæ*, firmly adopted and explained the Church's position on this point.[12]

Some of the votaries of the theory have nevertheless continued to try to advance it. The Church's response has been to reject the theory even more strongly and firmly, as Pope

---

[12] Congregation for the Doctrine of the Faith, *Personæ Humanæ*, December 29, 1975, no. 10.

John Paul II did in his 1993 encyclical on the Splendor of Truth, *Veritatis Splendor*.[13] The fundamental-option theory is not mentioned in the *Catechism* because it is contrary to the teaching of the Church. In the light of the specific magisterial pronouncements that exclude it, the disingenuous comment that the term "is not used" in the *Catechism* but that it has "gained acceptance among many moral theologians" evidently cannot repose upon any other theory but one that sees moral theologians as taking precedence over the Church's Magisterium.

The fact that two theology professors feel able to go on advancing the theory anyway, in spite of the Church's explicit rejection of it, in a work intended to familiarize people who teach the faith with what is in the *Catechism* illustrates rather dramatically the basic problem of how the *Catechism* is being received in the United States. The openness with which these two professors feel able to contradict the Church is symptomatic. They proceed as if this were now the established practice in theology. They have no doubt observed from fairly long practical experience that they are quite unlikely to be called to account or suffer any consequences for misrepresenting and undermining the Church's contemporary statement of what she holds and teaches, the *Catechism of the Catholic Church*.

IV

The examples we have cited up to this point from *The Catechism: Highlights & Commentary*, by Professors Hill and

---

[13] Pope John Paul II, encyclical letter *Veritatis Splendor*, August 6, 1993, nos. 65–67.

Madges, can surely serve to illustrate both the nature and the flavor of the book in question. Under normal circumstances, these examples would probably suffice to make the point we have been trying to make, namely, that the implementation of the *Catechism of the Catholic Church* is in too many instances being given over to professionals "in the field" who do not, in fact, accept the *Catechism*. To go on at length citing other examples in the same vein could, we recognize, open us up to the charge of beating a dead horse.

Unfortunately, the circumstances are not normal when what purports to be a "commentary" on an authoritative Church document actually serves to undermine and even contradict that same document—and nevertheless remains perhaps one of the most recommended and frequently used of all instruments in the United States for training DREs, teachers, and catechists in the significance and contents of the *Catechism*.

What this means, bluntly, is that the horse is not dead. As long as *H & C* goes on being used—or its serialized chapters in *The Religion Teacher's Journal*, or the video series based on it—at least some religious-education professionals will go on deriving their basic ideas about the *Catechism* from this source. Just as they will go on in their turn conveying these same ideas to those in their charge, whether catechists, volunteers, or even catechumens and children in the classroom. This is a situation that should be considered intolerable by the Church.

In order to preclude any possibility of a doubt about the things we have been saying, therefore, we feel constrained to cite a few more examples from *H & C*—examples that not only reinforce our contention that this book is unsuitable as a commentary on the *Catechism* but that also show that the book was surely intended by its authors to *replace* the *Catechism* in the hands of today's religious educators, substituting in the minds of the latter its variant message in place of the Church's message. *H & C*'s authors consistently appeal, and want their readers to be in the habit of appealing, to the findings of modern scholarship and modern social science rather than to the Catholic tradition. For them it is what the experts think, not what the Church has handed down, that is now to be transmitted.

To detail and explain all of the errors of *H & C* would no doubt require a book longer than the original. The excerpts that follow, however, should at least be sufficient to show that this kind of a book should be eliminated from any Catholic religious-education enterprise:

## The Use of Scripture in the Catechism

Over fifty years of contemporary biblical scholarship have provided insights that opened the way to newer and deeper understandings of the Catholic tradition. One wishes that contemporary exegesis would have been used much more extensively in the *Catechism*. Scripture in the *Catechism* tends to be used in the more traditional form of "proof texts."

## The Self-Awareness and Divinity of Christ

Both the divinity and the humanity of Jesus Christ are foundational to Catholic faith. Traditional Church teachings, and, to some extent, the *Catechism*, accentuate the divinity of Christ and lessen the emphasis given to his full humanity. Today, however, theologians often present an "ascending theology" which begins with the historical Jesus, his gradual awareness of his identity, the growing manifestation of God's power in his life, and the full validation by God of Jesus' life and mission in his resurrection.

### The Pope and the Bishops

Many theologians today maintain that apostolic succession does not refer to an unbroken line of officials going back to the apostles. Rather, they understand it as a way of seeing the teachings of the present church in continuity with the teachings that Jesus handed on to the original apostles.

The identification of the pope as Peter's successor also needs to be put into historical context. There is a broad consensus among biblical scholars that Jesus gave Peter a primary place among the apostles. At the same time there is the awareness that the position of the Bishop of Rome only gradually gained primacy over the other bishops.

### The Sacraments

"Institution by Christ" is understood differently today, now that the church recognizes the contribution of biblical criticism and historical studies. We now realize that the church's rituals and sacraments have all undergone change and development with the passage of time. From this point of view, one might say that the church and the Spirit of the Lord are co-authors of liturgy and sacraments. In effect, many theologians hold that the sacraments have been instituted by the church under the inspiration of Jesus Christ.

### The Catechism *Faulted for Not Showing Flexibility in All Areas of Morality*

Openness or flexibility is generally not evident in the *Catechism*'s treatment of sexual matters. It categorically condemns abortion, masturbation, homosexual acts, and artificial means of contraception. . . . Although moral theologians may affirm the formal norms or basic values underlying the specific prohibitions related to matters of sexuality—for example, the sanctity of life or the sacredness of heterosexual intimacy—some moral theologians claim that these values cannot be transformed into exceptionless moral laws. They insist that the church's sexual teaching needs to balance its attention to the act performed with attention to the particular individual performing the act. . . . Reading the reflections of contemporary moral theologians on sexual matters can not only illuminate the complexity of moral decision making in such matters, but also explain why differences in judgment in these matters are often sharp and heated.

## The Indissolubility of Marriage

Given the dynamic notion of sacrament found . . . earlier, reference to the sacrament of matrimony being accomplished by consent and consummation seems inappropriate. Many theologians maintain that the marriage bond evolves over time, and cannot be limited to such legal and physical considerations. Moreover, some question whether many of the baptized actually have the faith necessary to celebrate marriage as a sacrament.

Enough. It evidently does not matter to these authors what the Catholic tradition is or what the *Catechism* says; today's experts and specialists will in any case henceforth decide what we are to believe and do, and this is also what they will pass on to those to whom they have access. In citing these examples of the interpretations given to some of the *Catechism*'s authentic teachings by this *H & C* volume, we have selected only a few excerpts. We could have quoted questionable material from virtually any page. The "faith" being expounded by Professors Hill and Madges is not, in crucially important ways, obviously the same faith that is set forth in the pages of the *Catechism of the Catholic Church*.

Theirs is rather a "faith" based primarily on a supposed consensus of the acquired knowledge of modern scholars and scientists, which is to say, it is not a faith at all in the sense of *credenda* that the Church authoritatively proposes to us. Rather, it is a mere collection of opinions that, tomorrow, could well be different from what they are today. The idea that anybody could ever be "saved" by such opinions is derisory on its face, but then it is not clear the degree to which today's Neomodernists even believe in salvation any longer anyway.

So little do Professors Hill and Madges regard the Church's settled decisions on faith and morals, apparently, that they even at one point place the term "Protestant errors" in quotation marks. Nobody is in "error", theologically speaking, it seems, since it is scarcely even to "theology" that anyone looks any longer, but rather to the discoveries of psychology, sociology, anthropology, and other secular sciences, the better to understand the phenomenon of "faith". (These disciplines, of course, should be appropriately used by people of real faith, but Hill and Madges, like many modern writers, do not seem to notice when supernatural faith affirmations simply become obliterated by the supposed requirements of modern knowledge.)

Like many "social justice" advocates whose supernatural faith has apparently long been fading, this type of modern thinker often compensates by placing an exaggerated stress on building a better world, usually without reference to the problem of sin or the faith of Christ; and this, indeed, is the very thing catechists are now supposed to be stressing in the classroom. The "social gospel" evolved in a similar way in Protestantism, as the articles of traditional supernatural faith fell by the wayside, one by one. What have people got *except* a "social gospel", after all, if they no longer believe in sanctification and salvation in Jesus Christ in the sense in which the Church holds and teaches this?

In *H & C*, this same this-worldly, "social" bias is seen in the book's quite uncritical promotion of liberation theology. This highly questionable theory and movement is praised and promoted throughout the book. Liberation theology clearly does seem to represent a "faith" upon which the authors have pinned their hopes. There is not the slightest hint in any of their references to it, however, of how critically the Church's Magisterium has had to judge certain aspects of liberation theology.[14] Certainly it is not a topic that is given any attention in the *Catechism*, although the latter does give an accurate and even an admirable account of the Church's authentic social teachings.

But the fact that liberation theology is not a *Catechism* theme in no way embarrasses these authors of their supposed "commentary". In accordance with their typical practice, they simply relate that "liberation theology *goes beyond* the focus of the *Catechism* when it emphasizes Jesus' preference for the poor" (emphasis added).

The "suggested readings" provided in *H & C* are of a piece with the rest of the volume. The authors apparently see nothing irregular or incongruous whatsoever in recommending in what purports to be a commentary on the of-

---

[14] See especially: Congregation for the Doctrine of the Faith, "Instruction on Certain Aspects of the Theology of Liberation", August 6, 1984; and "Instruction on Christian Freedom and Liberation", March 22, 1986.

ficial teachings of the Catholic Church the books of authors who have been open and in some cases even belligerent dissenters from those teachings. Included among these dissenting authors are Fr. Charles E. Curran, Fr. Berard L. Marthaler, O.F.M. Conv., Fr. Richard McCormick, S.J., Fr. Edward Schillebeeckx, O.P., Fr. Gerard S. Sloyan, and Dr. Rosemary Radford Ruether.

What conceivable benefit, for example, could the catechist preparing to teach the faith derive from following *H & C*'s suggestion to read Sr. Joan Chittister's *Womanstrength: Modern Church, Modern Women*? The author is the religious sister who "preached the homily" at the 1994 Call to Action convention in Chicago.

"Chittister got a ten-minute standing ovation", *Call to Action News* later reported. "The electrifying effect on the crowd came not just from the novelty of hearing a gifted woman preach in a Church that disallows woman preachers. It struck resonant chords of faith in the congregation because it went back to the basics—the Gospel call of Jesus to the Church." The view of "faith" held by this group is surely as singular as its idea of what the "Gospel call" consists of.

In keeping with the spirit of a self-named "Catholic" group that openly and proudly does what it knows to be disobedient *because* it is disobedient, Sr. Chittister, "rephrased" the four marks of the Catholic Church found in the Creed —one, holy, catholic, and apostolic—as "ecumenical, spiritual, inclusive, and ministering."[15]

Is this the sort of author that should be recommended to catechists? Apparently it is, at least in the view of com-

---

[15] *Call to Action News*, January 1995.

mentators Hill and Madges, since they have most definitely included her in their list of "suggested readings". They are hardly adverse to a little "rephrasing" of things themselves, after all, as we have seen.

V

We have dealt at great length, and quite deliberately so, with *The Catechism: Highlights & Commentary* (*H & C*), by Brennan Hill and William Madges. For this is a book through which significant numbers of religious-education directors and teachers are currently being introduced to the *Catechism*. They are being quite expressly told that the *Catechism* is not really all that important for people "in the field", and that the "official" doctrine it lays out is just one "theology" among many others.

Furthermore, as we noted earlier, this Hill and Madges work is more than just a book. *H & C* formed the basis of seven catechetical training sessions sponsored and promoted by *The Religion Teacher's Journal* in the course of the 1994–1995 school year.[16] The text of *H & C* was substantially reprinted in monthly installments in this journal, published by *H & C*'s publisher, and widely read by DREs, teachers, and catechists. The articles, as they appeared in the RTJ, were illustrated, significantly, by a special logo-like design heralding "the Old Teaching and the New", the "old teaching" presumably being all that is now passé in the view of the present catechetical establishment. On the evidence of *H & C*, of course, it is precisely the contents of

---

[16] *The Religion Teacher's Journal*, published during the school year by Twenty-Third Publications.

the *Catechism of the Catholic Church* itself that is frequently considered to be passé and has to be "gone beyond".

Reprinted in *The Religion Teacher's Journal*, of course, *H & C* will undoubtedly reach many who will never see the book itself. Moreover, the text was not merely reprinted in the pages of RTJ; the journal prepared and distributed special lesson plans to enable diocesan and parish DREs to use the *H & C* materials to train their teachers and catechists. These lesson plans were printed in a supplemental newsletter, *DRE Directives*, which RTJ supplies to subscribers to more than one copy of their journal—that is, most likely, to parishes, catechetical offices, and the like.[17]

From the average religion teacher's point of view, these lesson plans are actually quite helpfully and imaginatively done. Certainly they are in a format with which modern religion teachers are familiar. DREs are encouraged to assemble their catechists for an opening prayer service, along with a Bible, "a lighted candle, and any symbols that represent the presence of Christ, you and your catechists." The DRE is then supposed to lead the catechists in short prayers and readings in which the catechists participate. The whole thing comes across as quite a nice way of training and motivating catechists.

As the RTJ lesson plan proceeds, following the prayer service, further indications begin to appear that also remind us that we are, after all, dealing here with the new catechesis:

> Give each catechist one of the small slips of paper [which the DRE had been instructed to have on hand] and ask him or her to silently and briefly reflect on this question:

---

[17] See *DRE Directives*, Guidelines for Meetings Using *The Religion Teacher's Journal*, January 1995.

What is at the heart of the Christian faith for you? Explain that you are not looking for "right" answers and they need not sign these slips. When they have finished writing, have them take their slips and tape them inside the heart on your poster [which the DRE had also been instructed to have]. (*Allow three minutes or so for this.*)

We should note that the emphasis here is on what faith means "for you" and that indifference to "right answers" is conscious and explicit—the imagination strains at trying to wonder what the prophets or Jesus himself would have thought of the idea that revealed faith is a subjective feeling or "right answers" are not important.

It is at this point in the lesson plan that we come to a section entitled "What the *Catechism* Says". When we see how *this* subject is handled, we can no longer be in any doubt that we are indeed dealing with the new catechesis here:

Now ask catechists to turn to "The Heart of Our Faith" (January *Religion Teacher's Journal*). Encourage catechists to mark passages they don't understand or have questions about, and allow sufficient time for this.

When all have finished reading, ask them to gather in grade-level groups of three or four to discuss these questions:

—What do you think the expression "Christian Mystery" means?

—Does your own experience of liturgy make God's saving events "present and real today"? In what ways?

—Do those you teach experience liturgy as an encounter with Jesus Christ and his Holy Spirit? How can you tell?

—Does the music and singing in your parish express the "beauty of prayer, the participation of the community and the solemnity of the celebration"? If not, is there anything you as a catechist can do about this?

And so on. The emphasis is on "experience" and on what catechists "think" the "Christian Mystery" means, not on what it does mean. The questions deliberately lead the catechist away from what the *Catechism* says and encourage them to focus on their own experience. The very notion that it is one of the functions of a teacher to convey knowledge to other minds is almost wholly obscured here as well, as it is so often in the new catechesis generally. The practice of dividing everybody up into "small groups" in order to "share questions and concerns" (as the lesson plan later instructs the DRE to do) is similarly one more indication of how the new catechesis is almost wholly involved with "process" and not with "content"—even when, as in the present case, the subject *is* content ("What the *Catechism* says").

When looking at a lesson plan such as this, it is discouraging to reflect that one of the reasons why the new catechesis has been able to establish itself so firmly today is that the new catechists customarily put together their concepts and approaches for teachers in such prepackaged formats. This is one of the marks of modern "professionalism" in catechetics; experts, consultants, and publishing houses have sprung up all over to provide these ready-made lesson plans and teaching guides to Catholic schools and CCD programs.

Publishers of religious-education materials solidly based on the teachings of the Church sometimes do not compete well in this regard. This may be because they have often tended to think it enough simply to present the authentic faith without all the paraphernalia of lesson plans, precanned questions, "activities", and the like, which the new catechesis never fails to provide. Actually, the Church herself, in issuing the *Catechism*, in certain ways seems to regard the task as essentially done, now that the authentic faith has been laid out. This is to fail to reckon with the well-established custom of DREs and teachers to look almost automatically to already prepared religious-education materials as the basis of their teachings, not to what the pope and the bishops may have issued.

The average teacher or catechist today is, typically, grateful for the help in organizing classes, formulating the questions to be asked, and so on, that comes with using a regular series of religion books and materials. This average teacher or catechist does not normally reflect on the fact that this emphasis on "process" in no way insures that the content presented will be doctrinally sound.

The same thing, unhappily, is true of the six video presentations produced and distributed by Twenty-Third Publications at the time *H & C* came out. This video series is entitled *The New Catechism: Catholic Faith Today*,[18] so there is definitely a claim being made to present the *Catechism* in this series, as well as a claim to expound the Catholic faith.

Moreover, this claim is evidently taken quite seriously. This video series has been favorably reviewed in the current catechetical literature, one review calling it "a lively and interesting look at a very interesting text" (meaning the *Catechism*). "Parish DREs and pastoral leaders need all the help they can get in making the *Catechism* accessible to a broader Church audience", this review opines.[19]

This video series was expressly designed to be used along with the Hill and Madges volume, *H & C*. In the typical fash-

---

[18] Brennan Hill and William Madges, *The New Catechism: Catholic Faith Today* (video cassettes "designed to be an aid to those desiring to use the *Catechism* for teaching"), Twenty-Third Publications, Mystic, Conn.

[19] See review in *The Catechist*, January 1995.

ion of modern religious-education materials, the brochure accompanying the videos provides a ready-made "model program", as well as "suggested questions for discussion and reflection". As we have noted, the catechetical establishment in the United States has rarely failed to understand the very real need of the average religion teacher for outlines, prepared lesson plans, discussion questions, and so on. Beautiful and compelling as the true faith of Christ presented by the Church is, it does not always win out over catechetical revisionism in a culture that otherwise thrives on packaging, process, and pizzazz.

And so the Hill and Madges videos, too, come with all the usual modern catechetical accoutrements, not excluding detailed directions about how the catechists using the materials are to proceed ("Catechists might at this point cluster according to the grade level they teach and discuss practical methods and activities"; "Adult education groups may also divide into smaller groups to share their stories and reflections on the videos").

When the videos themselves are viewed, the inevitable first impression is that there simply could not be two nicer guys than Professors Hill and Madges. The same thing is true of their copresenters, two religious sisters who also teach at Xavier University: they are all thoroughly nice people. The whole approach seems to be for the presenters to come across as relaxed, warm, friendly, nondemanding, non-dogmatic people. Nothing about them could even remotely suggest today's modern media stereotype of religious people as tense, shrill, intolerant, and judgmental. Whatever else these videos achieve, they certainly avoid these stereotypes (religious habits, Roman collars, and other symbols of authority and rigidity are similarly absent, for the most part, from these videos).

As to the discussion about the *Catechism* itself, it is quickly made clear, in the video entitled "Introduction to the *Catechism*", that this magisterial document itself actually represents a *process* of instruction. The focus is on discussing Vatican II and contemporary thinking, the sharing of one person with another, and feeling comfortable in a personal relationship with God. There is mention of the *Catechism* too, of course, but what is said about it is evidently intended to be more soothing than challenging.

In the midst of all the bland discussion, however, the presenters do manage to establish that no catechism from Rome is ever going to preempt "ours". There will definitely have to be developments and changes; and here the "inculturation aspects" are presented as especially "invigorating".

Each of the six video presentations has its own theme: Faith in God and Christ, the Holy Spirit and the Church, Liturgy and Sacraments, Morality and Social Justice. But the actual substantive discussion of all these topics is in fact quite sparse throughout the entire series. Typically, the presenters mention what the theme is. But then, very quickly, they fasten upon a favorite subject such as, for example, "experience". Then they proceed to develop that: how Karl Rahner established that our own reflection on our inner experience gives us access to God, for example; how all we have to do, in effect, is to be open to the God within us.

The claim is even made, in passing, that the *Catechism* itself begins with "human experience". (Not exactly: while the *Catechism* properly discusses the human *capacity* for God, it also stresses how it is really God who first comes to man; man's proper relationship to God is a *response*. See part 1, section 1, chapters 1–3 of the *Catechism* itself. As Archbishop Schönborn has characteristically pointed out, the first word in the *Catechism* is "God", and roughly two-thirds of its text is also devoted to God.)

When such a method as this is followed, the *Catechism* itself, and what it says, quickly recedes into the background. And, although some truths do occasionally get stated, such as the fact that faith is a gift from God, the real emphasis is placed on our own experience and how even revelation itself is not just something that happened two thousand years ago. It is something that is ongoing; it is around us and in us. Hence we need to look into the real-life stories of people today for the confirmation of our faith. This, essentially, is how the presenters proceed throughout.

It is not clear how these presenters would interpret the teaching of Vatican II—the Council about which they otherwise talk so much—to the effect that revelation, properly speaking, ended with the advent of the Christian economy as the New Covenant; and that "no new public revelation is to be expected before the glorious manifestation of our Lord, Jesus Christ."[20] Obviously, this is also the teaching of the *Catechism* (CCC 66). Of course the *Catechism* also points out that revelation, while it is complete, is not yet always fully explicit. This is where "development of doctrine" legitimately comes in; but this does not mean just adopting many modern ideas wholesale, as today's Neomodernists often seem to imply.

Viewing this particular segment of these video presentations, one of the present authors wrote down in his notes at this point: "They pretend they are talking about the *Catechism*, but they are really talking about themselves and their experiences." The idea of the series, precisely, seems to be,

---

[20] Vatican Council II, Dogmatic Constitution on Divine Revelation, *Dei Verbum*, no. 4.

while mentioning the *Catechism* from time to time, to get away from it as soon as possible and get into "stories", and "community", and "sharing".

This proved to be a consistent pattern extending throughout all six of the video presentations, taking up a wholly disproportionate share of the video time in a series nevertheless billed as being about the *Catechism*. In addition to the presenters themselves, other participants were brought in to provide audience reaction and to share stories and experiences: undergraduate and graduate theology students, DREs, teachers, and so forth, all apparently chosen carefully according to contemporary canons of "political correctness": there were males and females, old and young, clerics and lay people, naturally of *several* different races.

Another advantage for the presenters in having such a plethora of "audience reaction" is that the presenters then subtly become no longer quite as responsible for what is said. Although the whole presentation was always deliberately bland and low key, there were nonetheless a number of explicit anti-Church and anti-*Catechism* sentiments expressed by various participants in the course of the six videos, such as when scriptural readings were characterized as "highly offensive to women", the purpose of marriage characterized as "well being", or the Creed described as now "changed". One woman went on at length on the subject of "reconciliation" between friends, as if this were equivalent to the sacrament of the same name.

In general, all the participants seemed well grounded in the philosophy of Hill and Madges. And far be it from the presenters on the videos ever to *correct* any of the "shared faith experiences" when the participants diverged from the teaching of the Church as plainly set forth in the *Catechism*. Correcting misconceptions about the faith and reiterating authentic doctrine would no doubt have broken the spell of relentless niceness that characterized all of these video presentations. After all, as one of the "audience reactors" expressed on one of the tapes, speaking of moral behavior: "If people cannot live up to an ideal, then those who fail feel excluded."

Incidentally, if any reference was made, anywhere, on any of these six videos, to the name or teaching of Pope John Paul II, then we missed it. The Pope who promulgated the *Catechism*, a towering figure on the world scene today, was evidently not one of the topics about which any "stories" or "shared reflections" were considered worthwhile. Meanwhile, the story about how the mystical experiences on his deathbed brought St. Thomas Aquinas to the conclusion that all his writings were "straw" was recounted mainly in order to bring out the opinion that knowledge and learning are *not* all that important.

Any impartial judgment about these six video presentations, supposedly designed to help religious educators introduce the *Catechism of the Catholic Church*—the promotional brochure about them advertises: "everything you need to know about the new *Catechism* in a user-friendly video series"—would have to conclude that they quite lamentably fail to fulfill their announced purpose. Rather, these videos seemed to us to have been almost designed and intended to downgrade the importance of the new *Catechism* in favor of business as usual as the catechetical establishment has been accustomed to conduct it. They essentially present a hodge podge of all the failed theories of the past thirty years that have afflicted the new catechesis, while very, very little that was either accurate or attractive was ever presented about the *Catechism*.

If the Hill and Madges book, *The Catechism: Highlights &*

*Commentary*, along with the lesson plans and video presentations based on it, represent a typical response of today's catechetical establishment to the *Catechism of the Catholic Church* —and unfortunately it is hard to doubt that it is anything but typical—then we have to conclude that the *Catechism* is not being received by the catechetical establishment in the United States.

This is a very sad outcome, of course, because catechists are surely among the most important of all the apostles "sent out" by the Church. This is true in the very nature of what is involved in the teaching of the faith. Some of today's professional new catechists, however, on the evidence of this commentary and the videos based on it, seem not very concerned even to attempt to conceal their reluctance to be apostles of the authentic faith of the Church and of Christ that is found in the *Catechism of the Catholic Church*.

# CHAPTER SIX

# A Theological Establishment Response to the Catechism

## I

If the catechetical establishment in the United States does not much like the *Catechism of the Catholic Church* and has been expending considerable energies preparing commentaries and training materials evidently aimed at neutralizing if not replacing it, what does today's theological establishment think of the new *Catechism*? It is a fairly well-known fact that the modern catechetical movement has regularly looked to prominent theologians and scholars, not only for much of its inspiration, but even for some of its approaches, methods, and techniques.

Reliance on the work of theologians began for the modern catechetical movement as far back as the 1930s, when Fr. Josef Jungmann, S.J., was calling for a more "kerygmatic" approach to teaching the faith based on a more Scripture-based "proclamation" (Greek *kerygma*) of it, together with greater attention to actual life situations. Fr. Jungmann's kerygmatic method seemed—and seems—to be quite a good approach to teaching the faith. Unfortunately, the method could not survive the increasing skepticism of some later Scripture scholars, who have progressively undermined in the minds of many new catechists the affirmation that what the Scriptures say is *true*. It would be rather difficult in the best of circumstances, after all, to be "proclaiming" as salvific what had come to be understood as mere ancient Near Eastern "myths".

One of the more prominent theorists of the new catechesis, Fr. Berard L. Marthaler, O.F.M. Conv., has expressly underlined the close relationship between today's catechetical and theological establishments. "The catechetical movement over the past fifty years or so", Fr. Marthaler wrote in his introduction to the *Sourcebook for Modern Catechetics*,

> has had a symbiotic relationship with biblical scholarship, the liturgical movement, and the "new theology." It has been able to assimilate and use the practical insights of learning theory based on experience and the findings of developmental psychology. Borrowing from anthropology, sociology, and psychology, it has come to have a better understanding of how individuals and groups appropriate symbols to establish a sense of identity and a world of meaning and value."[1]

If the new catechesis had managed to prove itself, perhaps such a close, indeed "symbiotic", relationship with the new theology and the new exegesis could have been said to be a good thing. Since the new catechesis has manifestly not been able to prove itself, however—judged by the standard of how well its recipients know and practice a Catholic faith that is authentic—then its close relationship with the new theology and exegesis becomes a considerably more questionable proposition.

---

[1] Berard L. Marthaler, introduction, *Sourcebook for Modern Catechetics*, ed. Michael Warren (Winona, Minn.: Saint Mary's Press, Christian Brothers Publications, 1983), 19.

Conversely, it may not even be going too far to assert that the value and validity of the new theology and the new exegesis can themselves be called into question on the basis of how poorly they have played themselves out in the very practical, down-to-earth world of the teaching of the faith. Perhaps its heavy reliance on contemporary theology —not to speak of its reliance on anthropology, sociology, and psychology—was a mistake from the beginning for the new catechesis.

It did not have to be so. The Catholic Church in all ages has amply demonstrated both her ability and her willingness to take what is good from external sources, be they secular or pagan, and then to "baptize" them. The "baptizing" of Greek philosophy and Roman law are only among the more outstanding examples of this in history. The Church has similarly been open to the adoption and use of modern knowledge and techniques compatible with her faith. Many valuable acquisitions have been—and can still be—adopted from other disciplines by a faith otherwise bound, of course, to maintain its own truth and authenticity.

But what about taking things from these external sources and then *failing* to "baptize" them—failing to realize, perhaps, that some things need to be "baptized"? What about adopting key concepts and findings from modern disciplines in a way that could allow or cause a watering down, or even a denial, of the faith? What about adopting things that are simply incompatible with the faith, meanwhile imagining that this is somehow required by "science" or "scholarship"? This is preeminently the case with some of the modern acquisitions that have been attempted in the postconciliar era.

Of course the deleterious effects of adopting things that are alien to or incompatible with the faith remain the same, even if these incompatible features came into catechesis indirectly via the new theology or the new exegesis. This would simply mean that the alien things in question had earlier been wrongly adopted by the new theology or the new biblical scholarship, that these disciplines themselves had become tainted with ideas and methods taken from modern secular culture and science incompatible with the faith and then had in turn passed these tainted goods on to the new catechesis.

It is no secret that some of today's new theologians and exegetes have taken positions at variance with the Church's declared faith, as now set forth authoritatively in the new *Catechism*. It is similarly no secret that some of these same dissenting scholars have nevertheless sometimes remained pillars of today's theological establishment in the United States and elsewhere. Some of them are frank and open dissenters, declaring that what the theologians decide *is* the new norm for the Church. Others blur the issue and may even perhaps condescendingly refer to the Church's authentic faith (again, as it is now contained in the *Catechism*) as being merely the "official theology" among other "theologies", or as the "Roman theology" as opposed to other theologies considered more modern and creative.

There seems to be general agreement in the current theological establishment, though, that it is the theologians themselves, and not the Magisterium, who are to be the final judges in all that pertains to the Catholic faith, including, naturally, the *Catechism*.

As one instance of how a typical member of the current theological establishment views the *Catechism*, we may take the views of Fr. Francis Buckley, S.J., a professor of systematic and pastoral theology at the University of San Francisco. Fr. Buckley was one of the Woodstock group of scholars who attacked the draft catechism in the book entitled *The Universal Catechism Reader*, which, as we noted in Chapter Three, found the draft "fatally flawed".[2] His negative view of the completed *Catechism* proved to be equally pronounced. In an article entitled "What to Do with the New *Catechism*", Fr. Buckley declares that "it would be a mistake to hand the text of the new *Catechism* to everyone. It does not distinguish between matters of faith and theological opinion." He probably means the *Catechism* teaches as part of the doctrine of the faith things the new theologians consider "opinion" and hence subject to change by them.

"Catholics without professional theological training could be confused," Fr. Buckley complains, "thinking that all doctrines mentioned in the *Catechism* are matters of faith." Again, "professional theological training" proves to be the key for him even to having access to what the faith is. "The *Catechism* could have been written before the Second Vatican Council", he goes on to state. "Its doctrinal treatment of angels, human nature, and sin (to mention only a few areas) is seriously flawed by a failure to apply contemporary biblical criticism when appealing to biblical texts." Only the *Catechism*'s part four on Prayer, apparently, meets his exacting standards and makes it possible to use the volume as something besides "a doorstop", in his own colorful characterization. In the end he sees the *Catechism* as usable only "if supplemented by strong commentaries on Scripture and the documents of Vatican II".[3]

Thus, a typical member of the theological establishment sees the *Catechism* in the same way the catechetical estab-

---

[2] See n. 3 to Chapter Three *supra*.

[3] Rev. Francis J. Buckley, S.J., "What to Do with the New *Catechism*", *Church*, summer 1993.

lishment tends to see it: it simply cannot be used as is; it must be adapted, brought under control, "domesticated", as it were. Perhaps the worst thing that could happen would be for the faithful to receive the *Catechism* as it comes to them from the hands of the Church. What is needed are "strong commentaries" on it—the same thing Professors Brennan Hill and William Madges decided the catechetical establishment needed to have, as we saw in the last chapter.

Is there also a commentary on the *Catechism of the Catholic Church* in which prominent representatives of the current theological establishment give their views on it? As it happens, there is. It also happens to be one that is international in both its authorship and its publisher(s), and hence its range extends considerably beyond that of the theological establishment in the United States alone. But there is no doubt that the most visible members of the theological establishment, whether here or abroad, know exactly what they think about the *Catechism*. And that, as it turns out, is not terribly different from what the catechetical establishment thinks about it.[4]


## II


Even before the *Catechism* itself became available in an official English text, both the Liturgical Press in the United States and Geoffrey Chapman in Britain announced the publication of a formidable volume entitled *Commentary on*

---

[4] The remainder of this chapter appeared in slightly modified form as an article in *The Catholic World Report*, April 1994.

*the Catechism of the Catholic Church.*[5] This *Commentary* appeared to be a very ambitious international undertaking. Although a nucleus of its contributors, including the volume's editor, Michael J. Walsh, are or have been connected with Heythrop College, University of London, the twenty-five contributors are, variously, American, Belgian, British, Canadian, Dutch, French, German, and Irish. Most of them are theologians, some of them prominent theologians, and all of them occupy, or have occupied, positions on recognized Catholic faculties, presumably in good standing with the Church, including even the faculties of Roman ecclesiastical universities.

Although making no claim to be "official", this *Commentary* can scarcely avoid appearing to be something very like that, and not just because of its title. Both the British and the American publishers of it number among the official publishers of the *Catechism of the Catholic Church* itself, for example. To all appearances, the contributors are recognized —in some cases, eminent—Catholic authorities on the subjects they treat. A trusting and unsuspecting reader would have to be pardoned for accepting this *Commentary* at face value and taking it to be, if not an official, at least a reliable guide to the *Catechism*.

Such a trusting and unsuspecting reader would be mistaken. Although three or four of the twenty-five contributions in this *Commentary* are not bad, or are at least innocuous, most of them are serious and determined efforts to call into question and undermine the authority and credibility both of the *Catechism* itself and of the Magisterium of the Church that issued it.

---

[5] Michael J. Walsh, ed., *Commentary on the Catechism of the Catholic Church* (Collegeville, Minn.: Liturgical Press, 1994).

The publishers' announcement advertising the *Commentary* asks: "How well does [the *Catechism*] represent the faith which it is meant to encapsulate?" But are authors and publishers now to be the judges of this? The *Pope* declares it to be "a statement of the Church's faith and of Catholic doctrine, attested to or illumined by Sacred Scripture, the Apostolic Traditions, and the Church's Magisterium".[6] But the publishers boast instead that they have assembled "a team of distinguished Catholics drawn from theological faculties . . . around the world . . . [to] enter into critical dialogue with the text and relate its strengths and weaknesses".

"Critical dialogue." The pattern has become only too familiar in the postconciliar era in the Church: the Magisterium issues a statement or ruling, and immediately some Catholic theologians rush to enter into "critical dialogue" with it. Christ called "blessed" those "who hear the word of God and keep it!" (Lk 11:28). Today we are into "relating its strengths and weaknesses".

Judging by the *Commentary* they have produced, we can only conclude that these theologians have a generally low opinion of the *Catechism*. One of them, Fr. Dermot A. Lane, of the Archdiocese of Dublin, where he has been associated with the Mater Dei Institute of Education, writes that "the treatment of faith, like the rest of the *Catechism*, is highly condensed and as such calls out for commentary and clarification. The language is very traditional and will therefore be taxing to contemporary readers," he claims, "with very few concessions made to style or imagination."

---

[6] Pope John Paul II, apostolic constitution *Fidei Depositum*, on the Publication of the *Catechism of the Catholic Church*, October 11, 1992, no. 3. This apostolic constitution is printed in the front of all of the editions of the *Catechism* available in the United States.

"Readers should prepare themselves for something of a cultural shock as they are conveyed abruptly back to the thirteenth century", writes Fr. Gabriel Daly, O.S.A., a lecturer in systematic and historical theology at Trinity College in Dublin.

One of the Heythrop College theologians, Fr. John McDade, S.J., believes that "in the composition of the *Catechism*, the best theological resources of the Church have not been utilized." Dr. Monika K. Hellwig, of the theology department at Georgetown University in Washington, D.C., finds that the *Catechism*'s treatment of the sacrament of Penance is "clearly not a text to be used directly in the preparation of children . . . [and it is] quite confusing if followed too closely in an adult initiation program", thus eliminating, it would seem, the *Catechism*'s usefulness here for both children and adults. Dr. Hellwig believes the whole thing "leaves a great deal that must be supplied from elsewhere."

Another American, Fr. James L. Empereur, S.J., for many years a professor at the Jesuit School of Theology in Berkeley, California, finds the text on the sacrament of Anointing "too general to be a source of theological reflection . . . [and] too minimal to be of any pastoral assistance", thus again eliminating both the theological and pastoral value of this particular text.

Solution? Fr. Empereur declares that he himself "will fill out the text to enhance it", that is, he will write what the authors of the original text *should* have written if only they had possessed his particular insight. With this attitude, it is hardly a surprise that Fr. Empereur concludes in the end that "the real catechism of the Roman Catholic Church is still to be done."

Yet another contributor and Heythrop College Jesuit,

Fr. Philip Endean, S.J., similarly decides to provide his own "alternative account of the relationship between prayer and theology" in order to remedy the *Catechism*'s perceived deficiencies on this topic. Dr. Joseph A. Selling, chairman of the Department of Theology at the Catholic University of Leuven in Belgium, confirms the judgment of most of his colleagues when he writes concerning the *Catechism*'s treatment of morality that "even the most 'traditionalist' (moral handbook) theologian will have to be disappointed by the lack of nuance exhibited by this text." He adds: "One does not teach by uttering clichés, perpetuating slovenly language, and succumbing to popular misunderstanding."

It quickly becomes evident that these writers believe the *Catechism* would have been better off if it had never been written. The next best thing that suggests itself to them is that correctives be provided for it. "Local catechisms will have to compensate for the shortcomings of this *Catechism*", concludes Catherine Mowry LaCugna of Notre Dame University in South Bend, Indiana.

Can this be true? That distinguished Catholic theologians belonging to recognized Catholic faculties and being published by firms that publish the *Catechism* itself—and which here are similarly claiming to be publishing something "Catholic"—have instead produced a volume openly attempting to *discredit* and *subvert* the *Catechism*, in the guise of providing a "commentary" on it?

Yes: this is exactly what we have in this *Commentary*. This can be surprising only to those who have not read Pope John Paul II's recent encyclical *Veritatis Splendor*, in which the Pontiff points out what most serious observers of the postconciliar Catholic scene have long known, namely, that today Catholic doctrine risks "being distorted or denied *within the Christian community itself*. . . . It is no longer a matter of limited and occasional dissent," John Paul II says, "but of an overall and systematic calling into question of traditional . . . doctrine" (emphasis in the original).[7]

Although the Pope was talking about moral teaching in his encyclical, his characterization applies to this *Commentary*'s treatment of the Catholic doctrine generally to be found in the *Catechism of the Catholic Church*. In vain, apparently, did the Pope declare that the work contains "what the Church believes", for we have here some twenty-odd Catholic theologians from around the world, most of whom would not too politely beg to differ with him. They reserve the right to decide for themselves "what the Church believes"; and therefore also to decide what kind of "reception" should be accorded to this *Catechism* as well.

Unfortunately, in the circumstances of today, a commentary such as this probably represents an all-too-typical example of the reception the *Catechism* is likely to receive in more than a few areas in the Church in the English-speaking world. It could even come to be considered something of a standard commentary in spite of its manifold defects.

Advocates of the new theology are only too likely to lock in on this *Commentary* like a guided missile on its target, using it henceforth as an authority on how the *Catechism is* to be received and then, in effect, promptly set aside.

## III

From what standpoint does a group of academic theologians, even if described in the publishers' blurb as "distin-

---

[7] Pope John Paul II, encyclical letter on the Splendor of Truth, *Veritatis Splendor*, August 6, 1993, no. 4.

guished", presume to judge and find so drastically wanting a *Catechism of the Catholic Church* issued by the supreme authority in the Church? How do they manage or contrive to be taken seriously? How do they manage to get published by seemingly mainstream Catholic publishers?

We need to bear in mind what we covered in the first two chapters.

—The *Catechism of the Catholic Church* was requested by the 1985 World Synod of Bishops.

—It was commissioned by the Supreme Pontiff.

—It was overseen at every stage by a special commission of twelve cardinals and bishops headed by the prefect of the Congregation for the Doctrine of the Faith.

—It was carried through *ten separate drafts* by an editorial committee composed primarily of seven diocesan bishops and one priest who enjoyed expert theological advice and assistance at every stage.

—It was edited carefully at every stage by another bishop who is also a distinguished Dominican theologian.

—The *Catechism* was submitted for review to all the Catholic bishops of the world, to all the bishops' conferences, and to major Catholic universities, with the result that nearly twenty-five thousand separate proposed amendments (*modi*) were sent back and carefully considered (and many times incorporated) by the editorial committee; this was *the first time in the history of the Catholic Church* that a major teaching document such as this was ever subjected to such a massive, worldwide consultation process.

—The final draft was then personally reviewed by the Holy Father, who called for certain modifications (he later commented that he had corrected the drafts himself!).[8]

---

[8] Pope John Paul II, "Address on the Occasion of Approving the

—Finally, the completed *Catechism* was promulgated and given to the world with the full authority of the Church behind it.

This is impressive; the document resulting from this process would be entitled to respect by any standards. Anyone who believes in the divine mission and commission of the Catholic Church, and in the promises given to her by Jesus Christ, however, would repose even greater confidence in any result stemming from a process including all the above steps. Conversely, those who rush to judge the *Catechism* only to find it so drastically wanting would appear not to believe very strongly in the divine mission and commission of the Catholic Church or in the promises given to her by Jesus Christ.

In fact, many of those who do not like the *Catechism* do not seem to like the Catholic Church herself very much, either. This can be quickly verified by looking at most of the contributors to this *Commentary*. No matter that virtually all of them hold full-time positions in Catholic institutions: they *still* do not like the Catholic Church.

And it almost goes without saying that most of the contributors consider theological dissent from the teachings of the Church's Magisterium to be, not merely permitted, but both legitimate and necessary. They do not so much assert such a right to dissent as they simply exercise it and take it for granted, although one of the contributors from Heythrop College, University of London, Fr. Gerald J. Hughes, S.J., does sharply contest the *Catechism*'s teaching that "rejection of the Church's authority and teaching" would constitute an instance of "erroneous judgment" (CCC 1792). How dare

---

Final Version of the *Catechism of the Catholic Church*", *L'Osservatore Romano*, July 1, 1992.

the *Catechism* itself attempt to do what these theologians presume to do on every page of their *Commentary*, namely, issue adverse judgments? Fr. Hughes calls this teaching of the *Catechism* "scandalous" (at the very time when, it had come to seem, the very concept of "scandal"—at least theological scandal—had disappeared from Catholic discourse forever). The same author criticizes the *Catechism* for using in its paragraph 2270 a citation from Jeremiah 1:5— "Before I formed you in the womb I knew you"—as one of the reasons for opposing abortion on moral grounds.

Another contributor, Fr. Gerald O'Hanlon, S.J., from Dublin's Milltown Institute of Theology and Philosophy, actually complains about what he alleges is a contemporary "lack of tolerance for theological discussion and dissent". "The Church can become oppressive in a way that needs challenging", Fr. O'Hanlon asserts. Actually, the publication of this *Commentary* is itself proof of the contrary: Is there *anything* that cannot be published today under "Catholic" auspices, with little or no fear of any ecclesiastical or hierarchical challenge?

The typical attitude toward ecclesiastical authority of most of the contributors to this *Commentary* can perhaps best be seen in the tranquil way in which they regularly proceed to *correct* the *Catechism* wherever they believe it needs correcting. Thus, Dr. Lisa Sowle Cahill, professor of theology at Boston College, in Massachusetts, and past president of the Catholic Theological Society of America, judges that "the *Catechism*'s insistence that the teaching on the sacramentality of all marriages between baptized persons has been a part of Christian belief from the New Testament onward, and that even creation as presented in Genesis clearly requires monogamy and indissolubility, is *fallacious*" (emphasis added). *Ipsa dixit.*

Professor Sowle herself holds that indissolubility of marriage is "impossible" as well as "inequitable". Again, talk about dogmatic statements handed down from on high! The plain words of Christ to the contrary, so many times confirmed both by the Church's Magisterium and her pastoral practice, she believes, as do so many non-Catholic Christian communions, to be merely "ideals", like the counsels offered in the Sermon on the Mount.

This is a view readily echoed by Fr. Gerald J. Hughes, S.J., already quoted above, who declares that "as is not uncommon with Vatican documents, the [*Catechism*'s] article on conscience sometimes states as facts what are, alas, no more than ideals."

A further example of the way in which these commentators simply proceed to "correct" the *Catechism* at will is the statement of the Belgian theologian Fr. Jacques Dupuis, who is on the faculty of Rome's Gregorian University. Fr. Dupuis holds that the *Catechism*'s teaching (CCC 609) that the cry of Jesus on the Cross was made "in our name" is "both unfortunate and far-fetched".

This same Roman university professor finds the teaching of the *Catechism* in paragraph 474 to the effect that "the human knowledge of Jesus enjoyed in all its fullness the knowledge of the eternal design he had come to reveal" to be "unwarranted by the evidence which is cited". The "evidence cited" in this particular case happens to be two scriptural passages. But what is singular about the opinion of Fr. Dupuis here is his apparent assumption that the Church's Magisterium can only make statements for which it proposes evidence that is satisfactory to him.

However that may be, Fr. Dupuis fails to abide by the same standard he demands of the *Catechism*. He asserts, without evidence, that the statement of Jesus in Mark 13:32

—that "of that day or that hour no one knows, not even the angels in heaven, nor the Son, but only the Father"—is an example of "true, not feigned ignorance". The *Catechism*, however, cites Acts 1:7—"It is not for you to know times or seasons which the Father has fixed by his own authority"—as its authority for declaring that when it is said that Jesus did not "know" something, it means he did not have the mission to reveal it.

Admittedly, the question of the knowledge of Jesus, who was true God and true man, is a very difficult one to understand and explain. One of the striking things about this example from the *Commentary*, however, is how quickly certain scholars today are apparently prepared to make their own flat, dogmatic-sounding statements on the basis of modern study of an issue, while denying to the Magisterium of the Church the right to make any such statements "without evidence", even when the Magisterium is merely transmitting a long-held traditional belief of the Church.

The Magisterium—Catholics believe and the *Catechism* reiterates—enjoys the special assistance of the Holy Spirit. However, this does not appear to impress these commentators. They do not grant to the teaching Church what they claim in practice for themselves.

Meanwhile, their skepticism with regard to the Magisterium at least raises the question of the solidity of their own Catholic commitment, that is, of any real belief in the Church as what Vatican II's Declaration on Religious Liberty, *Dignitatis Humanæ* (no. 14) called "the teacher of truth".

Many other instances of the same phenomenon of demanding "evidence" for magisterial statements could be cited. Fr. Dermot A. Lane, for example, reproaches the *Catechism* for including in its paragraph 149 what he styles "the historically unverifiable statement that Mary's faith never wavered and never doubted"—as if this kind of statement of the Church's immemorial tradition now has to be "historically verified". A very different criterion from the Church's ancient standard of adhering undeviatingly to the testimony handed down is quite patently being assumed and applied by these commentators. It is a standard that, if consistently and rigorously applied, could leave us very little firmly "verified" knowledge of any kind coming down from antiquity.

Yet the contributors to the *Commentary* do not hesitate to question even solemnly defined teachings of the Church in this way. Georgetown University's Dr. Monika Hellwig, for example, believes that it is "unfortunate that the text . . . still uses the expression 'Christ instituted the Sacrament of Penance'", because, according to her, "diligent Scripture study cannot find in the New Testament" any evidence for this. The fact that the seventh session of the Council of Trent solemnly *defined*, in a canon with anathema attached, that Christ instituted all seven of the sacraments[9] and the further fact that no scholar has, or could possibly have, any "evidence" that Christ *did not* do this—all this availeth naught in the present-day climate where "diligent Scripture study" now takes precedence over irreformable conciliar decisions of the Church's solemn extraordinary Magisterium.

Similarly, Fr. J. M. Tillard, O.P., of the Dominican Faculty of Theology in Ottawa, Ontario, thinks the *Catechism* "fails to give sufficient weight to historical evidence" when it quotes in its paragraph 834 the seventh-century Greek

---

[9] The General Council of Trent, seventh session, Decree on the Sacraments, canon 1, in J. Neuner and J. Dupuis, *The Christian Faith in the Doctrinal Documents of the Catholic Church*, rev. ed., (Westminster, Md.: Christian Classics, 1975), 352.

theologian St. Maximus the Confessor, who applied to "the great Church" of Rome Christ's promise to Peter that the gates of hell would not prevail. Fr. Tillard finds the inclusion of this quotation from St. Maximus the Confessor "inexcusable", and asserts that "most scholarly exegetes refuse to interpret the passage in which Matthew alludes to the gates of hell (Mt 16:18) as containing a reference to the Church of Rome."

For a Catholic theologian, however, this question cannot be limited to what "most scholarly exegetes" think, since the First Vatican Council, in its dogmatic constitution *Pastor Æternus* (no. 1), teaches that Christ's promise to Peter "has always been understood by the Catholic Church" to apply to the Church of Rome.[10] But apparently a conciliar teaching such as this does not impress modern Catholic theologians enthralled by modern scriptural exegesis. Far from being a source of almost any kind of exact knowledge, biblical scholarship actually constitutes one of the most speculative fields it is possible to imagine. This is not to say that the results of modern biblical scholarship are without value; but it is to say that they do not—and cannot—constitute the basis for anybody's faith.

A similar skeptical attitude toward historical magisterial decisions is exhibited by the Irish Augustinian Fr. Gabriel Daly, already quoted above as warning the reader of the *Catechism* to be prepared to be transported back to the thirteenth century. One of the things he was referring to was the profession of faith issued by the Fourth Lateran Coun-

---

[10] Vatican Council I, Dogmatic Constitution on the Church of Christ, *Pastor Æternus*, chap. 1, in *Documents of Vatican Council I*, sel. and trans. John F. Broderick, S.J. (Collegeville, Minn.: The Liturgical Press, 1971), 54–55.

cil in the year 1215 and confirmed by Pope Innocent III.[11] This was, and remains, one of the Church's solemn professions of faith (creeds). Among other things, it specifies that God created both spiritual and corporeal beings. Paragraphs 327–28 of the *Catechism* cite the authority of this Lateran IV profession of faith in declaring the existence of angels to be "a truth of the faith".

The *Catechism* then goes on, in its paragraph 336, to quote St. Basil the Great in support of the Church's belief in guardian angels. These affirmations are unlikely to shock many Catholics, who are usually very aware that the Church has *always* believed in angels and still does. The only ones likely to be shocked by this are those who have apparently come to believe, for whatever reason, that the Church does not really mean what she says.

On this whole subject, however, Fr. Daly delivers himself of a number of comments and observations that need to be quoted *in extenso*:

> What are late twentieth-century people to make of all this in a *Catechism* which has so little to say about the relationship between faith and science, ecology and other matters which many will think more pressing? Those who are used to symbolic thinking and to the interpretation of myth will have few problems with biblical references to angels as messengers of God. What *is* a problem, however, is the removal of mythological language from its natural literary context and its subsequent reduction to literalized dogmatic statement. Images which properly belong to poetic narrative cannot simply be reduced to prosaic, allegedly factual descriptions, which then become dogmatic statements. The authors of the *Catechism* show no sign of

---

[11] The Fourth Lateran General Council, Symbol of Lateran (1215), in Neuner and Dupuis, *Christian Faith*, 14–17.

recognizing that there are serious hermeneutical problems involved in dogmatizing figurative (and especially apocalyptic) language and that the revelatory intent of such passages has to be discerned *within* the poetic language before being reduced to flat dogmatic pronouncements.

This all sounds very scholarly and moderate and, at first glance, may appear to be a "valid" modern way of understanding ancient faith affirmations, such as the belief in angels, which the modern world sometimes finds so hard to swallow. Certainly some of the points made here do apply to some or even much of biblical language that is "poetical" or "mythical." However, it would appear that Fr. Daly has lost sight of at least one important fact: the fact that we are not talking here just about "biblical references to angels as messengers of God".

We are talking here about the solemn decision of the extraordinary Magisterium of the Catholic Church speaking with the assistance of the Holy Spirit in the year 1215 of our era. The problem is not merely whether or not "images which properly belong to poetic narrative [can] . . . be reduced to . . . dogmatic statements." The fact of the matter, in this case, is that the Fourth Lateran Council *did it*: it defined the existence of angels as a truth of the faith, as the *Catechism* properly records. And the pope of the day promptly confirmed the conciliar text in question. Anyone who grants that the Catholic Church has a Magisterium has to accept that this was a solemn act of that Magisterium. To deny the existence of the superior spiritual beings traditionally referred to as "angels" is really to deny the Catholic system, since the Church's Magisterium has once and for all affirmed the existence of these beings in her most solemn possible way.

Moreover, a pope of *our* day has confirmed the *same* conciliar teaching from Lateran IV. In his contemporary profession of faith known as the *Credo of the People of God*, solemnly pronounced on June 30, 1968,[12] Pope Paul VI cited the earlier profession of faith from 1215 as the authority for *his* explicit—modern—teaching that God created "pure spirits which are called angels". The *Catechism of the Catholic Church* simply confirms the tradition on this point.

It is no doubt true enough that Pope Paul VI's *Credo of the People of God* is scarcely today's most popular magisterial source in the eyes of theologians who like to consider themselves up-to-date; it almost never appears on the typical radar screen of today's theological discourse. However some theologians may protest, though, it surely forms an integral part of the Church's Magisterium. The *Catechism of the Catholic Church* cites this modern *Credo* of Pope Paul VI as an authority no fewer than fourteen times. Paragraph 192 lists *both* Paul VI's *Credo of the People of God, and* Lateran IV's profession of faith, as among the Church's authentic creeds.

Fr. Daly's reservations about the *Catechism*'s—and the Church's—affirmations concerning the existence of angels ("prosaic, allegedly factual descriptions"), then, if consistently applied in the way he evidently means to apply them here, would dissolve *numerous* elements of the Church's faith and creeds. This seems to be exactly the conclusion many of the theologian-contributors to this *Commentary* have reached. Fr. Daly himself, in a second contribution to this volume, appears to deny outright the defined Church doctrine of Original Sin. He avers that this doctrine "in its

---

[12] The text of Pope Paul VI's *Credo of the People of God* can be found, among many other places, in Austin Flannery, O.P., ed., *Vatican Council II: More Postconciliar Documents*, (Northport, N.Y.: Costello Publishing Company, 1982), 387–96.

traditional formulation invites disbelief" (in the same way, no doubt, that the declaration of Jesus in John 6 that he himself was the bread of life "invited disbelief").

Remarkably, most of the writers of this *Commentary*, even though they refuse to be held to any standard of belief in the Church's teaching themselves, nevertheless appear to believe themselves to be the final arbiters both of what the faith is and of how it is to be expressed. In other words— for this is what the whole thing really amounts to—they appear to believe that *they*, not the pope and the bishops, really do constitute the Church's Magisterium.

## IV

On what basis do the theologian-writers of the *Commentary on the Catechism of the Catholic Church* presume to criticize so radically, and proceed on their own to correct, a foundational teaching document issued by the supreme authority of the Church? Apparently on the basis of their own academic study of the faith—that is, on their learning, scholarship, science—or on their citation of what other scholars or specialists have allegedly established.

We live in the age of the expert. In every field of human science or endeavor, the authority of the expert is sought in order to supply whatever answers are thought to be required. It is thus easy to adopt the position, sometimes without even realizing it, that in matters of faith, too, we must now look to the experts, to the theologians, to supply the answers to all questions that arise. Even the traditional authority of the hierarchy of the Church is now seen as having to yield without question to the more modern and "scientific" authority of the specialist.

People today often lose sight of the fact that Jesus rather pointedly did not select any of the trained people in the establishments of his own day to preserve and perpetuate the faith he revealed to us while he was among us. Acquired expertise, however dazzling it might appear to the uncritical eye, is not—and cannot be—the standard by which the Catholic Church lives.

Yet another one of the contributors to this volume, Fr. Brian E. Daley, S.J., of the Weston School of Theology in Cambridge, Massachusetts, remarks that the *Catechism*'s view of the human body and soul rests on a theory that "many modern scientific and philosophical theories would not accept". In an era of more robust faith and strong Catholic identity, a believing Catholic would have been apt to reply to such a statement by saying "so much the worse for all those modern scientific and philosophical theories then!" Today, however, the prestige of science is such that even many believers are uncomfortable with anything that appears to go against current scientific fashions, even if the latter are shown to be highly questionable if not actually untenable themselves.

It is in any case widely believed, although usually only in a vague, general way without much precise, concrete data, that modern science and scholarship have "proved" that many "traditional" positions of the Church are now "outmoded" or "untenable". Science and scholarship have "proved" no such thing, of course, but the attitude that it is the Church that must always "change" persists anyway. When the Church, for her own reasons, inaugurates her own era of *aggiornamento*, of updating, mandating many official changes, as happened with Vatican II, the idea that everything is henceforth changeable unfortunately becomes almost irresistible for some. Certainly this mania for change has immeasurably affected the discipline of Catholic theology. When, in such a climate, the idea takes hold that henceforth faith questions, too, are to be decided by specialists on the basis of the discoveries, real or supposed, of science and scholarship, we arrive at something very like what is so regularly reflected in the pages of this revisionist *Commentary*.

The assumption that, as masters of the new science, theologians are now to be the arbiters of the faith—to constitute what may be called a "theological magisterium"—is an assumption that appears to be shared, at least in some degree, by most of the contributors to this *Commentary*. Some of them merely assume the position and act in accordance with it. Others expressly articulate it, even in the face of Vatican II's clear teaching that the Magisterium resides in the hierarchy of the pope and the bishops (see, *inter alia*, *Lumen Gentium* no. 25 and *Dei Verbum* no. 10).

Another one of the Heythrop College theologians, for example, Fr. Robert Murray, S.J., although he says he accepts the fact that "the Catholic bishops in communion with the pope have inherited apostolic authority and exercise this in teaching and interpretation", still believes this teaching authority is necessarily a "shared ministry". There is no warrant for this in official Church teaching; nevertheless he asserts that it is shared. And it is shared, he believes, with the theologians. Vatican II's teaching that the authentic interpretation of revelation has been entrusted to the Magisterium alone he finds "hard to verify from history"—but to *require* it to be verified from "history" is, precisely, to assert the priority of the claim of the specialist, in this case the historian, who supposedly verifies it from the study of history.

Fr. Murray is actually one of the "moderates" in this

volume, by the way, and he delivers himself of one of its more memorable lines when, in effect, he confirms Pope John Paul II's observation that Catholic doctrine is being distorted and denied *within* the Church today. Fr. Murray says: "It is true that some exegetes have come into tension, in some cases unresolvable, with orthodoxy." This is as close to a little honest "peer review", by the way, that any of the theologian-contributors to this volume ever really comes.

Another contributor, Fr. Philip J. Rosato, S.J., an American who is currently on the faculty of Rome's Gregorian University, commenting on the *Catechism*'s treatment of the sacrament of Orders—a treatment he judges "conceptually inadequate and spiritually uninspiring"—writes that "most members of the *theological magisterium* would not consider . . . female ordination and priestly celibacy . . . dogmatic issues but canonical ones open to further revision as social conditions and pastoral needs change. Yet the editors"— he means the bishop-authors of the *Catechism*—"following the *official magisterium*, do not make such a clear distinction between matters of faith and matters of law, with the result that the question of female ordination seems linked inextricably to Christology and that of priestly celibacy to eschatology" (emphasis added).

There is not in the Church, of course, any such thing as a "theological magisterium" parallel with the "official magisterium". There is only a "Magisterium" *tout court*—what Fr. Rosato calls here the "official magisterium". Moreover, whether they are matters of faith or matters of law, female ordination is excluded and priestly celibacy enjoined by one and the same Church authority, called "Magisterium" in its teaching aspect. (Yes: doctrines do "develop" and practices may be "changed", but both these developments and these changes must be approved by the legitimate authority of the Church; they are not just decided upon by free-wheeling theologians.)

The *Catechism* traces both the selection of men alone for sacred ordination and the discipline of celibacy, which has always pertained to this particular sacrament, back to the choice and preference of the Lord himself. Paragraph 1577 says that the Church "recognizes that she is bound by the choice of the Lord [that] the ordination of women is not possible." This, by the way, is clearly a doctrinal and not merely a canonical declaration. It is understandable that theologians and others who have come to think the ordination of women inevitable should recoil in shock at such an unequivocal statement to the contrary by the teaching Church.

The *Catechism*'s paragraph 1579 goes on to say that priests are "chosen from among believing men who are celibate and intend to remain celibate 'for the sake of the kingdom of heaven' (Mt 19:12)". The book thus correctly portrays the Church doing here what she has always done: practicing and handing on intact what she has received.

This has been a characteristic of the Church from the beginning: "For I delivered to you . . . what I also received", St. Paul wrote in 1 Corinthians 15:3. The Church invariably does the same; the *Catechism* proves this again in our own day. In the present case, the Church has always selected only men for ordination and has insisted that they agree to follow the manner of life of the virginal and celibate Jesus, in whose place they will stand. This does not mean, again, that the Church never changes; it means that what changes are made have to be decided upon by proper Church authority. But Fr. Rosato judges this to be a grave deficiency. He complains that "the editors . . . were constrained to limit themselves to the pronouncements of the official magisterium" and were not "permitted to engage in theological reflection". But this is to misunderstand entirely the nature of what a *Catechism* is.

"A catechism", according, once again, to Pope John Paul II's apostolic constitution *Fidei Depositum*, which promulgated this *Catechism*, "must present faithfully and organically the teaching of sacred Scripture, the living Tradition in the Church, and of the authentic magisterium, as well as the spiritual heritage of the Fathers and saints of the Church, in order to allow the Christian mystery to be better known and to revive the faith of God's people."[13]

Nothing about any "theological magisterium" here; nothing about any requirement for the *Catechism*'s authors to "engage in theological reflection". There is not even any mention of theology or theologians, as a matter of fact. Rather, what is mentioned is: "sacred Scripture", "living Tradition", "authentic magisterium", "the Fathers", "the saints": *these* are the sources through which the Church affirms and confirms the faith she has preserved and handed down from the time of Jesus. These are the things on which the *Catechism of the Catholic Church* necessarily concentrates and from which it draws the content of its teaching.

One of the *Commentary* authors complains about the *Catechism*'s "excessive preoccupation with the content of the faith", but, again, that is what a catechism *is*: a compendium of *doctrine*. And neither the doctrine of the faith itself nor any catechism that reflects and expounds it for the benefit of the faithful is based, or could be based, either on the discoveries of science or scholarship or on the reflections or speculations of theologians.

Most of the theologian-contributors to this *Commentary* have quite patently lost sight of what a catechism is.

---

[13] *Fidei Depositum*, no. 2.

Fr. Dermot A. Lane faults the document for lacking modern "conceptualities such as the turn to the subject and historical consciousness, the framework of modernity, process thought, and the emerging reconstructed postmodern ecological frameworks". The same author is also to be found writing another sentence calling for new "languages of faith such as the existential, the experiential, the anthropological, shared praxis, narrative and story variety".

Fr. Gabriel Daly, O.S.A., similarly regrets that the modern "turn to the subject"—this is currently a fashionable jargon-phrase, both in modern theology and in modern catechetics—is not reflected in the *Catechism*. He doubts the document's usefulness for what he calls "an honest, critically aware faith". "Neither process thought nor feminist critique has had the slightest moderating influence . . . on the *Catechism*." As far as Fr. Daly is concerned, "the greater part could have been written hundreds of years ago." Fr. John McDade, S.J., similarly remarks: "The exposition it offers could have been compiled at any stage of Christian history."

Precisely. The *Catechism of the Catholic Church* aims to hand down, and does hand down, nothing else but "the Catholic faith that comes to us from the apostles". It does so—as we have just quoted John Paul II as saying in *Fidei Depositum*—in order "to allow the Christian mystery to be better known and to revive the faith of God's people". This does not mean that it is not also entirely up-to-date in the things it is supposed to be up-to-date on, namely, how the traditional faith that has been handed down from the time of the apostles has also been developed and interpreted under the guidance of the Magisterium with the assistance of the Holy Spirit. As a matter of fact, the *Catechism* is outstanding in this particular regard: including and explaining modern developments.

Nevertheless, the *Catechism* is still what it is: a statement of the Church's faith. Is it possible to imagine *anyone's* faith being "revived" by, say, "process thought" or "the turn to the subject"? Or anyone being converted to Christ by "the existential" or "the experiential"? Where in the Gospels did Jesus ask for "critically aware" faith? How can the "feminist critique" be incorporated into Church teaching when the feminist critique essentially rejects Church teaching?

The poverty of imagination evidenced by these scholars and the severe limitations of their vision render them quite unfit to pass judgment on the masterful presentation of the living Catholic tradition of faith set forth in the *Catechism of the Catholic Church*. The entire original conception of the *Commentary* is deficient because it is based on a fundamentally deficient conception of the faith. The editor of the volume, Michael J. Walsh, a former member of the Society of Jesus and now librarian at Heythrop College, University of London, began with the assumption, as he rather ingenuously relates, that the text of the *Catechism* places "far too much emphasis on the authority of the magisterium . . . and far too little on the role of the Holy Spirit in the life of the Church". That is, on what he *calls* "the role of the Holy Spirit": invoking the Spirit in this way has become one of the standard excuses of those determined to rebel against the legitimate authority of the Church; it is encountered more than once in the contributions to this *Commentary*.

Walsh goes on to specify that the assigned task of each of the various authors of the *Commentary* was to enter "into critical dialogue with the text upon which they were commenting"—the same phrase used by the publishers in their announcements of the Commentary. "Critical dialogue", it would seem, is practically synonymous with "faith" in the minds of the writers of this *Commentary*.

What are Walsh's qualifications as editor of a volume whose principal aim, evidently, is to judge the qualifications of the Church and her Magisterium to produce a catechism? His qualifications, as it happens, may perhaps be gauged by a "definition" of the Church's Magisterium that he himself offered in his book entitled *Opus Dei: An Investigation into the Secret Society Struggling for Power within the Roman Catholic Church*. In it, the author succeeds in demonstrating neither that Opus Dei is a "secret society", nor that it is "struggling for power" within the Church. What he does succeed in doing is betraying his own inability to believe that anyone today might possibly take seriously the traditional tenets of the Catholic faith or be willing to subject themselves to serious spiritual direction. The things in his heaven and earth, it seems, are mostly those dreamt of in modern liberal ideology. Anyway, this is how he explained "the Magisterium" in his book:

> "Magisterium," simply translated, means "teaching," but its overtones are rather less neutral than that. . . . In this usage, it means the teaching, not of the Church at large but of the bishops, and, more particularly, of the Pope and his Curia in Rome: what is known to theologians as "the ordinary magisterium." No one suggests that such teaching is, in the full share of the word, "infallible," but many Catholics regard it as authoritative, even though, used in this way, it is untraditional, a creation of nineteenth-century ultra-papal sentiment."[14]

Mr. Walsh correctly though simplistically does get it right that "the pope" and "the bishops" are the Magisterium. Be-

---

[14] Michael Walsh, *Opus Dei: An Investigation into the Secret Society Struggling for Power within the Roman Catholic Church* (San Francisco: Harper, 1989), 89.

yond that affirmation, and the affirmation that "many Catholics" regard the Magisterium as "authoritative", he gets virtually everything else wrong.

The whole thing is so garbled that it is difficult to know where to begin to correct it. "Magisterium" does *not* mean "teaching" but "teaching authority"; there is no separate, distinct teaching of "the Church at large", separate from that of "the bishops" and of "the Pope and his Curia", because *they* teach *for* the whole Church, and there is no Church "teaching" at all apart from what they teach. Nor is the pope's "Curia" separate from *him* in its teaching function; Vatican II made it clear that the Curia legitimately speaks and acts for the pope when directed by him.[15]

Again, the teaching of the Magisterium *is* "authoritative", but not just because "many Catholics regard it as authoritative"; it enjoys special assistance from the Holy Spirit in ways the Church has carefully spelled out. Under certain specified conditions, it is even "infallible". Finally, the Magisterium is in no way an "untraditional creation" of the nineteenth century, although the *word* "magisterium" came into prominent use from approximately that time on. The *teaching authority of the Church*, which the word "magisterium" signifies, has been around at least since the time of the Council of Jerusalem described in Acts 15. The acts of the great Church councils of the first four or five centuries eminently illustrate the existence of such a definite Church Magisterium, or specific teaching office; so do the great interventions of the popes, such as the famous *Tome* of Pope St. Leo the Great acclaimed at the Council of Chalcedon in 450. So the "Magisterium" has been around all along;

---

[15] See Decree on the Pastoral Office of Bishops in the Church, *Christus Dominus*, no. 9.

even so, the word did *not* come into use as a result of what is miscalled here by Walsh "ultra-papal sentiment".

And so on. Does *this* inaccurate, misleading paragraph indicate any level whatsoever of theological competence on which a *Commentary on the Catechism of the Catholic Church* could properly be planned and executed?

Readers who would like to know what the Magisterium of the Church really is are urged to peruse for themselves chapter three (nos. 18–29) of Vatican Council II's Dogmatic Constitution on the Church, *Lumen Gentium*, and/or 871–96 of the *Catechism of the Catholic Church*.


# V


Heythrop College Librarian Michael Walsh proudly describes this *Commentary on the Catechism of the Catholic Church*, of which he is the editor, as "an up-to-date survey of the expert teaching of theologians on those topics in Catholic theology which are touched upon, often all too inadequately, by the *Catechism*." This statement, by itself, would seem to constitute a claim that there exists a "theological magisterium" corrective of the Church's actual Magisterium.

On the evidence, however, many of the contributors to this volume have *not* turned in a very plausible theological performance, as can be readily gathered from some of the quotations already included up to this point. We could quote many more. If these are the kind of people Catholics have to depend upon in order to get the faith right, we are in trouble.

Ironically, not a little of the scholarship in this book—in which the believing Catholic is now apparently supposed to

repose a kind of confidence that is to be denied to the pronouncements of the Church's Magisterium—is really quite
mediocre, as we have already seen. The Gregorian University's Fr. Philip J. Rosato, S.J., to give another example, cites
a single reference from Pope St. Leo the Great referring
to the election of presbyters as proof of what he describes
as "an anthropological principle underlying the concept of
ministry in the first millennium", namely, that priests were
the *delegates* of the faithful (presumably in the "democratic"
sense).

The same author regrets that "deaconesses are not mentioned at all in the *Catechism* although they constituted an
order throughout the first millennium." This latter statement is not only false but bespeaks an ignorance of the whole
subject of deaconesses. One of the two present writers was
the translator into English of the best authoritative modern work on this subject, Aimé-Georges Martimort's *Dea-*
*conesses.*[16] This book establishes that deaconesses have *never*
constituted an "order" in the history of the Church. The
very word "deaconess", which is simply derived from the
Greek word for "service", has actually been used to describe
very different types of "service" to the Church performed
by women at different periods in the Church's history.

Other examples of similar questionable scholarship from
this *Commentary* could be cited if space allowed. Enough
has surely been said already, however, to render highly
doubtful one of the key assumptions behind this whole volume, namely, that Catholics should transfer the allegiance
they have traditionally accorded to the Magisterium of the
Church over to the findings of selected modern scholars

---

[16] Aimé-Georges Martimort, *Deaconesses: An Historical Study*, trans.
K. D. Whitehead (San Francisco: Ignatius Press, 1986).

and exegetes. This would be to sell their birthright for a *real* mess of pottage.

## VI

The authors of the *Commentary on the Catechism of the Catholic Church* continually make reference to what Fr. Dermot A. Lane calls the "challenges of communicating truth to the modern world". The main challenge, as Fr. Gabriel Daly expresses it, is how to appeal "to the average modern believer of good will and critical intelligence". He wants to avoid having what he calls "unnecessary dogmatic obstacles placed in the path of thoughtful believers or would-be believers". This immediately raises the matter of deciding *which* of the Church's dogmas are "unnecessary" and have to go by the board. And this, of course, would appear to be precisely the task that the authors of this *Commentary* have arrogated to themselves. *They* will decide which Church doctrines must now be downgraded or thrown out. This appears to be one of the important ways the so-called "theological magisterium" of the Church, which they fancy they represent, should function.

It is almost superfluous at this point to remark that most of these commentators do not believe that the *Catechism of the Catholic Church* has succeeded very well in meeting the challenges the Church faces in trying to make her ancient faith credible to the modern world. Dr. Monika Hellwig finds that its treatment of Penance, for example, "does not support a catechism arousing vision, enthusiasm, and commitment"—which she believes we need if we ever hope to maintain "a faithful community".

Fr. Gerald O'Hanlon, for his part, thinks " 'churchy' lan-

guage such as 'redemption,' 'atones' (CCC 517) and 'reca-
pitulation' (CCC 518) . . . require . . . breaking down into
a more contemporary idiom by the theologically informed
catechist if they are to be fruitful mediations of the faith."

There are frequent similar statements scattered through
the texts of the various authors, all quite critical of how the
*Catechism* presents the faith to the modern world. At the
same time, it is strongly implied that these authors do know
how to present the faith properly and effectively to modern,
late-twentieth-century hearers.

What is the truth of the matter? What is the *record* of
such academics in evangelizing, catechizing, and otherwise
spreading the faith? What is the general state of the faith in
the present era in which they occupy such prominent positions on Catholic theology faculties? The sad fact is that the
knowledge and practice of the Catholic faith have fallen off
more catastrophically during these very years than during
any comparable period in the Church's history. The tragic
fact is that the formal teaching of the Catholic faith in Catholic schools and religious education classes has hardly ever
been less effective than in the very years that the training
of catechists and religion teachers has been so largely in the
hands of people such as these.

No doubt the root causes of the crisis of faith in our day
are extremely complex and varied and cannot be ascribed to
any single cause, let alone laid at the door of any particular
group of people in the Church, even the "new theologians".
Nevertheless the fact is plain and indisputable that they have
been a significant contributing factor. At bottom, these experts are peddling their own ideas, not the Church's faith.
They see themselves as modern, up-to-date, and relevant,
while they see the Church as ignorant, backward, myopic,
and outside the mainstream as well as behind the times.

The issuance of the *Catechism of the Catholic Church* by the Church's highest authority obviously marks a discouraging and very serious setback for the kind of revisionist theology that experts such as these had long since hoped and expected to see the Church adopt. Their disappointment is patent throughout this whole book. As the authors relentlessly point out in the pages of this *Commentary*, the Church has not adopted any Neomodernist positions. Indeed, the Church has quite conspicuously not adopted *any* of the typical revisions and modifications in the faith that these theological dissenters have been so tirelessly promoting over the past quarter century.

With this particular *Catechism*, the Church has instead restated and reiterated her authentic ancient faith, even while thoroughly and marvelously updating it in the authentic sense of that word. The revisionists claim that it slights Vatican Council II, but the *Catechism of the Catholic Church* cites the Council as its authority no fewer than 767 times, *far* more than any other source except the holy Scriptures themselves. This book thus represents one of the richest, most varied, and most nuanced statements of the Church's faith ever produced; but it *remains* a statement of her faith.

Although it is hardly their intention, the authors of the *Commentary* themselves provide some of the best hard evidence for the *Catechism*'s authenticity. Most of the comments, complaints, and criticisms the authors make indicate precisely this: the *Catechism* is not what they wanted. They are dismayed, in fact, for it reinstates, sometimes on a stronger basis than ever, doctrines that these people believe should have been dropped long ago.

On the subject of feminism, for example, a significant number of the contributors make reference to such things as the "difficulty many experience in addressing God as Father" (O'Hanlon) or to what is styled the actual "*oppres-siveness* of the use of Father" (Mowry LaCugna)—as if the Church, in response to the demands of a radical modern ideology, could ever give up one of the fundamental features of God's own revelation of himself, namely, that he *is* a Father, whom Jesus himself taught us to address as "Our Father". We saw in the last chapter how this scriptural image of "Father" so fittingly expresses the *transcendence* of God the Creator. We cannot change the traditional images and expressions of the faith in accord with the demands of modern ideologies without serious repercussions for the faith itself.

Similarly, a surprising number of contributors also invoke the concept of "the hierarchy of truths" as an excuse for downgrading the importance of some of the doctrines included in the *Catechism*. This, as the reader will remember, had also been the subject of much discussion in the earlier attack on the draft *Catechism* launched by the *Universal Catechism Reader*, which was written by theologians of much the same persuasion and even some of the very same authors we find here.[17]

As a result of the steady complaints of all these theologians, even the Holy See and the editorial committee of the *Catechism* felt obliged to make far too much of this concept of the hierarchy of truths than was ever necessary. In Chapter Three, we have already taken note of the lucid explanation of the concept made by Archbishop Christoph Schönborn.[18]

Properly understood, of course, the idea of a hierarchy of truths is a legitimate concept. Vatican II, in *Unitatis Red-*

---

[17] See n. 3 to Chapter Three *supra*.
[18] See n. 2 to Chapter Three *supra*.

*integratio,* taught that "in Catholic doctrine there exists an order or 'hierarchy' of truths since they vary in relation to the foundation of the Christian faith."[19]

Thus, a number of the contributors here, too, do not fail to seize upon the concept. In their minds, the phrase evidently means that some truths are "less true", or, at any rate, "less important", than others. Interpreted in this way, the idea is used as a means of setting aside—so that one can simply forget about—those traditional Catholic beliefs that today are thought to be inconvenient or even embarrassing. For if these doctrines can be considered "lower down" in the hierarchy of truths, then they need no longer be emphasized, and perhaps some of them are even entirely dispensable—so runs the revisionist line.

What the expression "hierarchy of truths" really means in authentic Church teaching, however, is that some truths are *derived* from other truths (or, as Archbishop Christoph Schönborn put it, some truths are central, others grouped around them). *Unitatis Redintegratio* (no. 11) itself specified that truths "vary in their relation to the foundation of Christian faith". But this does *not* mean that some truths are less true or less important than others.[20]

The impression is inescapable that the contributors to this *Commentary* expected and wanted certain Catholic doctrines to be downgraded or eliminated in the *Catechism*. When this did not occur, they necessarily found themselves constrained

---

[19] Vatican Council II, Decree on Ecumenism, *Unitatis Redintegratio,* no. 11.

[20] For a further discussion of how "the hierarchy of truths" has been used in the controversies surrounding the *Catechism*, see Msgr. Michael J. Wrenn, *Catechisms and Controversies: Religious Education in the Postconciliar Years* (San Francisco: Ignatius Press, 1991), esp. 59–64.

to try to shape the future of Church teaching in other ways. One of these ways was to invoke such subterfuges as the hierarchy of truths as justification for selecting which doctrines should be retained and which downgraded or eliminated.

Another and much more significant way to try to shape the future of the Church was to establish themselves as the "official"—or at least the most prestigious—interpreters of the *Catechism* itself. This appears to be the principal aim of the preparation of this *Commentary*. If the *Catechism* is as deficient as they say it is, then obviously their intervention is going to be required in order to set things right; *they* can decide which of the doctrines it contains are to be emphasized in academic theology and, particularly, in the training of catechists and religion teachers.

Or—even better from their point of view—they can decide and persuade others to believe that the *Catechism* itself does not even have to be used much, if at all, in spite of all the trouble the Church has gone to in order to produce it. All this *can* be managed and arranged, *if* theologians of this stripe continue to be tolerated in their various university faculties—and *if* a volume such as this *Commentary* is allowed to be presented to the unsuspecting Catholic faithful as a legitimate commentary on the *Catechism of the Catholic Church*.

There may have been a time when dissident and revisionist authors and theologians such as these could continue to maintain at least the appearance of remaining Catholic, even while consistently undermining or even contradicting known teachings of the Magisterium. There may have been a time when they could continue to maintain the appearance of being Catholic, in other words, even while coming "into tension", in the colorful phrase of Fr. Robert Murray, "in some cases unresolvable, with orthodoxy". In fact, they were often able to do this simply by putting forward their dissident or revisionist positions as *interpretations*, say, of Vatican II. Everyone knows that Vatican II meant "change", after all, and so everyone's own favorite "change", even in doctrine, could always be put forward under that label. Since all these same dissidents and revisionists tended to remain in place, moreover, whether on university faculties or in institutes or on the editorial staffs of theological journals, without ever being challenged, rebuked, silenced, or removed by ecclesiastical authority—itself neutralized, as often as not, merely by being *accused* of being oppressive— the reigning appearance could only be that their peculiar "interpretations" of Catholic doctrine indeed somehow remained within permissible bounds for Catholic theologians.

No longer. The *Catechism of the Catholic Church* has now come out, reiterating the Church's ancient faith and, for the most part, simply *passing over in silence* most of the dissident and revisionist positions of the past generation, which were supposed to have been so far on the way to official adoption in the brave new Church of the future. In many other cases, the *Catechism* specifically rejects favored modern notions. Virtually nothing of what the revisionists wanted happened.

Nevertheless, the advocates of all these same erroneous positions have not yet given up, even though they stand exposed and condemned by the words of the *Catechism* itself, which steadily reaffirms what they have so long openly tried to modify or drop. They do not intend to go quietly, however. This *Commentary on the Catechism of the Catholic Church* is only the latest of their efforts to steer the Church down the same wrong road they have been trying to get her to travel virtually since the end of the Second Vatican Council.

They failed in a number of rather strenuous previous efforts to prevent this *Catechism* from being written or published; they failed in similar attempts to water down its text.

Now they have tried to discredit the *Catechism* by coming out with a *Commentary* that criticizes it so severely that it will be neutralized—at least in the minds of some. The hope is, apparently, that it will be seen as unusable and then will just have to be put on a shelf somewhere and forgotten. And to the extent that these same people continue to teach religious educators, they can sometimes, unhappily, *insure* this outcome.

The odds in the long term, however, are that they will fail in their enterprise, for the simple reason that Christ's promise to the Church still obtains, as, indeed, the production and promulgation of this *Catechism* at this time under these circumstances almost miraculously confirms. How could the Church have produced such a splendid, entirely orthodox statement of her faith when a majority of her theologians, judging by the predominant tendencies of the contributors to this volume, were evidently urging her to travel in a wholly different direction?

In the short term, though, the odds are that many will unfortunately be deceived by this very defective *Commentary on the Catechism of the Catholic Church*. It *seems* fine, and it has been written by such "distinguished" theologians; and it has been brought out under such respectable "mainstream" auspices by publishers such as Geoffrey Chapman and the Liturgical Press. Nevertheless it is a very far cry from being the reception of this *Catechism* that the Catholic faithful both require and deserve.

And what is even more astonishing about it than the volume itself, perhaps, is the fact that this *Commentary* was very favorably reviewed in *The Living Light*, the official publication on religious education and pastoral ministry of the Department of Education of the U.S. Catholic Conference; it was favorably reviewed as if it were now established Church policy and practice in the United States to accept open denigration of the teachings of the Church as just one more expression of legitimate "theological opinion".

"The essays as a whole are constructive, thorough, and fair", the reviewer in *The Living Light* opined, and added: ". . . the authors successfully offer readers thorough examination of the *Catechism*'s strengths and weaknesses"—apparently taking it wholly for granted that the task of theology is to criticize and "correct" the magisterium. This particular reviewer was able to reach these particular favorable conclusions about this *Commentary* even as he quoted comments on the *Catechism* from it as bad or worse than some of those we have quoted above (for example, Fr. Gabriel Daly found in the section on creation and original sin "a near total disregard for the difficulties and doubts which beset" modern man; and Monika Hellwig found that the section on Penance "achieves a burdensome and depressing effect which cannot be helpful to catechesis").[21]

Unfortunately, this complacent acceptance of dissent and dissenters in the Church as natural and normal and legitimate by this reviewer is hardly unique to this issue of *The Living Light*; it seems to be standard fare in this "official" catechetical journal. The executive editor of the publication, Fr. Berard L. Marthaler, was one of the original twenty dissenting "subject professors" at the Catholic University of America during the controversy over the papal encyclical

---

[21] Review of *Commentary on the Catechism of the Catholic Church* by Morris Pelzel, Saint Meinrad School of Theology, Saint Meinrad, Indiana, in *The Living Light*, fall 1995.

*Humanæ Vitæ* back in 1968.[22] But this fact never seems to have prevented him from being one of the leaders most in view of the modern catechetical movement in the United States; nor has it, apparently, ever raised any serious questions anywhere about his suitability to be the editor of the USCC's official journal on catechesis and pastoral ministry; evidently one does not have to accept the faith oneself in order to be considered an expert in the teaching of it.

The anonymous author of the book *DOA*, on the initial reception of the *Catechism*, recommended that publication of *The Living Light* under official Church auspices should simply be terminated.[23] That might be a good beginning.

Meanwhile, when we see what the theological establishment is like today, we begin to understand more clearly some of the things that are wrong with the catechetical establishment. If the new catechists have so often shown themselves to be reluctant apostles, there is serious question whether some of these theologians, as evidenced by this *Commentary on the Catechism of the Catholic Church*, can be considered apostles in any sense at all: evidently many of them no longer even accept that they are "sent out" by the *Church* in any important way; it is all just a matter of one's "discipline".

---

[22] See Charles E. Curran, Robert E. Hunt, and the "Subject Professors", with John F. Hunt and Terrence R. Connelly, *Dissent in and for the Church: Theologians and Humanæ Vitæ* (New York: Sheed and Ward, 1969).

[23] See *DOA: The Ambush of the Universal Catechism* (by "Catholicus") (Notre Dame, Ind.: Crisis Books, 1993), 167–68.

CHAPTER SEVEN

# Can Such Things Be?

I

When the *Catechism of the Catholic Church* was issued in
1992, the document described itself as "an organic synthesis
of the essential and fundamental contents of the Catholic
doctrine, as regards both faith and morals, in the light of
the Second Vatican Council and the whole of the Church's
tradition" (CCC 11). This would seem to be a pretty clear
statement of what the *Catechism* is and what it contains, and
the document would surely seem to be what anyone would
think those professionally involved in Catholic theology or
religious education would normally welcome as an essential
and fundamental sourcebook for their fields.

But the times are not normal, and the evidence continues
to mount that some Catholic theologians and religious education leaders, far from welcoming the *Catechism* with open
arms, have instead been rather openly striving to downgrade
the importance of the document and to limit its role and
use. They seem to have been especially anxious to ensure
that, where the work is used, *they*, the experts, will be the
ones to dictate how it will be used (this must not be consid-

This chapter appeared in part in the *Fellowship of Catholic Scholars
Newsletter*, fall 1995.

ered as difficult or as far-fetched as it might at first sound, when we consider some of the positions in the Church's educational structure occupied by many of the malcontents and revisionists of this type).

These same people appear very uncomfortable with the idea that the book can just be purchased and used by, well, anybody; and that it can be consulted at any time to provide an authoritative statement of what the Church teaches in any given area. How can the religious-education establishment maintain its effective monopoly on religious education in such a situation? It has thus become very important in certain quarters that the *Catechism* not be seen as authoritative or, indeed, as anything very special at all.

As one catechetical expert wrote in a publication intended for, and primarily read by DREs, catechists, and those in what is increasingly today being called parish "ministry", the *Catechism* is merely "a point of departure". This expert, who is a professor of religious-education at the university level, confidently assures her readers throughout the Church's religious-education system that "the *Catechism* is primarily a reference book."[1]

The author of a column in a series syndicated for use in parish bulletins adopts roughly the same view and appears to reflect the current consensus of the catechetical and theological establishments when he writes that the *Catechism* is "not a static end result. Since by its very nature the CCC is a reference work, it is not intended, e.g., for use in parochial schools, in its present form. . . . The CCC is rather meant to encourage and assist in the writing of new local catechisms." Here the Pope's *Fidei Depositum* promulgating the

---

[1] Mary C. Boys, S.N.J.M., "Tradition: Ordered Learning", *The Catechist's Connection*, May 1993.

*Catechism* is actually quoted, but in a way that implies that the writing of new local catechisms is intended to be the *only* use of the *Catechism*. Since the whole project of a universal catechism started, in fact, it has been standard operating procedure for certain theologians and religious educators to quote the Pope and other high Church officials, with a great show of loyalty, on the current need for local catechisms, especially those "inculturated" in a particular region or country; in the meantime, the suggestion always is, the present *Catechism* by itself will simply not do.

"Future catechisms will capture the rich experience of their own Church as it continues to dialogue with a pluralistic society", the parish bulletin writer just quoted informs his readers in no doubt hundreds of parishes around the country. "Theologians, biblicists, historians, linguists, catechists, etc., will be asked to pool their talents for the good of the community." Apparently the pains already taken by the Pope and the hierarchy over more than seven years to produce and issue an accurate and comprehensive summary of Catholic teaching for all the faithful is not nearly good enough, and so now all these other experts are going to have to be called in. This same writer for parish bulletins is quite explicit about this: the good of the community "will . . . demand their *improving* certain areas in the CCC" (emphasis added). "What is most needed", according to this writer, is "the courage to change".[2]

Evidently this fairly uniform message has gone out about as widely as it has been within the power of the theological and catechetical establishments to disseminate it: the new

---

[2] John F. Craghan, "The *Catechism* and Future Catechetics", column distributed by Liguori Publications in the Bulletin of the Church of Mary's Nativity, Flushing, New York, February 26, 1995.

*Catechism* is really not all that important; if the Catholic bishops of the world have not labored entirely in vain on this project, they have apparently labored to little real valid or durable purpose; it all has to be reworked—such is the message.

It is a fairly consistent message too. For example, one of today's typical catechetical workshop "facilitators" told a conference in the midwest consisting of DREs, youth ministers, school teachers and principals, priests, and religious that "the *Catechism of the Catholic Church* is only one resource and was not written for everyone. . . . It is not even the full expression of our faith either", she said. This particular "facilitator", who has a doctor's degree in catechetics from the Catholic University of America and is currently a faculty member at St. John's University in Collegeville, Minnesota, said that she didn't "think catechetical materials would change much . . . because there is nothing new in the *Catechism*".[3]

This same message is not only disseminated, it is also received—at least some of the time. At the particular workshop in the midwest just mentioned, one of the participants was quoted as saying: "It helped me to see where the *Catechism* fits into Church and society. *It's not the answer*; it's a tool to help with faith" (emphasis added).[4]

It also seems to be a tool that many specialists in the craft of catechetics seem strangely reluctant to use. Sometimes it is eye-opening to read a popular-press account of a catechetical conference such as the one we have just quoted. A

---

[3] The speaker was Dr. Jane E. Regan, quoted by Laurie Chen, "Speaker: New *Catechism* Just One Resource for Catechesis", *The Sunday Visitor* (Diocese of Lafayette, Indiana), June 19, 1994.

[4] Ibid.

reporter writing down exactly what is being said, perhaps without realizing the larger significance of it, can highlight points that would perhaps otherwise be obscured by the in-group jargon that the new catechists normally employ to describe what they are doing. In the case of this particular catechetical conference in the midwest, it seems quite evident from the press report of it that the participants clearly got the message that the new *Catechism* contains nothing new, is far from being our only or perhaps even most important catechetical resource, and, in any case, is not even a full expression of our faith.

Furthermore, the significance of what appears to be a systematic downgrading and undermining of the *Catechism* here by this facilitator extends beyond the bounds of a particular catechetical conference that happened to take place in the summer of 1994. For the facilitator of the conference in question, it seems, is also one of the more prominent new catechetical professionals. It turns out that she has presented numerous day-long conferences to diocesan and pastoral leaders throughout the midwest, and thus her decidedly negative message about the *Catechism* has reached more than just one small audience. We learn all this from the foreword to a book she has written about the *Catechism*.

Yes: she is the principal author of one of the first commentaries on the *Catechism* to appear in English. She is Jane E. Regan, author of a book entitled *Exploring the Catechism*.[5] This book, written with several collaborators, is specifically aimed at introducing religious educators, youth ministers, and others to the *Catechism*; it is intended to be part of the

---

[5] Jane E. Regan, *Exploring the Catechism*, with Michael P. Horan, Timothy Backous, O.S.B., Francis Kelly Nemeck, O.M.I., and Marie Theresa Coombs (Collegeville, Minn.: Liturgical Press, 1994).

"implementation" of the document. If we want to know what a lot of people are learning about the book, especially those who themselves have responsibilities of various kinds and at various levels in religious education, we need only look more closely at Jane E. Regan's *Exploring the Catechism.*

Actually we have already encountered both this book and this author. In Chapter Two, we quoted from *Exploring the Catechism* in order to illustrate how the new catechesis so often downplays formal instruction in Catholic doctrine by, first, "naming the [whole] community as the agent of catechesis", in Jane Regan's words. Then catechesis itself is defined as not "simply instruction", again in her words, but as coextensive "with the ways in which faith comes to expression within our community—communal living, proclamation, teaching, liturgy, and service—and seeing those as both the context and expression of catechesis as well as its *content*" (emphasis added).[6]

It is true that all the expressions of faith in the life of the Church enumerated here are important and indeed necessary; they support and reenforce and bring alive the instruction in the faith imparted in catechesis. Pope John Paul II himself makes this same point in *Catechesi Tradendæ*, mentioning many other such supports and reinforcements of catechesis in the life of the Church such as pilgrimages, missions, participation in prayer groups, charitable activities, Catholic action groups, and so on.[7]

Nevertheless, catechesis in itself remains primarily *instruction* addressed to the mind. This remains true even when, as is generally the case in the United States, reli-

---

[6] Ibid., 18–19; see also n. 6 to Chapter Two *supra.*

[7] Pope John Paul II, apostolic exhortation *Catechesi Tradendæ* on Catechesis in Our Time, October 16, 1979, no. 47.

gious educators are also responsible for the greater part of sacramental preparation. Even here, they are teaching their *confirmandi*, catechumens, or first communicants *about* the sacraments and their effects. The *General Catechetical Directory* actually narrows catechesis down to one form of the ministry of the word in the Church. According to the GCD, catechesis has to be distinguished from other forms of the ministry of the word such as evangelization (or missionary preaching), liturgy of the word, and theology.[8]

Thus, catechesis is *not* coextensive "with the ways in which faith comes to expression within our community"; certainly these things do not constitute its "content". Trying to make the whole "community", in all of its life and activities, "the agent of catechesis", as Dr. Jane E. Regan wishes to do, is already to lose the sharp focus that catechesis needs if it is to be effective. This becomes even more true when the doctrinal content of whatever actual instruction remains is further neglected or watered down, as is the case with much of our typical modern catechesis. This is no way to produce believing and practicing Christians, as the results of the new catechesis over the past thirty years attest. To say, in effect, that everybody is responsible for catechesis is like saying that everybody is responsible for alleviating poverty or curbing violence. In practice it too often means that nobody in particular is responsible, and hence nothing gets done.

The *General Catechetical Directory* has made the important point that catechists, because they are responsible for imparting a living faith, must indeed be more than mere teachers of a particular subject matter, even though the im-

---

[8] Congregation for the Clergy, *General Catechetical Directory*, April 11, 1971, no. 17.

parting of such a subject matter—the doctrine of the faith —is indeed their primary task. "They are responsible", the GCD says, "for choosing and creating suitable conditions which are necessary for the Christian message to be sought, accepted, and more profoundly investigated."

It often seems that "choosing and creating suitable conditions" are the very things many catechists are most often involved in today, sometimes to the exclusion of the Christian message itself. Many of the new catechists seem to have heard only part of the GCD's message. Too often these new catechists seem to see their principal task as creating "experiences" that are supportive of faith; but meanwhile they sometimes forget that the faith has to be there first (by means of instruction) before it can be fortified. "Choosing and creating suitable conditions", however important, is not a *substitute* for instruction. The GCD takes for granted that instruction is primary and prior; and it further points out that "adherence on the part of those to be taught is a fruit of grace and freedom, and does not ultimately depend on the catechist; and catechetical action, therefore, should be accompanied by prayer."[9]

And not only by prayer, we might add, but by the confidence that the true word of God will make its own way if only it is properly made known. Catechists do not have to be concerned with constantly providing "experiences" to their charges for fear the latter might become "bored". Nothing is less boring than the true faith, the story of our salvation, as a matter of fact, and it is this that has to be imparted. Moreover, now it is all there, in the *Catechism*; and so the task is to impart the *Catechism*, not to seek ways to avoid using it or perhaps even mentioning it.

---

[9] Ibid., no. 71.

How anyone could imagine that instruction is not necessarily central or that "the life of the community" could somehow become the equivalent of the *content* of the faith, as Dr. Regan asserts, is one of the mysteries of the new catechesis that few outside its own ranks have been able to comprehend. We clearly need to examine further this particular specialist's book *Exploring the Catechism* if we want to know what some of the new catechists are doing with the *Catechism*.

## II

The book *Exploring the Catechism* treats in greater detail some of the same themes and principles that stand behind its author's catechetical-workshop assertions that the new *Catechism* is only one catechetical resource, that it was not written for everyone, that there is nothing new in it, and that it is not a full expression of our faith anyway. That someone holding such views on the *Catechism* should nevertheless be thought suitable to prepare a book about it might at first seem unusual; but her motives do become clearer as her particular approach to the *Catechism* is more clearly spelled out. "Each chapter is written with pastoral ministers in mind," the author explains, "supporting them as they *critically read* the *Catechism*" (emphasis added).

This is how Church teachings are now to be received at all levels, apparently: "critically". Religion teachers in the classroom are now apparently supposed to *be* mini-practitioners of the new theology and of the historical-critical method— yet one more way in which the catechist's role and function precisely as *teacher* of the faith has been misunderstood and misapplied by the new catechesis.

Jesus is never depicted in the Gospels, by the way, as

proposing his teachings for further discussion and possible criticism. No: Jesus customarily *proclaimed* his teachings to be accepted, assimilated, and acted upon. Whatever else the phrase "to teach as Jesus did" (the name of a pastoral letter of the U.S. bishops of a few years back) might mean, it cannot possibly mean to propose the truths Jesus revealed for "critical examination". Jesus taught "with authority" (Lk 4:32). The Church too has traditionally proclaimed the teachings of Jesus in the same manner, "with authority", inviting and accepting the same response of faith and action. That, indeed, was what the kerygmatic movement in catechesis was originally all about.

Yet some people today decline simply to accept Christ's teachings as they are authoritatively proclaimed by the Church, most recently in the new *Catechism*. The virus of theological dissent has penetrated so deeply into the Catholic consciousness today that many people now appear honestly to believe—mistakenly, of course—that Christ's teachings must necessarily be subjected to "critical analysis" rather than received and made the basis of one's life.

Unfortunately, many of these same people are to be found in the ranks of religious educators with formal responsibilities for teaching the faith to others. It is no wonder that some of them fail as badly at their task as the modern statistics show; for they have long since been trained to consider the Church's teachings as so much raw material to be processed further by *them*. *They* are now to be the final arbiters and judges of what the faith is. In Martin Luther's day, this was called "private judgment"; among modern new theologians and new catechists, it is often styled "mature faith". This is the approach that characterizes *Exploring the Catechism*.

The principal author of *Exploring the Catechism* tells us that "each person approaches the reading of the *Catechism of the Catholic Church* from his or her own perspective. . . . As theologian, I ask a number of questions. . . . What theological perspective is reflected there? . . . What does the text mean for *me*?" (emphasis added).

Or again: "What is the connection between a catechism and *my* ecclesiology, *my* sense of the nature of the Church?" This is surely private judgment with a vengeance. Dr. Regan does sometimes pose real questions, such as: What is the nature of the Church? or: What is the role of the Magisterium of the Church? It is just that she does not seem to see the *Catechism* as in any way providing the answers to such questions. Indeed she explicitly rejects the idea that the book could provide "the answers to our questions".

She claims at the same time to reject going to the other extreme as well; that is, she does not include herself among those deploring and denying the idea of any catechism at all, those in her description who scorn a catechism as laying down a "party line". Oh no! the Church may issue a catechism if that is what the Church wishes to do; it is just that someone with a Ph.D. from the Catholic University of America, apparently, need not be bound by what the Church does.

In fact, at one point Dr. Regan betrays only too tellingly her real sympathies when she characterizes the *Catechism* as something that really might bring about the possibility "that the life-giving spirit of inquiry within a pluralistic Church will be silenced".

"The life-giving spirit of inquiry within a pluralistic Church"—as if it were any "spirit of inquiry within the pluralistic Church", and not Christ and the *real* Spirit, which "gives life" within the Church! Old Voltaire and his Enlightenment friends surely did not labor in vain; a couple of centuries later, their disciples are apparently to be found in the ranks of the Church's trained and working theologians.

Dr. Regan's book on the *Catechism of the Catholic Church* includes several introductory chapters on the background of catechesis, catechisms, and the new *Catechism*. These contain standard material and are competently done, for the most part; there is no need to dwell on them. What is interesting from our point of view is that the author often cannot avoid displaying her own theological orientation and bias even when she is treating purely factual material. She comments, for example, that while a catechism is concerned with "uniformity", a directory allows for the possibility of "unity with diversity" (probably because a catechism explains doctrines so plainly that it is no longer easy to explain them *away*; it is always easy, on the other hand, to "interpret" the general "guidance" that a directory gives, that is, it is always possible to decide not to be guided by the guidance provided).

This same general approach is evident when Dr. Regan criticizes medieval society for trying "to present the Christian mystery as distinct propositions suitable for memorization"; or as being "entangled in lists and propositions unconnected with lived faith". As it happens, of course, the "lived faith" of medieval society raised up artistic monuments to faith that have never been equaled either before or since. Anyway, the present age is surely not in any position to be criticizing the "lived faith" of anybody. The present era can hardly pretend to give lessons to any other era at all, considering how little faith is generally respected today, or how little it is apparently able to affect our decadent society in any real way.

The first part of *Exploring the Catechism* sets the work in context and was written by Dr. Regan herself. In the second part of the book, she includes four other authors, who help provide the commentary on the four pillars of the *Catechism* itself, the Creed, or Profession of Faith, the Sacraments, the Commandments, and Christian Prayer. Dr. Regan herself wrote the commentary on the Sacraments, entitled the "Celebration of the Christian Mystery", as well as providing an overview of the whole. In the latter, she explains that the aim of her commentary is "to probe", to undertake a discriminating reading of the *Catechism*. She and her colleagues hope to present "theological concepts or understandings that are presumed in the texts but not always clearly explicated".

Thus, "theology" is what is presumed to be at the heart of this modern compendium of the Church's faith. Instead of accepting gratefully the gift that the teaching Church has presented to the faithful of our own and future eras, Dr. Regan sees her primary task and that of her collaborators as entering "into the multifaceted dialogue that exists between the text of the *Catechism of the Catholic Church* and the thoughts of contemporary theological discourse, between the theological presentation"—she apparently means the *Catechism*'s presentation of the Church's faith—"and their own *experience* as people of faith" (emphasis added). Once again, the "experience" of people is considered to be on a par with what has been revealed and handed down in the Church.

One possible explanation for this seemingly "naturalistic" approach comes from Dr. Regan's commentary on the Sacraments included in the book. In discussing grace, she gives fairly short shrift to what the *Catechism* itself says about it in comparison to what Jesuit theologian Karl Rahner has to say. The latter is quoted as saying that grace "is the comprehensive radical opening up of the person's total consciousness in the direction of the immediacy of God, an opening up that is brought about by God's own self-communication".[10] Where this leads, in Dr. Regan's view, is to the conclusion that "grace can be experienced."

While an attempt is made to express this in the "nuanced" terms that modern theology claims to favor—after all, the truth of this kind of statement does depend upon what one *means* by it—the fact nevertheless remains that, in a commentary on a catechism, or authoritative statement of the Church's faith, there is at least one fairly serious problem about pursuing such a line of thought in the way Dr. Regan does pursue it. For the *Catechism* teaches very plainly that: "Since it belongs to the supernatural order, *grace escapes our experience* and cannot be known except by faith. We cannot therefore rely on our feelings or our works to conclude that we are justified and saved" (CCC 2005; emphasis in the original).

The Council of Trent, to which reference is made in this paragraph of the *Catechism*, teaches that "no one can know with a certitude of faith which cannot be subject to error that he has obtained God's grace."[11]

So which is it: Can grace be experienced or not? The *Catechism*, basing its teaching on a dogmatic decision of a general council of the Catholic Church says No. A single modern theologian is interpreted as saying Yes. Somewhere along the line the fact that certain solemn teachings of popes and councils are irreformable seems to have been forgot-

---

[10] Quoted from Karl Rahner, *Meditation on the Sacraments* (New York: Seabury Press, 1974), xi.

[11] "The General Council of Trent, sixth session, Decree on Justification, chapter 9, in J. Neuner and J. Dupuis, *The Christian Faith in the Doctrinal Documents of the Catholic Church*, rev. ed. (Westminster, Md.: Christian Classics, 1975), 526.

ten. Actually, the Rahner view is, again, typically "nuanced". Dr. Regan cites another passage from Rahner which seems to indicate that what the Jesuit theologian thought could be experienced were really "moments of self-transcendence", in Dr. Regan's words. It is not clear whether this is the same thing as grace in Rahner's view. Still, how are catechists and pastoral ministers supposed to sort out this kind of thing? What is the point of a commentary that simply makes everything more complicated and at the same time seems to deny doctrines of the faith clearly stated by the *Catechism*?

It is not our intention here to enter into a debate about any part of the theology of Karl Rahner. The point we are concerned with here is that a commentator on the *Catechism of the Catholic Church* thinks it is her task to "correct" the *Catechism* using the opinions of a modern theologian as her pretext and authority. The average reader of her commentary, presumably one of our new catechists or modern pastoral ministers, is unlikely to end up with very much respect for a *Catechism* treated in such a cavalier manner.

Again, Dr. Regan appears to deny—although the denial is couched in another involved and "nuanced" statement—that the sacraments of the Church "give grace", as those instructed via the old *Baltimore Catechism* once learned. The new *Catechism* also very plainly says that, "celebrated worthily in faith, the Sacraments *confer* the grace that they signify" (CCC 1127; emphasis added); and that "the Sacraments are efficacious signs of grace . . . by which divine life is *dispensed* to us" (CCC 1131; emphasis added again).

In order to avoid misrepresenting what Dr. Regan appears to be trying to say on this subject, it is worth quoting a paragraph in her own words concerning how the *Catechism* presents what she calls the "theological concept" of the term "grace":

The *Catechism* seems to go back and forth between a quantitative notion of grace and the sense of grace that supports a renewed understanding of sacraments: grace as divine life that is always and everywhere present. To speak of the sacraments as conferring or dispensing grace can promote a less helpful perspective on the meaning of grace and potentially foster a magical understanding of sacraments. Missing from this notion of grace is the reality argued for in the *Catechism*: God is always initiating and inviting us to relationship; before we act, God is present.[12]

In other words, the *Catechism* has, once again, erred grievously; and above all, we must imperatively guard against any "magical understanding" of the sacraments!

It is extremely unlikely that either the bishop-authors who composed this *Catechism* or the commission of cardinals and bishops who approved it are ignorant of the thought of Karl Rahner. If, nevertheless, they decided not to include some of his views on grace in the Church's official modern account of her own faith, it would not be the first time that the Church has declined to take up the thought of one of her theologians. Some of the greatest saints and doctors of the Church have similarly been passed over in this manner when it comes to composing catechisms. In this situation, it ill befits theologians who are themselves supposed to be "sent out" by the Church to be second-guessing the Magisterium and adding in things that, in their opinion, should have been included. This would seem to be particularly inappropriate when what is added appears to *contra-*

---

[12] Regan, *Exploring*, 113. All further quotations from this commentary are taken from the volume itself; we shall not provide further page references.

*dict* what the *Catechism* says. In the nature of the case, this can only confuse the potential end-users of this commentary.

## III

The chapter commenting on the Creed in *Exploring the Catechism* was written by Michael P. Horan of the Department of Theological Studies at Loyola Marymount University in Los Angeles, California. Like Dr. Regan, Dr. Horan holds a Ph.D. in religious education from the Catholic University of America. It certainly cannot be said that CUA's School of Religious Studies is having no impact on the current religious-education scene in the United States.

Dr. Horan is a careful writer, and at first it appears that we really are going to get a genuine commentary on how the *Catechism* presents the Profession of Faith. He begins by correctly pointing out that the *Catechism*'s presentation of revelation is based squarely on that of Vatican II's Dogmatic Constitution on Divine Revelation, *Dei Verbum*. He calls this the "invitation-response" view of revelation; it draws heavily on the contemporary return to original scriptural and patristic sources—*ressourcement*—which preceded, accompanied, and has followed Vatican II. This approach links sacred Scripture inseparably with sacred Tradition. Unlike most other commentators, Dr. Horan actually praises the *Catechism*'s use of the historical-critical method so that both "the Jesus of history" and "the Christ of faith" are basically presented.

However, ominous early signs do appear in Dr. Horan's text. Among them are the author's reference to "the importance of human experience" and his disparaging observation that Vatican I's Dogmatic Constitution on the Catholic Faith, *Dei Filius*, displayed an understanding of revelation as "propositional" (why the human mind's natural tendency to organize and express knowledge and thought in "propositions" is not understood or admitted to be an integral part of "human experience" is rather difficult to fathom).

Dr. Horan traces back to the Enlightenment the modern view that the human being (which Christ became) is first of all "an individual in freedom". This is the reason, in his view, why theological work today must begin with the humanity of Jesus and work up "from below"—as if it were the Enlightenment and modern democracy, currently failing so badly to meet real human needs, that must necessarily govern the expression of a revealed faith handed down from a very different historical era. However that may be, Dr. Horan is critical of the *Catechism* for beginning with a "Christology from above". The following paragraph from the *Catechism* illustrates what he calls a "high-descending Christology":

> The Word became flesh to make us *"partakers of the divine nature"*: "For this is why the Word became man, and the Son of God became the Son of man: so that man, by entering into communion with the Word and thus receiving divine sonship, might become a son of God." "For the Son of God became man so that we might become God." "The only-begotten Son of God, wanting to make us sharers in his divinity, assumed our nature, so that he, made man, might make men gods."

In this single paragraph, the *Catechism* quotes Scripture, St. Irenæus, St. Athanasius, and St. Thomas Aquinas to make its point. Dr. Michael Horan nevertheless believes that starting with Christ's humanity instead would have been a more "creative use of theology". He evidently shares the same position articulated by Dr. Regan when she averred that pastoral ministers should "critically read" the *Catechism*. For his part, Dr. Horan believes that "catechetical leaders might well *review* the theology that shapes this document, as well as the Christology that would complement this work" (emphasis added). In other words, again, "catechetical leaders" —the professionals, the experts—are to have the last word, not the hierarchy, not the *Catechism*, not only about what is actually taught in the classroom but about what the faith is in its essence. Presumably, again, the hierarchy can issue all the catechisms it pleases containing the "official" teachings; it will then be for the "catechetical leaders" to "review" these teachings.

One of the things Dr. Horan himself appears to have decided about Christology is that "more information on the historical Jesus would help catechetical leaders who need to refer to a compendium of faith as Catholic minds currently analyze and articulate that faith." He himself singles out only two of many possible areas in which he believes modern scholarship has provided the wherewithal "to complement the approach and content of Christology found in the *Catechism*". They are: the Jewishness of Jesus and his commitment to the reign of God.

Actually, it is not clear who would wish to argue about the importance of either of these two themes. Least of all does the *Catechism* dispute them. Nor does it seem that modern scholarship has any monopoly on them. What we soon discover, though, is that Dr. Horan brings the first one up mostly in order to stigmatize "the sin of anti-Semitism among Christians" (which the *Catechism* naturally also condemns; see for example paragraphs 537 and 839). But it is hardly as if anti-Semitism were the main problem faced by Christians today, fifty years after the defeat and death of Adolf Hitler. The Holocaust that challenges us today is surely rather that of the unborn being legally slaughtered by the millions around the world. However, the moral problems to which Dr. Horan seems most attuned are likely to be the same politically correct ones stressed by today's secular liberals.

Similarly, his mention of the preference of Jesus for the poor as shown in the Gospels serves principally as the platform from which he can then recommend such aberrations as "liberation theology, feminist theology, and black theology" (his words), which, whatever else they may have accomplished, have surely done very little if anything for the real poor. On the contrary, it can be shown that they have surely done a great deal of harm.

In any case, the *Catechism* pointedly inculcates such things as active love for the poor (CCC 2443, 2462–63), the moral responsibility of wealthy nations (CCC 2439–40), poverty as an evangelical counsel (CCC 915 and 944), and poverty of heart in imitation of Christ (CCC 2544–47). It is the *Catechism*, not today's typical ideologues, that indicates the true Christian path to be followed in approaching the poor and downtrodden; the Church's own book is outstanding here in setting forth the Church's true social teachings. Nor is it clear that these things are in any particular need of being "complemented" in accordance with Dr. Horan's preferences. Has modern scholarship of the type Dr. Horan invokes really added anything new or unique here? Anything to justify the kind of free-lance "reviewing" and "complementing" of the *Catechism* he advocates?

Dr. Horan certainly seems to think so: "Biblical hermeneutics functions not only to enrich theological conversation", he writes, "but has a direct bearing on the pastoral life of the Church." In his view, the *Catechism* definitely requires "supplements and amplifications" on these and no doubt many other points.

It is astonishing what large and far-reaching conclusions some people believe can and must be drawn from the overall rather meager results of some two centuries of "biblical hermeneutics" and historical-critical method. Not that the Church opposes these things: on the contrary, she firmly encourages them and has recently issued a very fine document on biblical exegesis that, while carefully laying out all the advantages of the various approaches to studying the sacred Scriptures—a study she deems "indispensable"—at the same time understands that the principal aim of exegesis "is the deepening of faith. . . . Catholic exegesis does not have the right to become lost, like a stream of water, in the sands of a hypercritical analysis."

As for the historical-critical method, though it is necessary and valid for what it does achieve, it cannot, in the Church's view, "lay claim to enjoying a monopoly. . . . It must be conscious of *its limits*. . . . When historical-critical exegesis does not go as far as to take into account the final result of the editorial process but remains absorbed solely in the issues of sources and stratification of texts, it fails to bring the exegetical task to completion" (emphasis in the original).[13]

The bishop-authors of the *Catechism* were not unaware of the modern study of the Scriptures and of its most salient results. Most of these, where applicable, have been incorporated into the *Catechism*—as they were into the documents of Vatican II. Where the liberal exegetes appear to go wrong is in imagining that modern scholarship has re-

---

[13] *The Interpretation of the Bible in the Church* (Vatican City: Pontifical Biblical Commission, 1993), conclusion.

ally established anything that requires the traditional faith handed down in the Church to be *changed* in any important feature. It hasn't happened: the Church's faith has survived what in some cases was a very hostile onslaught carried on by a certain type of modern exegesis.

What is even more surprising is how exaggerated the claims can be today about just what it is that modern Scripture scholarship has accomplished. Today some exegetes believe, and catechists are encouraged to teach, some of the favorite conclusions of modern Scripture scholarship with the same certitude formerly reserved for dogmatically defined truths.

In spite of its achievements, modern Scripture scholarship nevertheless remains an inexact and indeed often highly speculative discipline. It cannot, for example, affirm with any real scientific certainty that the Gospels were not written until some thirty to seventy years after the events they recount, although this is almost universally claimed.[14] Nor can it prove that Mark's was the first Gospel or that there really was a "Q" document, another favorite theory usually taught as established truth.[15] It cannot really prove that John's is a "late, theological" Gospel or even that the Gospels were originally written in the Greek-language text that we possess.[16]

All these questions continue to be debated among competent scholars, and even those issues on which there is a

---

[14] See J. A. T. Robinson, *Redating the New Testament* (Philadelphia: Westminster Press, 1976).

[15] See William R. Farmer, *The Gospel of Jesus: The Pastoral Relevance of the Synoptic Problem* (Louisville, Ky.: Westminster/John Knox Press, 1994).

[16] See Claude Tresmontant, *The Hebrew Christ* (Chicago: Franciscan Herald Press, 1989).

"consensus" today among modern scholars are sometimes far from being established according to any really foolproof scientific methods. There is certainly no justification for teaching these theses to schoolchildren or catechumens as if they were supposed to supersede the Magisterium's authoritative statements of the faith.

After all, almost all the "historical facts" we possess about Jesus of Nazareth and the origins of Christianity are found in the New Testament itself. Christianity necessarily stands or falls on what is there. And we have therefore been in possession of most of these same "historical facts" since well before the historical-critical method was ever devised. Since this method has been developed, one of the most remarkable things about it is how many different interpretations of the "historical Jesus" it has come up with while studying essentially the same set of "facts". This has been evident at least since Albert Schweitzer published his *The Quest for the Historical Jesus* back in the early part of the present century. There was, for example, Schweitzer's own view of the Jesus who expected the end to come at any time (some of our new theologians and exegetes are still parroting this view today).

And there have been, to name only a few of the other pictures we have been given of the "historical Jesus", Jesus the dreamy Galilean romantic, Jesus the political revolutionary, Jesus the messianic plotter, Jesus the magician and wonder-worker, Jesus the Mediterranean peasant, and, lately, Jesus the marginal Jew.

Dr. Horan, referring to the *Catechism*'s paragraph 522, complains that the *Catechism* treats "the mysteries of Christ's life, not as they may have been historically, but as they are remembered and celebrated liturgically". Well? Which one of the above Jesuses would he have the *Catechism* adopt?

Merely to suggest that the Church's faith might possibly be grounded in any findings of modern historical-critical scholarship is already to demonstrate the essential foolishness and futility of such a project.

Rather, for the eyes of faith, the consistency and integrity with which the Catholic Church has continued to present the same Jesus she has always presented—including, most recently, in the *Catechism of the Catholic Church*—is a considerably more impressive and persuasive thing than all the modern achievements of "biblical hermeneutics" put together. (Of course, some of us continue to believe that the Church has had some special *help* in achieving this, as in some of the other features of her life and teaching!) The idea that catechists, instead of handing on the Church's faith, are now supposed to take their "content" from the theories of modern scholars and pass *this* on to their charges would perhaps be laughable if it had not already proved to be so tragically harmful to catechesis and to faith in our day.

In the rest of his commentary, Dr. Horan offers essentially the same criticism of the *Catechism*'s treatment of the Church as he did for its treatment of Christ. He finds that the document's treatment of the Church is, again, "from above". Moreover, in his view, the findings of modern scholarship once again have not been sufficiently taken into account. Even though he concedes that the *Catechism* follows Vatican II's *Lumen Gentium* when dealing with the Church, as it earlier followed *Dei Verbum* when dealing with revelation, he is unhappy because so much stress is laid on "the institutional and universal character of the Church".

For example, he notes that paragraph 765 of the *Catechism* depicts Jesus as founding his Church on the Twelve, thus "endow[ing] his community with a structure", whereas modern scholarship has supposedly "come to the knowledge that there were a variety of leadership models present" in the early Church.

But the same caution is necessary in dealing with historical scholarship as in dealing with biblical scholarship. The alleged "variety of leadership models" in the early Church often seems to be based on pretty slender evidence, sometimes on purely "negative" evidence (for example, on the fact that no "monarchical bishop" is mentioned in certain texts). But we have very few texts of any kind regarding the detailed structure of the early Church. The "model" of bishops, presbyters, and deacons that emerged and was quickly ratified by the universal practice of the Church is surely not incompatible with whatever "structure" Christ did endow his infant Church with. Such evidence as we possess does not seem to provide the basis for any revision of the authentic tradition of the Church in this matter, and it is this tradition that is ably and accurately reflected in the *Catechism*'s treatment of the whole matter.

Meanwhile, it is emphatically *not true* that modern scholarship has established that Jesus *did not* found his Church on the apostles; or that he *did not* intend that these apostles should be succeeded by successors, that is, the bishops. *Lumen Gentium* covered all of this same ground in any case, and so it is impossible to invoke Vatican II *against* the *Catechism*. Yet that is essentially what Dr. Horan does when he concludes his commentary on the Profession of Faith by remarking that the *Catechism* "should be used in the context of Vatican II".

"We might do well to understand that the *Catechism of the Catholic Church* is not the end of the search to provide catechesis", he writes. "It is a beginning. It is a source to which leaders may turn first, but they may not stop there."

We may be reasonably sure that Dr. Horan's "catechetical leaders" will see to that.

IV

The two remaining commentaries on the moral life and on prayer in *Exploring the Catechism* continue along the same freewheeling lines already established by authors Regan and Horan. We need not dwell upon these latter two commentaries at any length. The task of these commentators is thought to be to read the *Catechism* "critically" and, where deemed necessary, to provide a view "corrective" of it in accordance with the reigning opinions of the modern theological and catechetical establishments. There is no discernible perception among these authors that perhaps the Catholic Church has in any important sense "spoken" in the *Catechism of the Catholic Church*. Everything the Pope has said about it in promulgating and promoting it curiously seems not to count for anything with these authors.

The commentary on the *Catechism*'s treatment of the moral life, entitled "Life in Christ", is contributed by Fr. Timothy Backous, O.S.B. Fr. Backous is chaplain of St. John's University in Collegeville and has a doctorate in moral theology from the Alphonsianum in Rome. Like Dr. Regan, Fr. Backous is described as giving catechetical workshops around the country, so we should not underestimate the degree to which his views will be the ones absorbed by catechists being "trained" to "implement" the new *Catechism*.

Fr. Backous begins his contribution to this volume with a rather condescending reference to those who find the current state of the Church's morality to be in "crisis"; he remarks that these are the kind of people by whom the *Catechism* will be "enthusiastically welcomed".

On the level of theory, of course, one of those who finds the current state of the Church's morality to be definitely in "crisis" would seem to be none other than Pope John Paul II himself, who includes in his 1993 encyclical *Veritatis Splendor*, among other pointed comments on the same subject, the statement that "within the context of the theological debates which followed the Council, there have developed certain interpretations of Christian morality which are not consistent with 'sound teaching' (2 Tim 4:3)."[17]

On the level of practice, of course, one would not really have to go far beyond the current divorce or abortion statistics among Catholics to conclude that here, too, the Church's morality is surely in a very deep crisis situation. Or it is only necessary to recall the fact that today's Catholic politicians, speaking generally, apparently no longer believe that what they vote for need have any relationship whatsoever to the moral law of God as proclaimed by the Church. Indeed, many of them positively assert that they can and must vote for what the Church has definitively held to be *against* the moral law of God. And meanwhile, Catholic voters, who have surely heard all these issues publicly raised, go right on helping to return these same Catholic politicians to office. Fr. Backous would surely have a hard time making any case that the Church's morality is *not* in crisis; but then, of course, he does not try.

Very possibly, the current worldwide crisis of morality—one need think only of the agenda of the 1994 population conference in Cairo, for example—was one of the princi-

---

[17] Pope John Paul II, Encyclical Letter on the Splendor of Truth, *Veritatis Splendor*, August 6, 1993, no. 29.

pal reasons why the Pope and the hierarchy promoted the project of a universal catechism so vigorously in the first place. Merely to take note of the fact that a moral theology professor who also conducts catechetical workshops apparently *does not* think the Church's morality is in crisis today already provides at least the beginning of an explanation of what is wrong with this particular moral theologian's commentary on the *Catechism*'s treatment of the Christian moral life.

Generally speaking, Fr. Backous describes the *Catechism*'s treatment of morality accurately; he may even approve of it in certain respects. He properly points out how the *Catechism*'s treatment of morality closely follows that of Vatican II and is therefore "positive", emphasizing our vocation to beatitude, our freedom, and the necessity of developing virtues ahead of its treatment of sin (although the *Catechism*, of course, in no wise underestimates the reality, power, seriousness, and evil of sin). Fr. Backous further properly notes the emphasis of both Vatican II and the *Catechism* on social morality (but improperly appears to see this as lessening the importance of morality for the individual person).

Where his treatment most obviously goes wrong is in his basic attitude toward the *Catechism* (and hence, necessarily, toward the Church's Magisterium, which lies behind it): he appears to share the view of many theologians today that the primary theological task is to serve as the final, decisive arbiter in religious matters. The theological task, in a word, is to *correct* the *Catechism* where it is seen to have gone wrong or fallen short. Thus, he criticizes the *Catechism* for remaining "act centered" in moral matters, rather than person centered. And, characteristically, he quotes in this connection one moral theologian who thinks that the Church's responsibility is to provide "consolation" for the divorced and remarried and another moral theologian who thinks that the Church's judgment that certain acts such as blasphemy, perjury, murder, or adultery are intrinsically wrong is "too fixed and that more openness to uncertainty is in order".

In criticizing the *Catechism* for being act centered, incidentally, he apparently fails to grasp that, if it did not have this particular focus, it could scarcely draw the distinction—of which he strongly approves—between homosexual persons, who continue to possess goodness and human dignity, and homosexual acts, which are always disordered and evil. Similarly, he is precisely wrong, especially in a sex-obsessed society, in downgrading the gravity of sins such as masturbation (here he introduces his own word, "shaded", instead of the usual "nuanced"; the latter word has become the typical Wagnerian *Leitmotiv* in the contemporary theological literature whenever modern theologians want to water down the Church's authentic moral teaching considered by them too harsh and judgmental).

Fr. Backous faults the *Catechism* further for not being as open to the modern world as he thinks Vatican II was. Apparently he has little noted the modern world's precipitous slide, precisely in the years since Vatican II, into an unprecedented moral decadence that Pope John Paul II has rightly now had to label a "culture of death". Indeed, it would seem that the Pope has now consciously added to the Church's list of "intrinsically evil acts" three new ones by the solemn manner in which, in his 1995 encyclical *Evangelium Vitæ*, the "Gospel of Life", he has condemned abortion, euthanasia, and the killing of the innocent.[18]

---

[18] Pope John Paul II, Encyclical Letter on the Gospel of Life, *Evangelium Vitæ*, March 25, 1995, esp. nos. 57, 62, and 65.

Fr. Backous also sets up an artificial conflict in the *Catechism* between "obedience" versus "responsibility". Certainly "responsibility" is a positive factor that is rightly to be stressed and fostered whenever possible. But it is in no way *opposed* to obedience. On the contrary, it is our responsibility to be obedient—obedient to the calls and commands of the living God. We are all strictly called, for example, to the "obedience of faith" (Rom 1:5; 16:26); the *Catechism* notes that this is the *source* of our moral life (CCC 2087). Jesus Christ himself "learned obedience through what he suffered" (Heb 5:8). The *Catechism* teaches that "the obedience of Jesus has transformed the curse of death into a blessing" (CCC 1009). What is the *problem* some modern theologians always seem to have with obedience?

Deplorably, Fr. Backous quotes here in support of the false dichotomy he has erected between obedience and responsibility two dissenting California Jesuits, Fr. William Spohn and Fr. Francis Buckley, both of them contributors to the *Universal Catechism Reader*, the attack on the draft of the *Catechism* sent out to the bishops for comment in 1989.[19]

In keeping with his apparent view that the ultimate "magisterium" belongs to theologians by virtue of their learned expertise, Fr. Backous quotes theologians such as these quite indiscriminately. The mere fact that they are theologians apparently entitles them to his respect; certainly he does not read them "critically" in the light of the Church's true Magisterium. And so it is no surprise that he ends up citing and recommending such open and persistent public dissenters from authentic Church teaching as Josef Fuchs, Charles Curran, Richard Gula, Richard McCormick, and Bernard

---

[19] See n. 3 to Chapter Three *supra*.

Häring. In short, what we have in this commentary is a fundamentally *irresponsible* treatment of part three of the *Catechism*—hardly anything the catechist in the classroom needs to be "trained" in, alas!

# V

We may bring our examination of *Exploring the Catechism* to a conclusion by a very brief look at its final commentary, this one on part four of the *Catechism*, which deals with the subject of Prayer. The joint authors of this commentary are Fr. Francis Kelly Nemeck, O.M.I., and Sr. Maria Theresa Coombs, both of the Lebh Shomea contemplative-eremetical house of prayer in south Texas. Judging by the bibliography that is included, we conclude that these two are the joint authors of a number of books on spirituality and prayer; the same bibliography indicates that they are also familiar with an almost bewildering variety of other writers and topics, some perhaps sound from a Christian point of view, others very decidedly not.

Their ineluctable orientation toward the usual fashionable modern causes and isms quickly becomes evident through their calls for more attention in spirituality circles to such things as psychology, ecology, feminism, and the like. Their view of the *Catechism*'s widely praised treatment of prayer is both negative and hostile. As authorities against it, they often quote their own books. In general, they find the *Catechism*'s part four on Prayer to be "a smorgasbord of ideas about prayer, few of which are developed".

It gets worse. They write:

> On the whole, unless the readers of the *Catechism* already possess considerable experience in praying, coupled

278 / Flawed Expectations

with a reasonably well-developed theological framework in which to appraise the diverse modes and expressions of prayer, they will probably end up more befuddled than catechized by Part Four. Yet, those who do have both sufficient experience in praying and an adequate theological framework will find the *Catechism* woefully deficient. Sad to say, the masses of Catholics of all ages who are yearning for in-depth catechizing in prayer will not find it in this *Catechism*.

Noting that the *Catechism* "contains no meaningful discussion on Progress in Prayer", Fr. Nemeck and Sr. Coombs compose their own. *It* strikes *us* as a "smorgasbord of ideas about prayer".

The arrogance in considering themselves able to do what they think the Church signally failed to do in the *Catechism* is surely singular enough. Yet it is matched by the very plan and execution of the whole book, whose principal author, Dr. Jane E. Regan, concludes the work by announcing breathlessly how:

> As a map, the *Catechism* serves as an important reference tool for later maps. Our own journeys of faith—as individuals, as communities of faith, as a universal Church—will push at the *Catechism*'s boundaries. Our journeys of faith will go into regions to which this map has no reference. We will re-think and re-explore regions that the writers of the *Catechism* think are settled. As we continue to live out of and reflect upon the theology that underpins and flows from the Second Vatican Council, we must continue to return to the *Catechism* to change it, clarify it, make it more readable, and more usable for the next generation. Eventually . . . we will have to come up with a new text.

There we have it: the *Catechism* has to be "changed",

"clarified", and made more "readable" and "usable"; what is needed is a "new text".

# VI

Can such things be? That some of the very people who are writing the commentaries and conducting the workshops implementing the *Catechism of the Catholic Church* do not themselves accept it in a fundamental way? That it is *not*, in fact, being received in some of those very circles where it should perhaps have been most enthusiastically received, namely, among those who have been "sent out" by the Church as teachers of the faith to others? That, before its ink is even dry, some of these same people really aim to replace it with their own versions of the faith?

We have now looked at several different commentaries by various members of today's theological and catechetical establishments. On the evidence of all of these works, the conclusion is pretty hard to avoid that their real aim is to subvert the *Catechism*, not to implement it.

How widespread is the problem? In the absence of a methodical scientific survey, it is difficult to say. But if seemingly "standard" commentaries produced by faculty at supposedly Catholic institutions and published by putatively "mainstream" publishing houses that otherwise do a lucrative business in the Catholic market can seriously offer to the Catholic public as "commentaries" on the *Catechism* the works we have been examining in these pages, then quite a few things would seem to be rather seriously wrong in the way the *Catechism* is being implemented.

Moreover, the problem *is* widespread, even if we cannot say exactly how widespread. In the remainder of this chapter, let us look—more cursorily—at yet another one of the commentaries that has appeared in English on the *Catechism*, this one produced in Australia about the same time that the *Catechism* itself became available in English in June 1994. This commentary is entitled *The New Catechism: Analysis and Commentary*.[20]

Once again, this commentary is more than just another published book or academic exercise; the papers comprising it were mostly prepared by faculty members of the Catholic Institute of Sydney for a two-day in-service seminar on the *Catechism* for the clergy of the Archdiocese of Sydney. So the book represents yet another example of how people—in this case clergy—are actually being "trained" to regard and use the new *Catechism*.

Moreover, this commentary has not gone unnoticed in the catechetical world generally. It was reviewed, on the balance very favorably, in the summer 1995 number of *The Living Light*, where the reviewer remarked that, as one of the first commentaries on the *Catechism* produced in English, it "enjoys pride of place. Later commentaries of this genre will turn to it. No library or catechetical center should be without it."[21]

The editor of the volume, Fr. Andrew Murray, S.M., immediately sets what will be the fairly consistent tone of *A & C* (as we shall designate it for convenience's sake). "The *Catechism* is best seen", the editor avers, "as something that has been proposed by the Magisterium for reception in the Church. It has arrived and has to be dealt with."

---

[20] *The New Catechism: Analysis and Commentary*, ed. Andrew Murray (Manly, Australia: Catholic Institute of Sydney, 1994).

[21] Mark Heath, O.P., review of *The New Catechism: Analysis and Commentary*, *The Living Light*, summer 1995.

At least he is frank. We also note that he thinks that it has merely been *proposed* by the Magisterium for reception. Nor will he and his colleagues be loath to decide what they will or will not receive in it, either—always in their own fashion, of course. Fr. Murray warns the reader in advance about what he calls "the difficulty of making an *acceptable* compendium of the totality of Catholic teaching" (thus signaling at the outset that this *Catechism* is *not* acceptable). And he is similarly quick to point out how lamentably, in his view, the book "has failed to take into account modern learning and circumstances".

"The *Catechism* itself carries Roman authority", he specifies (whatever that means). "This will lead some, no doubt, to claim almost infallible status for it", but "nothing could be further from the truth", he quickly assures his reader, as if the Church's infallible teachings were the only Church teachings that have to be assented to and believed by Catholics. In justification for his position on this, he falls back on the new theology's tired and tendentious interpretation of Vatican II's teaching on "the hierarchy of truths", which we have encountered before, notably in the last chapter. Invoking the hierarchy of truths has practically become a mantra for some modern theologians, but Fr. Murray seems to be entirely unaware of any irony inherent in this.

Thus, it is already clear from the introduction alone that, in this volume, we are dealing with yet another commentary on the *Catechism* in which the theologians and experts in place have arrogantly set themselves up to mitigate what they see as the harm the *Catechism* will do. Indeed, they have set themselves up, again, to *correct* an unwanted document from the Magisterium.

Not all of the contributions to this volume are equally negative and hostile. A couple of the papers are straightforward and valid theological commentaries, but in the case of these authors, the question that has to be asked is: What are they doing in such company, if they really accept the *Catechism* as authoritatively coming from the Church with the guarantee of the Holy Spirit? Can orthodox commentators really be insensible to the *harm* their colleagues are inflicting on the very idea of an authoritative teaching Church by the critical way in which they approach this *Catechism*? Is academic prestige or standing so important to them that they can acquiesce in what they, precisely because they are trained theologians, must realize, are efforts to undermine the *Catechism* and the Magisterium? Why is there no "peer review" of the work of colleagues who seem to have departed in their work from the only possible basis from which anyone can legitimately "do" Catholic theology, namely, God's revelation to us in Christ as mediated to us by the Church?

We cannot get into a detailed analysis or critique of this volume. We can cite only a few of the statements made in some of the papers in order to demonstrate that the dominant theme in this commentary, as in the other commentaries we have examined, is the way in which the theologians and experts are the ones who must take charge of receiving the *Catechism* and who must see to it that this reception is basically negative.

The commentator writing on "Faith in the Creator God" in *A & C*, Fr. David Coffey, finds that "the *Catechism* is not notably successful, even in its own terms." This is so, in his view, because the Magisterium's own documents were relied on in the drafting of the work rather than the views of theologians such as Karl Rahner, Yves Congar, and John Courtney Murray. "The mentality of the *Catechism*", this author concludes, "is that of the Latin Roman theology manuals of the 1950s complete with their tendency to integralism, their lack of historical awareness, and their hermeneutical naivety." To put it bluntly: the *Catechism* "has been left behind by modern theology", according to Fr. Coffey.

"The good news", for this author, "is that episcopal conferences and dioceses are free and indeed encouraged to produce their own catechisms." We can imagine what these catechisms will be like if the bishops are so unwise as to call on their Fr. Coffeys to produce them!

Another contributor, Dr. Neil Omerod, writing on "The Narrative Christology of the *Catechism*", is quite favorable to the document's "biblical approach", as contrasted with what he calls the "more dogmatic, Scholastic approaches of past catechisms". Still, according to him, it "makes no significant attempt to make contact with contemporary culture"; and hence "there is a large task of inculturation that still needs to be done." The *Catechism* should definitely "not be seen as a 'stand alone' document".

Another one of the commentators, Fr. Richard Lennan, contributes a paper on the Church entitled "The Place Where the Spirit Flourishes"—an interesting characterization, considering the fact that the *Catechism* deals with the Church in the chapter on the Holy Spirit (no doubt because the profession of belief in the Church follows the profession of belief in the Holy Spirit in the Apostles' Creed). But in the midst of all the sometimes interesting questions that Fr. Lennan brings up, what really leaps to the eye is the realization that, if the *Catechism* is really as bad as he and some of his collaborators judge it to be, then the Holy Spirit is obviously *not* flourishing very effectively in the Church at the moment, at least as far as the writing of catechisms is concerned. Perhaps we are supposed to believe instead that the Holy Spirit *has* effectively provided to the theologians of the Catholic Institute of Sydney the proper guidance that the bishop-authors of the *Catechism* did not enjoy.

However that may be, the kinds of complaints found in this paper are only too familiar: "The *Catechism*'s failure to adopt a historical consciousness means that it cannot commend itself as a modern document. . . . It is also naive and reveals a lack of appreciation of contemporary society. It would surely be the task of any local catechisms to remedy this deficiency" Etc., etc.

Sr. Marie Farrell, R.S.M., in her contribution to *A & C* entitled "The *Catechism*'s Approach to the Blessed Virgin Mary", hopes that "during the preparation of local catechisms"—this is surely now being almost universally taken for granted as perhaps the *principal* result of the issuance of the new *Catechism*: namely, that substitutes are now to be prepared for it forthwith and everywhere!—"during the preparation for local catechisms," Sr. Farrell hopes, "issues raised by feminist theologians concerning Mariology will be given due consideration. . . . Criticism from feminist as well as ecumenical circles suggests that theological reflections on the quality of Mary's femininity be pursued along the lines of 'sisterhood,' since it allows for freedom in ways that 'motherhood' (which binds a child) does not."

Quite apart from the untold harm that the radical feminist concept of "sisterhood" has done not only to the religious life but also to marriage and the family and, most especially, to the status of the child (considered a burden on women instead of a blessing), Sr. Farrell's notion that Mariology should pursue this sort of thinking is also simply contradictory, when we consider that Mary's preeminent dignity resides, precisely, in the fact that she was the *mother* of God!

Another contributor, Fr. Gerard Kelly, specifically writing about "The Reception of the *Catechism*", believes that its "publication . . . should not lead to uniformity in the Church. . . . The words and expressions it uses are [not] always the most appropriate for the people who live in our particular culture at this time in world history. It may well say things that our people are not ready to hear." This, indeed, has been a problem for Christianity for a rather long time now: there are things in the Church's message that "people are not ready to hear".

Our particular culture, in fact, is probably especially prone to decide that the words of life that the Church transmits to us from Jesus constitute "a hard saying" (Jn 6:60), one to which our culture is not inclined to listen. But since when are Christians supposed to hold back on the message of Jesus on the grounds that there are some who do not want to hear it? What is probably unusual today, by comparison with some other eras in the history of the Church, though, is that many of the Church's own sons and daughters, including many of those specifically "sent out" to teach the faith, today seem inclined to side with the culture against the message of Jesus!

Can such things be? Can these really be the reflections of the faculty of a Catholic institute concerning a foundational document of the Catholic Church solemnly promulgated by the Church's supreme authority? We can only await with some trepidation the kinds of "local", "inculturated" catechisms that such people are likely to produce.

# CHAPTER EIGHT

# A New "Local", "Inculturated" Catechism?

## I

In promulgating the *Catechism of the Catholic Church*, Pope John Paul II carefully noted that "this *Catechism* is not intended to replace the local catechisms duly approved by the ecclesiastical authorities." On the contrary, he specified that "it is meant to encourage and assist in the writing of new local catechisms, which take into account various situations and cultures."

However, the Holy Father did include one important stipulation with regard to any such new "local", "inculturated" catechisms that might be prepared, namely, that they should "carefully preserv[e] . . . the unity of faith and fidelity to Catholic doctrine."[1]

The *Catechism* itself reiterates this same basic message when it declares that it "does not set out to provide the

---

An adaptation of this chapter was published in *Fidelity*, November 1995.

[1] Pope John Paul II, apostolic constitution *Fidei Depositum* on the Publication of the *Catechism of the Catholic Church*, October 11, 1992, no. 4 (*Fidei Depositum* is reprinted in the front of all the editions of the *Catechism* that have been published in the United States to date).

adaptation of doctrinal presentations and catechetical methods required by the differences of culture, age, spiritual maturity, and social and ecclesial condition among all those to whom it is addressed. Such indispensable adaptations are the responsibility of particular catechisms" (CCC 24).

From the moment the *Catechism* appeared, some Church officials have stressed the need for local adaptations of it, taking into account different ages, regions, situations, and cultures. Cardinal José T. Sánchez, prefect of the Congregation for the Clergy in Rome, which has responsibility for catechisms, has declared that the *Catechism* actually *"requires further inculturation on the local level"*.[2]

In April 1993, the Congregation for the Clergy sponsored a summit-meeting-type seminar on the *Catechism* in Rome itself, which brought together the heads of episcopal conferences and episcopal committees on education and other interested parties from the five continents to discuss how the *Catechism* could and should be locally adapted and inculturated in order to meet the needs of the people of various ages and conditions and in different geographical regions and cultures. This meeting declared that the *Catechism* was "not just one more text, but rather an *ecclesial event* rich in consequences"; it concluded that the "concrete manner of presentation" of any local, inculturated catechism would have to be "characterized by the groups to which it is directed: the community of believers, post-Christian society, or those who have not yet received the message of the Gospel"; but, finally, it specified that "no local catechism can contain any

---

[2] Cardinal José T. Sánchez, "Inculturation of the *Catechism* at the Local Level Is Necessary", in *Reflections on the Catechism of the Catholic Church*, comp. Rev. James P. Socias (Chicago: Midwest Theological Forum, 1993), 103.

element which is or may be interpreted as contrary to the teaching of the *Catechism of the Catholic Church*."[3]

Addressing this same seminar, Pope John Paul II declared that the *Catechism* itself would continue to be the "type" and "exemplar" for any other catechisms prepared for local use. "It cannot be considered merely as a stage preceding the drafting of local catechisms. [It] is destined for all the faithful who have the capacity to read, understand, and assimilate it in their Christian living." The Pope further emphasized that the *Catechism* itself necessarily remains "the support and foundation for the preparation of new catechetical tools which take the various cultural situations into consideration and together take pains to preserve the unity of faith and fidelity to Catholic doctrine."[4]

Thus, the Church has recognized from the beginning of the universal-catechism project that, however great its accuracy, comprehensiveness, and authority as a compendium of Catholic doctrine, the *Catechism* is not carved unchangeably in stone like the original Tables of the Law to be indiscriminately and unvaryingly imposed upon all of the faithful regardless of circumstances. Rather, the *Catechism* can and should be freely adapted, inculturated, excerpted, and summarized, *provided*—and this is an all-important provision— that it always remains this *Catechism* that is being adapted, inculturated, and so on.

It is necessary, in other words, that the *Catechism* itself always remain the solid basis of any claimed adaptation of

---

[3] Archbishop Crescenzio Sepe, secretary of the Congregation for the Clergy, "*Catechism of the Catholic Church* Must Serve as Model and Exemplar for Local Catechisms", in Socias, *Reflections*.

[4] Pope John Paul II, "*Catechism of the Catholic Church* Is a Gift for All", April 29, 1993, in Socias, *Reflections*.

it; that it always remain the basic authority, "sure norm", and "point of reference" for any doctrinal statements made in any "local", "inculturated" catechism prepared for specific use in a given country or culture; that the authentic Church teachings reaffirmed by the *Catechism* not in any way be diminished or watered down in order to suit a particular "culture"; and, finally, that the original *Catechism* itself continue to remain available "for all the faithful who have the capacity to read, understand, and assimilate it", as Pope John Paul II has specified.

To put it yet another way, there is no reason why there cannot be an American-style, graded religion textbook series based on the *Catechism* for use in Catholic schools and CCD programs. In fact, such a series would be highly desirable—provided, again, it is truly based on this *Catechism* and authentically imparts its teachings; and also provided that it does not, for instance, simply make reference to it occasionally or perhaps pay lip service to it from time to time, while really emphasizing other things.

There can and should be religion textbook series based on the *Catechism*, in other words, provided that any adapted version of it does not continue the unfortunate postconciliar tradition of content-deficient and doctrine-deficient texts that have nevertheless often *claimed* to be fully Catholic and in accord with Church directives such as the *General Catechetical Directory*.

Another requirement for any authentic "local", "inculturated" catechism—a requirement the Roman documents tend to assume as often as they actually spell it out—is that any adapted versions of the *Catechism* for a given age, locality, or culture, when completed, should themselves be specifically authorized and approved by ecclesiastical authority. Thus, *Fidei Depositum*, as we have already seen, speaks of "local catechisms duly approved by the ecclesiastical authorities", as if this were still observed in regular practice.

*Fidei Depositum* also speaks in this connection of approval by "diocesan bishops" and by "episcopal conferences", as well as of approval by "the Apostolic See". In his 1979 *Catechesi Tradendæ*, Pope John Paul II expressly said that "those who take on the heavy task of preparing catechetical tools, especially catechism texts, can do so only with the approval of the pastors who have authority to give it."[5] The meaning here would seem to be quite plain: no setting up on one's own to produce and sponsor local catechisms; the Church has to approve what is published.

Actually, the *General Catechetical Directory* had already long since required that "before promulgation, [local] catechisms must be submitted to the Apostolic See for review and approval."[6] It is far from clear, however, whether what seems to be a rather firm requirement here has really been honored.

Yet another difficulty in the way of producing acceptable local catechisms concerns the word and concept of "inculturation." This term has been often used and thus amply legitimated by high Church authorities, including both Pope John Paul II and Cardinal Joseph Ratzinger, among others. Nor have today's theologians and religious educators failed to latch on to the term. They have generally greeted the idea of inculturation with considerably warmer enthusiasm than they have ever apparently been able to muster for the *Catechism* itself. Indeed the whole idea of inculturation

---

[5] Pope John Paul II, apostolic exhortation *Catechesi Tradendæ* on Catechesis in Our Time, October 16, 1979, no. 50.

[6] Congregation for the Clergy, *General Catechetical Directory* (GCD) (Rome, 1971), no. 119.

seems to have already become a fad, if it has not become something of a tail now busily wagging the catechetical dog. In many discussions, what comes through most strongly is not so much that the message of the *Catechism* needs to be imparted but, rather, that the book needs to be, precisely, "inculturated".

There now appears to be, in fact, a clear and present danger that some important elements of the *Catechism* might well be attenuated or even lost in the process of "inculturating" it. It is therefore important to understand exactly what the Church means by "inculturation". In *Catechesi Tradendæ*, speaking about what he calls "the message embodied in a culture", Pope John Paul II writes as follows:

> We can say of catechesis, as well as of evangelization in general, that it is called to bring the power of the Gospel into the very heart of culture and cultures. For this purpose, catechesis will seek to know these cultures and their essential components; it will learn their most significant expressions; it will respect their particular values and riches. In this manner it will be able to offer these cultures the knowledge of the hidden mystery and help them to bring forth from their own living tradition original expressions of Christian life, celebration, and thought.

Such is inculturation as the Church most authoritatively understands it. Its point is to bring the gospel to the culture, not to allow the culture to modify or undermine the gospel. However, Pope John Paul II also adds two further indispensable qualifications, which he believes are essential to any effort to "inculturate" the gospel, that is, embody it in a given culture:

> On the one hand, the Gospel message cannot be purely and simply isolated from the culture in which it was first

inserted (the biblical world or, more concretely, the cultural milieu in which Jesus of Nazareth lived), nor, without serious loss, from the cultures in which it has already been expressed down through the centuries; it does not spring spontaneously from any cultural soil; it has always been transmitted by means of an apostolic dialogue. . . .

On the other hand, the power of the Gospel everywhere transforms and regenerates. When that power enters a culture, it is no surprise that it rectifies many of its elements. There would be no catechesis if it were the Gospel that had to change when it came into contact with the cultures.

Thus, the gospel cannot be separated from the original revelation that was accomplished in the cultural milieu of Jesus' time and place. We always have to refer back to that. We also have to refer back to the "culture" in which the authentic tradition of the Church has developed historically. Furthermore, it is not the gospel that has to change when it comes into contact with a given culture; it is the culture that needs to be changed. "To forget this", John Paul II concludes in this treatment of these points, "would simply amount to what Saint Paul very forcefully calls 'emptying the cross of Christ of its power' (1 Cor 1:17)".[7]

## II

The resounding popularity that the *Catechism of the Catholic Church* has enjoyed since it first appeared is in some ways surprising when we consider the low repute in which catechisms in general have supposedly come to be held in the

---

[7] John Paul II, *Catechesi Tradendæ*, no. 53.

postconciliar era. The fact that the *Catechism* has nevertheless proved to be so popular has probably set some people in the religious-education field thinking, even some of those who did not want to hear of catechisms any longer. Maybe there was something to be said after all about a catechism as an instrument for getting one's views across.

Moreover, with all the talk about "local" catechisms and "inculturation", even on the part of some of the highest authorities of the Church, the notion of producing a "local" American catechism, "inculturated" along the lines of modern American culture, rather soon came to be entertained by some of the people in the catechetical establishment. It could only be a matter of time before what was thought to be an attractive possibility would become a published and vigorously promoted reality.

No matter that the Pope has spoken of inculturation as bringing "the power of the Gospel into the very heart of culture". Most people are unfamiliar with the Pope's ideas about this. Inculturation could just as easily mean for them bringing the culture into the Church, which, since Vatican Council II, many of these same people have assumed to be more "open" to the world in precisely this way.

Perhaps the most frequently quoted passage in all of Vatican II is the beginning of *Gaudium et Spes*, which reads, in the Flannery translation, as "the joy and hope, the grief and anguish of the men of our time, especially those who are poor or afflicted in any way, are the joy and hope, the grief and anguish, of the followers of Christ as well. Nothing that is genuinely human fails to find an echo in their hearts."[8] This is both true and moving.

---

[8] Vatican Council II, Pastoral Constitution on the Church in the Modern World, *Gaudium et Spes*, no. 1, in Austin Flannery, O.P., ed.,

However, like other Church documents, like sacred Scripture itself, it always needs to be read in the context of the Church's whole teaching; it must not be read in isolation. In this specific case, it needs to be read along with the beginning statement of Vatican II's other great document on the Church, *Lumen Gentium*. This one reads: "Christ is the light of humanity; and it is, accordingly, the heart-felt desire of this sacred Council, being gathered together in the Holy Spirit, that by proclaiming the Gospel to every creature (cf. Mk 16:15), it may bring to all men that light of Christ which shines out visibly from the Church."[9]

This is the heart of Vatican II's idea of "inculturation". Yet the most persistent idea to be taken from *Lumen Gentium* appears, rather, to be that of equating the Church with the idea of "the People of God", which is only one of the models of the Church this Council document treats. It is true that *Lumen Gentium* includes an illuminating chapter on the People of God, a scriptural concept that goes back and includes God's original chosen people, with whom he made a covenant, and carries forward to include those who believe and are baptized into Christ today, the members of the Church.

As many are prone to forget, Vatican II also explicitly described this People of God as, necessarily, "guided by the sacred teaching authority of the Church (*magisterium*) and obeying it".[10] However, such nuances are generally lost upon today's progressive religious educators, who are usu-

---

*Vatican Council II: the Conciliar and Post Conciliar Documents* (Northport, N.Y.: Costello Publishing Company, 1975), 903.

[9] Vatican Council II, Dogmatic Constitution on the Church, *Lumen Gentium*, no. 1, in Flannery, *Vatican Council II*, 350.

[10] Ibid., no. 12, 363.

ally content merely to celebrate and promote the simplistic idea that "the people are the Church" (and for some of these same people it also seems to follow that *since* "the people are the Church", the hierarchy is *not* the Church).

If we put together the three, basic, simplistic ideas that the people are the Church, that the Church is now supposed to be open to the world, and that a "catechism" may be an effective teaching instrument after all, we could easily come up with what a number of prominent members of the current theological and catechetical establishments now *have* come up with: we could come up with *The People's Catechism: Catholic Faith for Adults*, a brightly colored paperback book that unselfconsciously claims on its outside front cover to be written: "By the People of God, for the People of God".[11]

That is exactly what it says on the cover: "By the People of God, for the People of God". It thus not only invokes Vatican II; it suggests the Gettysburg Address as well. And it probably represents the first volume off the press in the United States attempting to lay claim to being one of the new "local", "inculturated" catechisms following up on the *Catechism of the Catholic Church*.

Of course the book does have real authors besides "the People of God": six of them, in fact. They are all identified on the title page, and their smiling faces, along with those of the book's three editors, appear on the back cover. Most

---

[11] *The People's Catechism: Catholic Faith for Adults*. "By the People of God, for the People of God." Edited by Raymond A. Lucker, Patrick J. Brennan, and Michael Leach. Written by William J. O'Malley, S.J., Mitch and Kathy Finley, Kathleen Hughes, R.S.C.J., and Barbara Quinn, R.S.C.J., and Timothy E. O'Connell (New York: Crossroad Publishing Company, 1995).

of the names will be familiar to those who are acquainted with the contemporary theological and catechetical literature in the United States (although no one would probably have suspected any of them of being willing simply to equate themselves with "the People of God"). Of the book's three editors, by the way, one is a bishop.

The pretentious subtitle, "Catholic Faith for Adults", seems expressly intended to convey the notion that there is perhaps some other kind of "Catholic faith" out there besides the one presented in this book for adults, a faith presumably *not* for "adults", one that could *not* hope to merit the same designation as the "faith" of those who write, edit, and publish—and read!—this one. In fact, the very way in which this book has been written, published, and promoted, virtually on the heels of the *Catechism of the Catholic Church*, suggests that it is the faith set forth in the latter that is thought not to be for adults.

Jesus Christ said: "Truly, I say to you, whoever does not receive the kingdom of God like a child will not enter it" (Mk 10:15; Lk 18:17). The people responsible for this book instead pride themselves on "adult faith". Actually, applying the word "adult" to "faith" in this manner has become a fairly common code expression today for describing the typical Neomodernist version of the faith championed by today's self-designated "magisterium of theologians". It can hardly be said to refer to the concept of the "maturity of faith" that is set forth in the *General Catechetical Directory*.[12]

This book promotes itself with a couple of pages of enthusiastic blurbs inside, a number of them from well-known public dissenters from authentic teachings of the Church's real Magisterium. These blurbs bring out clearly why this

---

[12] GCD, no. 21ff.

book is likely to be a big hit with the current catechetical in-group: the book is "drawn from human experience . . . , written in modern idiom for real people . . . , a truly contemporary catechism . . . , an adult follow-up to the new *Catechism* . . . , directed to mature Catholics . . . , presents Catholicism as the living faith of a people", and so on. The immediate implication is that these same things cannot be said of the Church's *Catechism of the Catholic Church*. No doubt that is why a "follow-up" was thought to be necessary so soon after the Church had completed her own *Catechism*.

According to the editors' introduction, this *"People's Catechism* attempts to bring life and a fresh understanding of the truths of faith contained in the *Catechism of the Catholic Church*, [but is] presented in a style and format that makes it a useable tool in adult faith formation sessions, small groups or Christian communities, ministry training programs, and personal enrichment or study."

The book employs "a catechetical methodology . . . in each chapter, with relevant passages from Scripture; stories from contemporary human experience; the teaching of the Church presented in popularized, understandable, existential language; questions for discussion and faith sharing; suggestions for putting faith into action; and shared prayer". Again, the implication is that the *Catechism* is *not* a "useable tool", does *not* present the teachings of the Church "in popularized, understandable, existential language". And so on.

Actually, this book probably will appeal immediately to the average religious educator today. It has the requisite "catechetical methodology", the "questions for discussion", and the rest of the pedagogical apparatus that catechists today have come to expect.

The immediate appeal that the book will almost certainly

have, however, is unfortunate because this book is almost a caricature of nearly everything that is bad in modern religious education today. The Scripture quotations are often random and not necessarily or systematically linked with themes of the faith in the book, almost as if they were included merely to show that "Scripture" was indeed being included. The stories are often inferior fiction; often they seem pointless, and sometimes they even border on the vulgar. The teachings of the Church are presented only sporadically; sometimes they are seriously misrepresented and even contradicted.

The doctrinal omissions alone in this book are glaring. In no way can the book claim even to come close to presenting the *General Catechetical Directory*'s "global adherence to Christ's gospel as presented by the Church" or as "contributing to the gradual grasping of the whole truth about the divine plan".[13]

Given the slant of the book, the questions for discussion are heavily weighted toward the subjective and the impressionistic (for example, "In your *experience*, is God distant, silent, 'other,' or close, reassuring, a friend?"). Since a severely truncated version of the faith is being presented, the "faith sharing" is as likely as not to be "faith obscuring". Many of the suggestions for putting the faith into practice are wholly indistinguishable from secular liberal political activism. The prayers are limp and often banal.

This is a book by and for people who have precisely *lost* the excitement and romance of *orthodoxy*, as described in the famous volume of that name by G. K. Chesterton. These people secularize and trivialize the faith of Jesus Christ in exactly the same way that many modern religion textbooks

---

[13] See GCD, nos. 18, 24.

do. To believe the faith of Christ in its fullness, as it is now set forth in the *Catechism of the Catholic Church*, they prefer a version of the faith set forth by the modern "magisterium of theologians". They are apparently oblivious to the impertinence entailed in coming out with a volume such as this following the publication of the real *Catechism*. The editors actually describe the latter, in a typical jargon-phrase, as merely adding "foundational clarity to the essence of the Catholic expression of Christianity"—again, as if there were some other and better "expression" of the faith besides the Catholic one.

One of their principal aims seems to be to change the way Catholics have been catechized; they may not succeed in getting much across to their charges by their new methods, but at least they are *not* going to give them what they used to get. Traditional Catholics are simply considered "too rote in their faith or too non-reflective".

This book claims to challenge "its readers not simply to know about God passively"—but it is not really, and never was, a question of passivity versus activity. In their desire to promote "activity" and what they call a "living faith", the new catechists have succeeded at least in this, that they have produced an entire generation, and more, who do *not* know about God in the fullness with which the Church presents him. Nor will this book contribute much, if anything, toward remedying that state of affairs.

Unperturbed, the editors go on repeating the typical received maxims of today's theological and catechetical establishments, despite the fact that these have not been shown to work. For example:

> —"There will never be a definitive catechism since every age needs a fresh expression of the faith and applica-

tion of the Christian message to new circumstances"—so why not use the "fresh expression" of it that is currently to be found in the *Catechism*, instead of producing an inferior substitute for it such as this one?

—"There is one faith and many theologies"—but why does the particular "theology" found in the *Catechism* always, somehow, turn out to be the one that is not acceptable in catechesis today? That therefore has to be "corrected" by books such as this one?

—"No group in the Church of Jesus has a corner on the truth." So the editors of this volume sagely inform us, thus eliminating with a single *obiter dictum* the special importance the Magisterium has in the Church, including in the preparation of catechisms.

In keeping with this liberal view, this book was written, we are told, by representatives of the diverse People of God, including "laity and women"—again unlike the *Catechism of the Catholic Church*, since the latter was written by bishops and therefore obviously cannot claim to be as "representative" as this one. We begin to see what the editors apparently mean by "the People of God". What they mean is what in the culture is currently referred to by the expression "politically correct". We shall see that the book generally reflects this outlook. We therefore do not apologize for referring to this so-called *People's Catechism*, in the examination that follows, as *PC*.

## III

*PC* is not arranged in exactly the same four parts as the *Catechism of the Catholic Church*. The latter's part one on the Creed, or Profession of Faith, is covered by two different authors here in *PC*, one writing on the "Foundations of the Faith" and the other on the "Message". There is a part three on the Sacraments and a part four on the Moral Life. There is no separate treatment of Prayer in *PC*, however; apparently the prayers that are included in each chapter were considered sufficient.

*PC*'s "Foundations of Faith" section was written by William J. O'Malley, S.J., a teacher of English and theology at Fordham Preparatory School in the Bronx, New York, and a five-time winner of a Catholic Press Award. Actually, Fr. O'Malley is a skillful and entertaining writer, if that were the only or even the most important question involved in catechesis. His attitude toward the faith found in the *Catechism*, however, as evidenced by his contribution to this volume, is something else again. Moreover, his negative attitude appears to be of fairly long standing, since this same Fr. William O'Malley is another one of the writers who tried to ambush the draft *Catechism* in the notorious 1990 *Universal Catechism Reader*.[14]

Fr. O'Malley's basic approach is breezy and "with it", probably what is thought to be the most effective approach for prep schoolers nowadays. It is certainly the approach that many of today's new catechists try to take as well. They all seem quite undeterred by the fact that, on the evidence, this approach scarcely boasts a shining record of producing very many believing and practicing Catholics. Nevertheless, like George Santayana's famous "fanatics", they tend to "redouble their efforts after they have forgotten their aim".

Like today's new christologists, Fr. O'Malley typically starts "from below", with "our intelligence". Drawing on modern psychology, he tells us that "the function of adolescence is to *critique* certitudes uncritically 'taped' from par-

---

[14] See n. 3 to Chapter Three *supra*.

ents, teachers, peers, and the media, to find which square with objective reality and which do not." Apparently this is the way the faith is to be approached too. Jesus said: "Do not fear, only believe" (Mk 5:36). The Evangelist wrote in order "that you also may believe" (Jn 19:35). Father O'Malley, however, prefers to "critique certitudes". "Adult faith", he tells us, "is a calculated risk based on reasoning about objective facts."

No, it is not: the *Catechism of the Catholic Church* makes this unmistakably clear, echoing Vatican I: "What moves us to believe is not the fact that revealed truths appear as true and intelligible in the light of our natural reason: we believe 'because of the authority of God himself who reveals them, who can neither deceive nor be deceived' "(CCC 156; *Dei Filius* no. 3).

Fr. O'Malley has got it all wrong, clumsily attempting to inspire what he calls "adult faith" by equating it with the methods of scientific and inductive inquiry. Reason, both inductive and deductive, does play a role in the development of faith, of course; but Fr. O'Malley is out at sea about how it all works, having cast himself adrift from the moorings provided by the Church of God.

He does say a lot of nice things about God, Jesus, creaturehood, natural law, and so on. He really does still appear to be in some sense a sincere believer in Jesus and even to have retained something of a Catholic outlook, at least in some respects (although, Protestant-style, he will arrive at all his own conclusions regarding Jesus, thank you). Given the position independent of the Church that he has adopted, however, he says a number of other things that can in no sense be considered nice, or even acceptable, in a presentation that purports to be Catholic. Some of his assertions, in fact, contradict the *Catechism of the Catholic Church* as plainly as does the definition of faith we have just quoted from his account.

We could cite a fair number of similar aberrations, large and small. Considerations of length and space, however, must limit us to commenting upon only two of the other subjects he treats: (1) what he calls "the rock-bottom, non-negotiable beliefs of Christian doctrine"; and (2) his treatment of "figurative language" in Scripture.

The very concept of "rock-bottom, non-negotiable beliefs", of course, already suggests the existence of other beliefs that *are* negotiable. From the moment we adopt this point of view, we have already moved into the realm of pick-and-choose Catholicism. This, of course, is exactly the way many of those who like to invoke Vatican II's notion of a hierarchy of truths do approach things: while there surely are some beliefs that are nonnegotiable, they reason, others are not; they are therefore up for grabs. Which ones?

Or, more fundamentally: Who decides which ones? Once we have reached this point, we have already turned responsibility for deciding this over to the private judgment of theologians, if not, again Protestant-style, to that of simple, individual Bible readers. Henceforth the very concept of a Church Magisterium becomes devoid of any plausibility or meaning.

Fr. O'Malley's own choice of "rock-bottom, non-negotiable Christian doctrines" is comprised of the following four:

> [1] Jesus is the embodiment of God, God-made-flesh.
>
> [2] Jesus-God died in order to *rise* and share with us liberation from the fear of death and to offer us a share in the aliveness of God right now.
>
> [3] To engraft oneself into Jesus-God, one must give up the values of what St. Paul called "the world" ("me

first!") and take on the values of what Jesus called "the kingdom" ("them first"—God and the neighbor).

[4] We celebrate our oneness with Jesus-God in a community of service and in a weekly public meal.

It is hard not to notice how even the language of an otherwise good writer such as Fr. O'Malley becomes forced and stilted when he leaves the broad highway of the Church's authentic faith in order to go joy-riding on secondary roads of his own choosing. Fr. O'Malley goes on to explain and discuss his four core doctrines. He quotes scriptural proof texts that firmly establish them, in his view, and then he summarily calls for belief in them! Those who do not believe them are simply not Christian, he declares. He thus has his own clear doctrine of "orthodoxy" ("*anathema sit!*") based on these four doctrines. On the basis of them, he dares to say, in other words, what he and his confreres now deny the Church the right to say, namely, what orthodox doctrine is and who are and are not Christians.

Have we not arrived at a rather evident absurdity here? The Catholic Church can no longer teach with authority what her doctrines are or say who belongs to her communion, but an English and theology teacher at Fordham Prep can! However absurd it may seem, Fr. O'Malley is quite serious about it all, he who can so easily make light of Catholic teaching in general. He returns more than once to his "rock-bottom, non-negotiable doctrines" in the course of his narrative, explicitly using them at one point to justify the licitness of dissent from Catholic teaching:

Some devoted Catholics take strong exception to other Catholics' beliefs that conflict openly with the Vatican. Yet they remind us that, as long as we agree on the non-negotiables—the divinity of Jesus, the resurrection, the anti-materialism of the gospel, and worshiping and serving community—there is no need of schism, much less excommunication. And they remind us that God gave us intelligence before God saw need to give us the magisterium.

But what if someone disagrees with the nonnegotiables too? Surely, in today's climate, working theologians could be found at almost any convention of the Catholic Theological Society of America who might disagree with at least the first two of these four nonnegotiables. What standard does Fr. O'Malley have for judging in that case? Will "schism" and perhaps even "excommunication" have to follow *then*, even for *him*?

Otherwise, how is he going to be able to insist on maintaining the four nonnegotiables? How is he going to manage otherwise than the Church has had to try to manage when certain of her children have risen up against her and denied her teachings? How is mere "intelligence" going to resolve the problems posed in this case for Fr. O'Malley's "magisterium of one"?

Obviously, to ask these questions is to answer them. We are not sanguine that Fr. O'Malley himself is going to recognize the absurdity of his position; nevertheless we believe it is our plain duty to point out that nobody with such a position ought to be "catechizing" anybody else.

We can only make mention of one other issue raised by Fr. O'Malley's deplorable treatment of the "Foundations of Faith" in this *People's Catechism*: his views on "figurative language" in Scripture. He deals with the general subject of figurative language quite well and imaginatively, as a matter of fact, pointing out how often we regularly use figurative language in our speech and writing. This leads him to ask why, suddenly, everything has to be "literal" when it comes to sacred Scripture?

The answer, of course, is that it does not. Nor has the Church ever said that it did. The *Catechism* expressly says, for example, that "the account of the fall in Genesis 3 uses figurative language"; but the *Catechism* also goes on to affirm that this figurative language "affirms a primeval event, a deed that took place at the beginning of the history of man" (CCC 390). In other words, the *Catechism* teaches, language can be figurative all right; nevertheless some of the things expressed by figurative language can also be true and real. What things? The short answer, for Catholics, is: the things that the Church's Magisterium, guided by the Holy Spirit, declares to be real.

Fr. O'Malley's views on this end up diverging quite markedly from the *Catechism*'s. For him the main point about figurative language is that "stories can tell very real and important truths about human life without having literally, historically occurred." This is a true enough statement as far as it goes. He gives as examples Æsop's fables and similar folk tales. He could as easily have instanced the parables of Jesus, since presumably neither the Good Samaritan nor the Prodigal Son were real people.

But he decides to go much farther. He aims to show that some, or even much, of the Gospel narratives consist of "stories" that did not, in his view, "literally, historically" occur. He divides the Gospel accounts into "actual historical events", "obviously fabricated stories" (in which he does include the parables), and "stories the Catholic community made up".

How does he know all this? Modern Scripture scholarship, how else? We are back to the question of who decides. Who decides which scriptural accounts are actual historical events, which obviously fabricated, and which fabricated by "the Catholic community"? Again, modern Scripture scholarship is supposed to provide the answers. He tends to treat even the most tentative of scholarly hypotheses as so much established dogma, if only someone belonging to the "magisterium of scholars" has advanced the view somewhere: the Gospels were not written until A.D. 65 at the earliest, Mark's was the first Gospel, and so on. It is all depressingly conformist.

He quite confidently asserts, for example, that "Peter probably did *not* say, 'You are the Messiah, the Son of the living God' "—something for which, in the nature of the case, neither he nor any scholar will probably ever have any really decisive, probative evidence, either for or against, beyond the "evidence" we all possess, along with the Church, in the well-known plain words of the Gospel. Catholics do not believe the Gospels because modern scholars have turned up evidence that Jesus did or did not actually say this or that. Catholics believe the Gospels, as St. Augustine said long ago, on the authority of the Catholic Church.

In this particular case, the Church has solemnly taught, in a dogmatic constitution from one of her general councils, that she "has firmly and with absolute constancy maintained, and continues to maintain, that the four Gospels . . . whose historicity she unhesitatingly affirms, faithfully hand on what Jesus, the Son of God, while he lived among men, really did and taught for their eternal salvation, until the day he was taken up".[15]

Fr. O'Malley's narrative betrays no hint that he is even acquainted with Vatican Council II's *Dei Verbum*, where the Church has officially addressed all the major questions raised by the modern study of Scripture. The Church has also pro-

---

[15] Vatican Council II, Dogmatic Constitution on Divine Revelation, *Dei Verbum*, no. 19.

vided her own very careful and very plausible answers to these questions. Although difficulties, anomalies, and many unanswered questions will no doubt always remain in anything as varied and complex as the Bible, there can be no doubt at all that the Church's own witness in *Dei Verbum* to her steadfast and abiding faith in sacred Scripture, as it has been handed down to us, represents a much more impressive and satisfying account of the matter than all the modern theories and methods that continually attempt to deconstruct Scripture.

And the *Catechism of the Catholic Church* closely follows *Dei Verbum* in its treatment of Scripture, as even some of the *Catechism*'s detractors have admitted. A Fr. O'Malley, however, is evidently more interested in trying to weed out "literalists" or "fundamentalists" who might be lurking about, unconvinced of the blessings that have flowed from the use of the historical-critical method.

## IV

*PC*'s part two is on the subject of "The Message: the Nicene and Apostles' Creeds". The authors are husband and wife, Mitch and Kathy Finley. Mitch is a writer and five-time Catholic Press Award winner, and Kathy teaches in the Religious Studies Department of Gonzaga University in Spokane, Washington. The Finleys refer to and quote the Church's own words—notably, Scripture, the liturgy, Vatican II, and the *Catechism*—more frequently than the other authors, and they are also more likely to approve of what they quote, it seems. Their particular presentation exhibits the fewest signs that the real purpose of *PC* is to give the reader the honest lowdown about "adult faith" today, something the *Catechism of the Catholic Church* has supposedly failed to do in a manner acceptable to certain modern ideas about catechesis.

Where the Finley presentation chiefly falls down is in the disparate, disjointed, and even miscellaneous way in which it treats a topic that needs to be presented much more systematically. Their topic, after all, specifically treats the "Message", the Apostles' and Nicene Creeds. This subject matter takes in a lot of territory, which the Finleys manage to touch upon only in a few selected spots. While selection was surely necessary in the space allotted to them, their very method prevents them from getting very far into any of the themes they do broach.

Each of their chapters begins with a little story or vignette, sometimes composed by them: a husband and wife reflect on their marriage; a young man compares the splendors of the King Tutankhamen exhibit with the even greater splendors of God's creation; a woman discovers that her family inevitably goes along with her in spirit, even when she goes on retreat. Other times the stories or vignettes are summarized from known authors such as Garrison Keillor or Shusaku Endo. For the most part, there is nothing wrong with these stories. It is sometimes hard, however, to discern what connection they have with the doctrine that is supposed to be expounded but that is often, instead, barely touched upon in the authors' preoccupation with "human interest".

In general this approach to the Creeds fails to bring out either the depth or the meaning of the great mysteries of our faith, or sometimes even that fact that there are any such great mysteries: creation, sin, redemption, the mystery and mission of Jesus Christ, the Holy Spirit, and the Church.

While the exposition of the great truths contained in the

Creeds might normally be expected to elicit gratitude, wonder, and awe, the approach here is determinedly down-to-earth, folksy, and chatty: nobody here but the People of God! Contrary to the claims of the editors of this volume in their introduction, this is most emphatically *not* the way to teach the truths of the Creeds. Trivialization of them is almost impossible to avoid when they are approached in this fashion. The Finleys actually quote a number of advertising jingles to illustrate the topic of redemption, for example. The point in this case seems to be how badly today's popular culture misuses such words as "redemption" and "salvation". So it does; we always knew that. But that is no excuse to descend to the same low level, while ostensibly catechizing people in the truths of the Catholic faith.

Moreover, like all of the authors of this volume, the Finleys tend to be conventionally modern and quite secular in their orientation, even when explaining specific religious and theological themes. For example, in their treatment of sin, while they do carefully explain the difference between venial and mortal sins, what immediately occurs to them as an available remedy for sin is not the Church's sacrament of Reconciliation; they never mention it, in fact (although they do mention in passing that "in Baptism we die to sin"). Instead, in one of their "Faith in Action" recommendations, they invoke step five in the Twelve Steps of Alcoholics Anonymous, where reforming alcoholics are supposed to admit "to God, to ourselves, and to another human being the exact nature of our wrongs".

Our purpose in citing this example is not to belittle either the idea of making amends or the Twelve Steps of Alcoholics Anonymous; the latter have undoubtedly helped many people. But in what is supposed to be an exposition of the Christian message as professed by the Catholic Church in the Creeds, the fact that the authors do not even advert to sacramental confession as the Church's primary remedy for sin is only too symptomatic of the book's entire treatment: these authors are simply determined to be relevant and modern.

They are apparently equally determined to be politically correct. One of their introductory stories is about a young engineer who, as a result of reading Pope John XXIII's *Pacem in Terris*, comes to an acute crisis of conscience as a result of working in the U.S. defense industry (not that this viewpoint is necessarily to be despised; but it is in no way a clear-cut moral issue, either). The command in Genesis to exercise dominion over the earth inevitably suggests to them the importance of ecology: "We are to use the earth's natural resources gently and take care that we leave the environment the way we found it." The role of the Jewish people in salvation history immediately raises for them the question of the Holocaust, and Christians are admonished as severely as they are ever admonished about anything in this book to avoid anti-Semitism.

The point is not that we should not respect the environment, the Jewish people, or the consciences of individuals. The Church teaches that we should. Nor is there anything wrong with reiterating the Church's teaching about these things. But the whole presentation in this section is supposed to be about the *Creeds*! The ease and regularity with which the authors slip into the conventional, politically correct positions of the day, while talking about almost anything but the Creeds, is indicative of the relatively modest place to which they, like all the authors in this book, tend to assign questions of mere "doctrine". Why we get so little doctrine of any kind in what is supposed to be the major doctrinal portion of the book is a legitimate question.

Moreover, some of the doctrine that we do get is at times a bit shaky. Quoting paragraph 1250 of the *Catechism* on how baptism frees us from bondage to "a fallen human nature tainted by original sin", the Finleys go on to explain that this is "perhaps best understood not as a personal sin committed by a historical first man and first woman (Adam and Eve). Rather, the point of the Adam and Eve narrative in Genesis—and the concept of 'original sin'—is to acknowledge and explain the mystery of evil in human existence and in the world and its impact on us."

Unfortunately, as we have already seen in dealing with Fr. O'Malley's "figurative language" above, the *Catechism* unmistakably teaches that the Genesis story "affirms a primeval event, a deed that took place at the beginning of history" (CCC 390). How can they miss such things? Or be excused when they miss them?

Once again, in dealing with baptism, the Finleys begin their explanation by warning: "Baptism is not magic." Like Fr. O'Malley, they seem unusually concerned to correct possible misconceptions arising from the way Catholics were formerly—and the suggestion is, wrongly—catechized. For example, they remark that "earlier generations thought of the Church itself as the kingdom of God." Earlier generations? Vatican II plainly teaches that "the Church is the kingdom of God already present in mystery."[16]

It is hard to avoid the conclusion that what these *PC* writers really want is a very different kind of Catholic from the "passive", "accepting" kind, with his rosary beads and (as they tend to believe) his various hang-ups and guilt trips. They want modern up-to-date activists and do-gooders—without the encumbrance of what they evidently see as a lot

---

[16] *Lumen Gentium*, no. 3.

of dubious doctrinal baggage. *That*, unfortunately, is one of the principal "messages" that comes through in this part supposedly devoted to *the* message; but for the most part the latter gets lost along the way.

The new catechists appear to want to change the world into something not easily distinguishable from the modern secular liberal's vision of a changed world. In order to accomplish this, they believe they have to eliminate a good deal of what Catholics were formerly taught in favor of teaching positive, activist precepts. Were they ever to succeed with this approach, it is quite unlikely that the world would be significantly changed for the better. What the results of the new catechesis to date is likely to show, however, is that, continuing this approach, we are going to have nothing more than another generation committed to a vague and vapid do-goodism, with little attention paid to the great and awesome truths of our sanctification and salvation in Jesus Christ.

So much for the specifically "doctrinal" part of this pretentious *People's Catechism*: it is not a "message" that is likely to inspire very many people.

## V

*PC*'s part three on the Sacraments was written by two religious sisters, Sr. Kathleen Hughes, R.S.C.J., academic dean and professor of liturgy at the Catholic Theological Union in Chicago, and Sr. Barbara Quinn, R.S.C.J., a pastoral associate at a Chicago parish who is now also completing a doctorate in "ministry" at the same Catholic Theological Union. It is not reassuring to learn, after reading this part, that one of the coauthors, Sr. Hughes, is a member of the advisory committees for both the Bishops' Committee on the Liturgy and the International Commission on English in the Liturgy (ICEL). If the view of the sacraments expressed in this part is shared on either of those two committees, we are in trouble.

Sr. Hughes and Sr. Quinn are unfortunately no improvement on the Finleys in their use of little vignettes to illustrate their topics. The "sacramental principle" in their account is thus actually introduced by the citation of a letter from a "friend" testifying to how her deceased father's "presence" remained in the house after his death through the objects ("symbols") pertaining to his former life there. This analogy is both weak and misleading because sacraments, while being visible signs, truly do also confer something real, that is, grace, God's own life. The "signs" or "symbols" of the deceased father left behind, however, only represent or call to mind his *former* "real presence" in the house, while he was still living; but there is nothing real about these symbols themselves.

*PC*'s rather consistent fashionable political correctness is present in this part too. The topic of "Finding One's Place in the Church's Sacramental Life" is actually introduced by the story of Oskar Schindler of *Schindler's List*. Nearly all of *PC*'s applications of Christian beliefs and principles to life similarly turn out to be almost indistinguishable from the concerns of today's dominant secular liberal culture. This "catechism" is "inculturated" in the sense that it is consistently accommodating to the modern culture found today in the United States. *PC*'s authors are so "bold" and "prophetic", like those of *America* or *Commonweal* magazines, or the *National Catholic Reporter* newspaper, that they almost always exactly reflect the current secular liberal *Zeitgeist*.

Since this is the part of the book that is supposed to expound the Church's sacraments, though, the way in which these religious-sister authors do define and explain the sacramental system cannot but be disquieting. They adopt what has now become a standard technique by beginning with a correct definition, the old *Baltimore Catechism*'s definition of a sacrament as an "outward sign instituted by Christ to give grace". But it very quickly becomes clear that this definition, according to the authors, "must be expanded and enriched by contemporary phenomenological insights". This they undertake to do, and *voilà!*: a sacrament has suddenly become "an event, at decisive moments in the life of the *community* that celebrates in symbolic language the *experience* of encounter with God in Christ dead and risen, in the life of the community and its members" (emphasis added).

The authors emphasize that a sacrament is "an *event*, not a thing, but a vital action of the Church. . . . Sacraments are *celebrations*, which means that they give public, ritual expression to our human religious experience through patterned activity and *symbolical language* (words, gestures, objects, music, space and time)" (emphasis in the original).

Now not all of this is completely wrong; they could hardly get it all wrong and still be intelligibly talking about the same sacraments with which all Catholics are familiar. Nevertheless, the emphasis they adopt is misplaced, heavily stressing the symbolical and experiential aspects, while never directly stating that *it is God who gives his life to us in the sacraments*. This emphasis that they adopt cannot but end up giving a distorted view of the sacraments. Their view, in our estimation, is a markedly naturalistic one.

But then, in their view, the whole of reality is a "divine milieu" (Teilhard de Chardin). The worlds of nature and grace have become virtually indistinguishable. The sacrament of Reconciliation has become "starting over again after failure", in their words. "Jesus demonstrated no interest in lists of offenses", they remark a little later on the subject of this same sacrament, to which it can only be replied that Jesus expressly enjoined the keeping of the Commandments, which he went to the trouble of specifically enumerating (cf. Mk 10:19; Lk 18:20). And St. Paul, of course, was not at all loath to compile "lists of offenses". Indeed, one of his lists has become perhaps the classical, definitive one: "all manner of wickedness, evil, covetousness, malice, . . . envy, murder, strife, deceit, malignity, . . . gossips, slanderers, haters of God, insolent, haughty, boastful, inventors of evil, disobedient, . . . foolish, faithless, heartless, ruthless" (Rom 1:29–31). Such "lists" would seem to occupy a rather venerable position in the history of the Church; nor is it at all clear where the liberal dislike of "lists" arises from or what is wrong with them.

Speaking about the Eucharist, Sr. Hughes and Sr. Quinn mention the "simple meal" that the early Christians allegedly shared. "Could Jesus really have intended to leave us a last will and testament based on such an ordinary and necessary human activity?" This, of course, is exactly what the Last Supper was *not*: a simple meal. Nor is the Eucharist today to be equated with the "eucharistic meal" the authors keep referring to. "Could the way to God and the way to holiness truly be as close to us as sharing a meal with friends?" they ask artlessly.

The answer to this question is, of course, most emphatically: "No!" The Eucharist has never been a simple "meal with friends". From the beginning, the Eucharist has been a memorial ritual solemnly and strictly enjoined upon us in which Jesus continues to give himself to us in a unique way.

To imagine it as a mere "meal with friends" is to forget WHO JESUS IS.

Yet again, in another connection, these authors are able to ask: "Isn't Eucharist celebrated each time a family welcomes relatives at holiday time, when a maître d' creates an atmosphere of gracious dining that invites graciousness from those who gather, when a person goes without in order to send money to a relief fund for a famine-stricken people?" The answer, again, is: "No!" However meritorious these acts that they describe, they are most distinctly *not* "Eucharist".

We cannot go on at any length attempting to detail the many things that are either misleading or are quite simply wrong about this particular treatise on the sacraments. Suffice it to say that the same approach we have seen up to this point has been consistently followed by these authors: they state a thesis that is at least minimally intelligible to the instructed Catholic; then they go on to explain and qualify it virtually beyond recognition. The "institution of the sacraments by Christ" is yet another case in point.

This particular teaching is a rather hard one to get around without openly declaring that one has simply renounced the Catholic faith. For this teaching was solemnly defined by a general council of the Church, the Council of Trent, and the *Catechism of the Catholic Church*, echoing the Church's contemporary Magisterium, has not failed to restate it more than once (CCC 1084, 1114, 1117, and so on). Srs. Hughes and Quinn, however, do not allow this to bother them unduly. "Institution by Christ", they write, "simply means that the Church has evolved a pattern of sacramental activity over the centuries as it attempts to remain faithful to Jesus' life and ministry." In other words, "institution by Christ" evidently simply means for them "institution by the Church".

Their descriptions of the particular sacraments are consistent with this position. All the sacraments "evolved", it seems. Baptism, which they call "Initiation", was "forged as the community tried to address the growing numbers attracted to membership. . . . The community chose a rite of water and word. . . . Other questions and other needs gradually gave rise to other Sacraments." And so on. In this remarkable account, we even learn at one point that "Jesus Christ was not a priest" (the Letter to the Hebrews to the contrary!).

It is true that many unanswered historical questions do surround the development of the sacraments within the Church of Christ. There is perhaps little concrete evidence that some of them were understood and practiced exactly as we understand and practice them today. In the nature of the case, we may never possess the evidence that would be necessary in order to clear up some of the questions that have been raised. But, again, the "evidence" here is mostly negative: the historical record is simply silent about some of the questions that have occurred to us.

But the Church's firm tradition in this matter of "institution by Christ" cannot simply be laid aside on the basis of such arguments from silence. The utterly cavalier way in which Sr. Hughes and Sr. Quinn present a largely fanciful theory of how the Church herself instituted and developed the sacraments is not a legitimate stance for Catholic theologians to take. The Church has solemnly taught, and now in the *Catechism* has plainly reiterated, that the seven sacraments were "instituted by Christ". That is where a Catholic theologian is obliged to *begin*. However this phrase is to be explained, and whatever the historical evidence that can be brought to bear on it, it still necessarily constitutes the basis of any teaching about the sacraments that is truly Catholic—or else the Church herself is a fraud and a sham.

The fact that the authors, editors, and publishers of this *People's Catechism* apparently do not understand such an elementary point is just one more reason why this book is an unreliable guide to Catholic faith of any kind, much less "for adults".

# VI

*PC*'s part four on the Moral Life was written by Timothy E. O'Connell, Ph.D., who is a professor of Christian ethics in the Institute of Pastoral Studies at Loyola University of Chicago. He is the author, *inter alia*, of *Principles for a Catholic Morality*, and thus he appears to be a member in good standing of the current theological establishment.

After what we have seen in the first three parts of this book, though, we cannot be unduly surprised to learn that his presentation on the moral life begins with a reference to Disney's *The Lion King*. Unfortunately, too much of this part, like the rest of the book, is on this same level. The very next reference to contemporary culture in this author's presentation is to the absurd George Burns movie *Oh, God*. This kind of approach cannot but trivialize the subject matter, although Dr. O'Connell's contribution is an unusually earnest one when compared to those of some of the other authors.

He claims to believe in a "teaching Church", and, on a number of critical questions, he does state the Church's teaching, which he generally characterizes as "strong". He even includes a chapter on the great moral issues posed for society today by the legalization of abortion and euthanasia, issues that liberals of the type represented by the editors and authors of this book generally prefer to downplay or even bypass. More characteristically, though, he also includes "ecology" in the chapter dealing with these grave moral issues, as if the destruction of the environment, however valid a concern, were even remotely on the same moral level as the deliberate killing of human beings.

Even though he does raise the issues of abortion and euthanasia, he does not really engage them on any deep moral level. The challenge for Catholics faced with the legalization of these evils in the society in which they live, he writes, is "to remain involved in the community of moral discourse". Why could he just not say, as the Pope does in his recent encyclical on the Gospel of Life, *Evangelium Vitæ*, that these evils are intolerable for Christians and have to be opposed? For Dr. O'Connell, however, the "emphasis ought to be not on fervent questioning as on candid questioning". He is quite sure that most people involved in abortions "are not persons of intentional bad will", although it is not at all clear how he knows this.

His typical solution to the problem of the legalization of the sheer evil of euthanasia turns out to be his recommendation that people should be "challenged to develop technology and social structures to the point that euthanasia becomes obviously *inappropriate*" (emphasis added). "Inappropriate"? Euthanasia is gravely *wrong* and destructive of the very idea of human dignity. Why can something like this not be said plainly?

From his treatment of sin and evil, even though he freely concedes that such things do exist, and even discusses them at some length, it would be hard for the reader to conclude that sin and evil, at bottom, ever really are all that wrong.

For there are always explanations, mitigating factors (as even the Church recognizes, of course, but in a markedly different perspective from his).

In Dr. O'Connell's perspective, there is almost no recognition at all that God has actually *commanded* anything or that the Church truly *insists* on reiterating what God has commanded. The characteristic approach of the ancient prophets—"Thus saith the Lord!"—is entirely alien to his own approach to the moral life.

Similarly, he rarely indicates that the Church "holds" or "teaches" anything. His most characteristic way of indicating a Church position is to say something like "our tradition teaches." He is always talking about "our tradition" as if, since it is only "our tradition" after all, it could well be different from what it is—and, indeed, we can never forget also that there are all those other "traditions" out there as well. Marriage, for instance, is for him the "setting" within which "our culture" says sexuality may be legitimately exercised (he is going to have a problem with this one, considering that "our culture" has lately been steadily legitimizing the exercise of sexuality *outside* of marriage!).

The moral urgency for human beings of doing good and avoiding evil, which the Church's own moral teaching never fails to bring out, for instance, in the *Catechism of the Catholic Church*, is something that is notably absent from Dr. O'Connell's treatment of the moral life. In his treatment, morality becomes bland and attenuated. At the moment when St. Maria Goretti was about to give up her own life in defense of her chastity, she said to her assailant: "God does not wish it!"

Ultimately, down deep, this is the reason why all of us must always strive, with God's help and in the face of whatever difficulties, to try to do good and avoid evil: because

God *does* wish good for us and, at the same time, cannot tolerate evil from us. Nobody would ever be likely to sacrifice life or limb, as did St. Maria Goretti, or even convenience or advantage, merely because "our tradition" might wish it. Yet Dr. O'Connell explicitly states that the idea that God might ever "demand" anything represents what he calls "cheap legalism". This is fundamentally to misunderstand the nature of the Christian moral life.

The fact remains that the Commandments are from God, however this uncomfortable fact may displease some modern moralists. There are things God most emphatically does "wish" from us, and that is the basic reason the Commandments were given to the human race in the first place. Jesus specifically reiterated the same Commandments by name. The Church has similarly never failed to emphasize and lay them out, including, most recently, in the *Catechism*.

The approach of this modern author, however, like that of some of our other modern moral theologians, is deliberately to blur and obscure the sharp edges of the human moral life, to trivialize and homogenize the awesome nature of all our acts in the sight of God. Just as earlier authors in this volume came up with one of the Twelve Steps of Alcoholics Anonymous as a fitting remedy for sin, so Dr. O'Connell also comes up with the remedy of "counseling or participation in a Twelve Step Group" in the same way. Just as an earlier author came up with his own list of "rock-bottom, non-negotiable doctrines" in place of the Church's teachings, so Dr. O'Connell comes up with his own version of the moral life reduced to what he calls "children's categories" for "interpersonal living": these are, according to him: play fair, leave other people's stuff alone, tell the truth, don't snoop, keep promises.

Not that there is anything wrong with this list as far as

it goes. Children do often have a keen sense of morality and justice on which grace and proper catechesis can build. In this case, however, we have to ask whatever happened to the boast of this book that it represents "Catholic faith for adults"? How can he reduce the moral life in this way and imagine that this reduction is acceptable? St. Paul said: "When I became a man, I gave up childish ways" (1 Cor 13:11), and we can only wonder, confronted with this presentation, why some moral theologians apparently cannot manage the same transition.

## VII

In summary, what can be said about a book such as *The People's Catechism*, styled "Catholic Faith for Adults" and "written by the People of God, for the People of God"? This book is more than just trivial and pedestrian; it is more than just misleading and tendentious; it is simply wrong on many counts.

The sponsors and authors of it have a very serious reality problem. At the very moment when the Catholic Church, with the issuance of her new *Catechism*, has integrally reaffirmed her traditional doctrine and morality in the face of the increasingly disintegrating modernity she encounters in the world all around her, these people stand up and determinedly, almost frantically, come out, in effect, in favor of key aspects of that same modernity!

All of the editors and authors of *PC* hold official positions in ostensibly Catholic entities and institutions. One of them is actually a bishop (although one who previously signaled his negative attitude toward the *Catechism* by contributing a chapter to the notorious *Universal Catechism Reader*). The fact that *PC* is the work of such visible members of the current theological and catechetical establishments in the United States gives this book the appearance of credibility as a possible "local", "inculturated" catechism of the kind that even Pope John Paul II has said needs to be prepared.

But this book is not one of them. The kind of local catechisms John Paul II had in mind were to be based on the *Catechism of the Catholic Church*; they were to bring the Church's faith to the culture, not water down the Church's faith in the interest of accommodating the culture.

What the authors and editors of *PC* have produced, however, is a caricature of a real catechism, a parody. Just as Voltaire once quipped that the Holy Roman Empire was neither holy, Roman, nor an empire, so this book does not present the Catholic faith, nor is it for adults; nor, in fact, is it a catechism.

CHAPTER NINE

# "*What Shall We Do?*"
# (*Acts 2:37*)

I

A new bookstore recently opened on the lower level of the National Shrine of the Immaculate Conception near Catholic University in Washington, D.C. The shrine is visited by many thousands of pilgrims each year and has long since become one of the most visible and abiding symbols of the public affirmation of the Catholic faith in the United States. A quality bookstore offering good Catholic books on this site seems to fill an obvious need. The wonder is perhaps that a good Catholic bookstore was not a part of the Shrine complex from the beginning. When this bookstore was finally opened in 1995, it was dedicated with great fanfare by Cardinal James Hickey of Washington.

It was gratifying on one's first visit to the Shrine bookstore to see an enormous display table in the center of the store piled high with copies of the *Catechism of the Catholic Church*. There were stacks of them in the original hardcover and trade paperback editions and more stacks of the newer mass-market paperback edition. The *Catechism* was also available in Spanish. For more in-depth study, boxed copies were available containing the *Catechism*, together with the Ignatius Press Ratzinger-Schönborn *Introduction* to it,[1] and the same publisher's *Companion* volume,[2] containing the texts of the 3600 references in the *Catechism* to Scripture, conciliar texts, papal documents, and the writings of the saints and of the Fathers.

The whole display was another heartening sign that the *Catechism* continues to be taken very seriously by many Catholics in the United States—no sign of any neglect or downplaying of it here! It is to be hoped that the Shrine bookstore's diligence and imagination in mounting this display has been rewarded by hundreds of individual sales of the *Catechism* to the crowds of pilgrims from all over who regularly visit the Shrine of the Immaculate Conception.

Any genuine effort to promote the *Catechism*, of course, would also want to promote and provide the appropriate tools for further study and mastery of it. This proved to be the case here too. In addition to the *Catechism* itself, there were also stacks of the various commentaries on it that have appeared in English to date. The commentaries were neither as numerous nor as prominently displayed as the *Catechism* itself. Nevertheless they were there, and precisely for the serious student or reader who wished to go more deeply into the *Catechism*.

There was *The Catechism: Highlights & Commentary*, by Brennan Hill and William Madges.[3] There was the *Commentary on the Catechism of the Catholic Church*, edited by Michael

---

[1] Joseph Cardinal Ratzinger and Christoph Schönborn, *Introduction to the Catechism of the Catholic Church* (San Francisco: Ignatius Press, 1994).

[2] *The Companion to the Catechism of the Catholic Church: A Compendium of the Texts Referred to in the Catechism of the Catholic Church* (San Francisco: Ignatius Press, 1994).

[3] See Chapter Five.

J. Walsh.[4] There was *Exploring the Catechism* by Jane E. Regan.[5] Nor would this collection of "tools" to "help" the reader of the *Catechism* have been complete without Fr. Berard L. Marthaler's volume arising out of a conference on the neighboring Catholic University campus: *Introducing the Catechism of the Catholic Church: Traditional Themes and Contemporary Issues.*[6]

All these books were there. A couple of them were even featured in the Shrine bookstore's front display window, along with the *Catechism* itself. No one could have been faulted for imagining that all these volumes were wholly legitimate aids to the study of the *Catechism*. (*The People's Catechism* had not yet been published at the time of the visit to the Shrine bookstore.)

Of course the Shrine bookstore could never be criticized for stocking and displaying these commentaries, either. How could it be? They are currently standard items. No doubt they are to be found in many Catholic bookstores right alongside the *Catechism*. All of them are published, after all, by seemingly mainstream publishers who stay in business publishing Catholic books: the Liturgical Press, the Paulist Press, Twenty-Third Publications. Two of these publishers are actually copublishers of the *Catechism* itself, licensed by the U.S. bishops.

Anybody who has read the present book up to this point, however, now knows that all these commentaries, far from being "tools" to "help" anyone understand the *Catechism*, are wholly unsuitable for that purpose and seem to have been, in fact, deliberately written to subvert it.

---

[4] See Chapter Six.
[5] See Chapter Seven.
[6] See Chapter Three.

Knowing how easy it is for anyone who ventures to criticize the current theological and catechetical establishments to be labeled "uncharitable", "preconciliar", or even "extremist", we have not been content merely to state the case against these books. We have gone to considerable length to insure that the case is *proved* against them for anyone not antecedently unwilling to recognize that the present catechetical establishment simply does not much like the *Catechism of the Catholic Church* and does not intend to use it to any greater extent than it has to.

Moreover, it is quite evident from what we have seen that many in the current theological and catechetical establishments are using the positions they enjoy within Catholic academia and Catholic education to spread a very different message about the *Catechism* from the Church's message. As often as not, as in the conferences and workshops where they are speakers, or in the classrooms of the institutions where they have tenure, these people are doing this under at least semiofficial Church auspices.

Almost as a matter of course, these rebels against Church authority—for we have certainly shown them to be that— are being aided and abetted in their efforts at subversion of the *Catechism* by established institutions that insist on bearing the name "Catholic", and accepting contributions from Catholic donors, even while they reject any oversight from the Church. They are similarly being aided and abetted by mainstream publishers who benefit enormously from their sales in the Catholic market.

We need only consider the situation: the Pope and the bishops go to enormous lengths and exert huge efforts over nearly seven years in order to produce and publish a *Catechism*. No sooner have they solemnly presented the results of all their labors to the Catholic people and, definitively, said, "this is your faith", than prominent leaders among the very people the bishops have "sent out"—whose salaries for the most part continue to be at least indirectly paid by the contributions of the Catholic people—immediately have recourse to all means available to them to reply, in effect, "No, it is not!"

And again, it is this dissenting word, rather than the authentic word of the Pope and bishops, that gets out to many of the very people who are involved in religious education. At this point, there are no doubt already considerable numbers of catechists and pastoral ministers who now "know", as a result of the training given them under Church auspices, that the *Catechism* is really no big deal and that anybody who is really "with it" in religious education will want to continue looking elsewhere for the "answers" (if there are any "answers").

In public administration terms, what we have here is a case where many "staff", or members of specialized bureaucracies, have broken loose in significant ways from the oversight or supervision that the "line", or executive function, is supposed to exercise over them. In a formal sense and in some significant ways, of course, the executive function does continue to remain over them, if only in the sense that the Pope and the bishops still retain the ultimate power to appoint or dismiss them.

But in other important ways (that is, with respect to the content of the faith being imparted), the "staff", or bureaucratically delegated catechetical functions within the Church, are currently both disposed and able to escape effective "line" control on a fairly wide scale, indeed, just about wherever they decide to do it, it seems. In other words, the overseers are often not overseeing what is actually being taught; they are over*looking* it!

Instead of responding to the very clear direction the hierarchy of the Church has given in issuing the *Catechism*, many members of the Church's specialized knowledge class are instead looking to other specialists for their primary guidance and direction. Thus, the catechetical establishment currently looks to the theological establishment for its basic guidance, while the latter presumes to establish its own standards and criteria for faith, supposedly based on scholarly and scientific considerations and conclusions.

In the case of modern catechesis, other elements in the Church besides those directly involved in teaching can be equally deceived in the present climate. Catholic book publishers, for example, can be similarly co-opted and, as the most natural thing in the world, can begin looking to the current theological establishment for basic guidance concerning what should be published. There appears to be no indication whatsoever on the part of the publishers of the books we have examined in these pages, for example, that these publishers ever saw anything untoward at all in coming out in the wake of the *Catechism* with commentaries trashing it. Nor did the typical reviewers of these books apparently see anything unusual about it either.

There appears to be a whole "culture" out there, in fact, that now simply takes "dissent" and "private judgment" for granted where Catholic doctrine is concerned. And often nobody even appears to question this state of affairs; eyebrows are only generally raised, not at what the dissenters are doing, but at anybody who might venture to call attention to or to criticize *them*. The psychology is the same as that found in the First Book of Kings, where the people had turned away from the Lord to worship idols. When the prophet Elijah called attention to this unfortunate state of affairs, King Ahab taxed *him* with being the "troubler of Israel" (1 Kings 18:17).

How widespread is the overall problem of dissent and disloyalty in the Church's current religious-education system? As we have noted, this question cannot be answered with statistical accuracy. But we have surely demonstrated in this book that the problem is widespread enough to compromise significantly the implementation of the *Catechism* that is currently underway. Orders may have been issued to implement the *Catechism* all right, but how are these orders being carried out?

We do hasten to add, though, that the problem is not universal. The *Catechism of the Catholic Church* has already proved to be an outstanding success in the United States in incalculable ways, as it has been around the world. It has been widely received by the Catholic people with both gratitude and enthusiasm. It is manifestly going to make its own way in the world; it has already caught on in crucially important ways. Nor can all the subversive commentaries on it taken together even begin to compete with it (although they can, we repeat, do significant damage to the proper implementation of it).

It is also true, moreover, that the commentaries we have examined in this book are not the only ones available. There are some other commentaries out there that are quite good, expounding and explaining the document in a way that really is helpful to the loyal Catholic who wants to understand and assimilate the *Catechism*. There truly are, in other words, proper tools out there to help the bishop, pastor, teacher, or catechist desirous of understanding the faith better and teaching it authentically, according to the new *Catechism*.

In the category of good commentaries on the *Catechism of the Catholic Church*, we mention in particular the book

*Essentials of the Faith*, which Fr. Alfred McBride, O.Præm., originally wrote as a series of articles in *Our Sunday Visitor*.[7] There is also Fr. James Tolhurst's *A Concise Companion & Commentary for the New Catholic Catechism*, published both in the United States and in the United Kingdom.[8] It is gratifying to be able to report that both of these books were also available among those on display at the National Shrine bookstore. We earnestly hope that these two volumes have been outselling the other commentaries offered!

Another outstanding commentary, on the doctrinal part of the *Catechism* only, is the book published in Scotland by Fr. Aidan Nichols, O.P., called *The Splendour of Doctrine: The Catechism of the Catholic Church on Christian Believing*.[9] Fr. Nichols' thoughtful commentary clearly brings out what a solid and in-depth work the *Catechism* really is, in spite of the allegations of its detractors to the contrary.

For anybody involved in religious education who is serious about truly implementing the *Catechism*, two other books on display at the Shrine bookstore would also be helpful. One of them is the very concise and readable guide that Msgr. Francis D. Kelly has written entitled *The Mystery We Proclaim*.[10] Msgr. Kelly was one of the forty inter-

---

[7] Alfred McBride, O.Præm., *Essentials of the Faith: A Guide to the Catechism of the Catholic Church* (Huntington, Ind.: Our Sunday Visitor Publishing Division, 1994).

[8] James Tolhurst, *A Concise Companion & Commentary for the New Catholic Catechism* (Leominster, Herefordshire: Gracewing, and Westminster, Md.: Christian Classics, 1994).

[9] Aidan Nichols, O.P., *The Splendour of Doctrine: The Catechism of the Catholic Church on Christian Believing* (Edinburgh, Scotland: T & T Clark, 1995).

[10] Msgr. Francis D. Kelly, *The Mystery We Proclaim: Catechesis at the Third Millennium* (Huntington, Ind.: Our Sunday Visitor, 1993).

national consultors for the writing of the *Catechism of the Catholic Church.*[11] This little book not only warns about and gently steers the religious educator away from some of the excesses and errors of recent catechesis; it also outlines a solid and serious methodology for teaching the faith in the new era inaugurated by the *Catechism.* This is the kind of book that needs to be in the hands of all DREs in this new era.

Another book that turned out to be something of a pleasant surprise for the present writers is Fr. Robert J. Hater's *New Vision, New Directions: Implementing the Catechism of the Catholic Church.*[12] This book was commissioned by the National Conference of Catechetical Leadership (NCCL), one of the strongholds of the catechetical establishment, and it was published by a publisher whose catechetical offerings are not uniformly desirable, and so we were initially a little apprehensive about it. In fact, although it is still wedded to some of the typical new catechetical language and approaches, the book seems wholly accepting of the *Catechism* and prepared to implement it properly. Moreover, because of its NCCL sponsorship, it is likely to reach an audience that might not be reached by some of the other good commentaries on the *Catechism.*

These two books represent particularly hopeful signs, since both authors have been in some ways identified with the catechetical establishment in the past. Msgr. Kelly was for many years executive director of the Department of Religious Education for the National Catholic Education As-

---

[11] Listed in *Origins*, CNS Documentary Service, March 8, 1990.

[12] Robert J. Hater, *New Vision, New Directions: Implementing the Catechism of the Catholic Church* (Allen, Tex. and Chicago, Ill.: Thomas More/A Division of Tabor Publishing, 1994).

sociation (NCEA), while Fr. Hater is a professor of religious studies at the University of Dayton. The fact that both have now published important books seriously aimed at implementing the *Catechism* surely indicates that those we have been calling "the new catechists" do not have a monopoly on religious education in this country. Many who can help usher in the new day in religious education that the *Catechism* undoubtedly calls for are also at work and will make a difference in the end.

Yet another good sign that a new and positive spirit is perhaps arising within some of the Church's principal educational organizations is the recent spiral-notebook publication of the National Catholic Educational Association (NCEA) entitled *The New Catholic Catechism: Workshop Resources*, by Sr. Mary Ann Johnston. This is an excellent outline presentation designed to be given in workshops introducing the *Catechism* to teachers and others. Half the publication consists of graphic charts that can be easily reproduced as overhead transparencies; the other half consists of an outline that the presenter can follow in using these same transparencies to introduce the *Catechism*. The presentation is straightforward, accurate, and surprisingly complete. If all catechists were being introduced to the *Catechism* in this manner, we would not have the problem we have been describing in this book. The NCEA and Sr. Johnston have performed a most useful service here.[13]

And then, of course, we also have the fine commentary on the *Catechism* written by Cardinal John O'Connor of New York, based on the series of homilies on the *Catechism* that

---

[13] Sr. Mary Ann Johnston, *The New Catholic Catechism: Workshop Resources*, National Catholic Educational Association, 1077 30th Street, NW, Suite 100, Washington, D.C. 20007–3852.

His Eminence delivered from his cathedral pulpit in the course of the year 1994. This book is entitled *A Moment of Grace*.[14]

Thus, the various signs on the reception and implementation front for the *Catechism* are not entirely negative. In addition to the very imposing fact of the *Catechism* itself, its outstanding excellence and utility, the heartening popular reception it has enjoyed nearly everywhere and the commitment made by the Pope and the bishops to its proper implementation, it is also especially important that there is still to be found at least a nucleus among the Church's "staff" specialists today who are prepared to respond positively to the direction given by the Church's "line" executives, the Catholic bishops. This is something the Church can definitely build on.

## II

Although the reception given to the *Catechism of the Catholic Church* may be considered quite favorable from a certain point of view, the evidence examined and evaluated in this book points to a much more troubling overall conclusion. In spite of the favorable factors we have noted, significant numbers of theologians and religious educators who, in normal times, would have been considered the bishops' first line of support in implementing the *Catechism*, nevertheless today do not, on the evidence, appear to accept the *Catechism*. They not only do not accept it; they do not intend to implement it in any real sense; some of them intend to

---

[14] Cardinal John O'Connor, *A Moment of Grace* (San Francisco: Ignatius Press, 1995).

prevent or subvert its proper implementation to the extent they can.

The evidence we have accumulated in these pages in support of this negative conclusion is quite strong. We could have, and we could still, adduce yet further evidence in the same vein. Any expectations the Catholic bishops or the Catholic people may have entertained that the present theological and catechetical establishments would accept and automatically help implement the *Catechism* can now be seen to be flawed expectations.

Those within the Church's professional or knowledge classes who do not accept the *Catechism*—or, alas, among the Catholic people who follow their lead—basically do not accept the *Catechism* because they no longer accept the Catholic Church. Or, to be a little more specific, they do not accept the Church for what she really is.

It was Vatican Council II that said it: "The Catholic Church is by the will of Christ the teacher of truth. It is her duty to proclaim and teach with authority the truth which is Christ and, at the same time, to declare and confirm by her authority the principles of the moral order which spring from human nature itself."[15]

This is what the Council teaches, but today's typical dissenters, with all their talk about implementing Vatican II, no longer really accept that what the Church teaches is, precisely, truth. In their view, the Church can no longer issue catechisms that bind or obligate people for the simple reason that the Church can no longer teach binding truth at all. The Church may all the while remain a "community of believers" in some sense, never well defined; but, like some

---

[15] Vatican Council II, Declaration on Religious Liberty, *Dignitatis Humanæ*, no. 14.

Protestant communions that reject any official Church Magisterium, or teaching authority, the *regula fidei* that is still supposed to be professed by this "believing community" is no longer really enforceable. Nor, prudently, does anyone attempt to enforce it. Nor, sadly, do many of those who perhaps go on professing their belief in "the holy Catholic Church" when they recite the Creed any longer think real belief in what the Church teaches to be a requirement for membership in the "believing community".

What this means is that truth can no longer be defined and proclaimed with any certitude. Henceforth truth is understood as something that is merely sought after or searched for, usually by employing scientific methods of inquiry and verification. God forbid, however, that anyone should ever claim to have found truth! Or should ever claim to be able to teach it, as the Church in fact claims to be able to do. These things are held by the modern mind to be contradictions in terms.

This view of truth has pretty much reigned in our society at large since the eighteenth-century Enlightenment. The Church has strongly and steadily resisted it, but it nevertheless gained a substantial foothold among Catholics, particularly educated Catholics, at the time of Pope Paul VI's 1968 encyclical *Humanæ Vitæ*. When the Pope publicly reiterated the Church's constant teaching condemning artificial methods of birth control, and declared that each and every marriage act must be open to the transmission of life, he obviously went against the nearly universal contrary opinion of the modern world.

"And they laughed at him" (Mt 9:24; Mk 5:40; Lk 8:53): the position the Pope espoused against artificial birth control was considered to be not only false but almost too ludicrous for words. Open dissent against this papal teaching proved to be nearly as massive inside the Church as it was outside the Church, although the position on birth control that the Pope was reiterating had been the universal position of all Christian believers up to the year 1929, when the Church of England's Lambeth Conference broke ranks on it for the first time in Christian history. Since then, of course, most Christian denominations have been tripping over each other in the rush to approve the contemporary secular view of birth control as a great boon to humanity. The Holy See was virtually alone in its opposition to that view, a position providential for the Catholic Church as a whole.

Many Catholic theologians and many others in the Church's knowledge class, however, instead judged the Church's stand on birth control to be anachronistic if not simply ridiculous. Many of these same people soon decided that what the whole *Humanæ Vitæ* affair really proved was that the Church's Magisterium could err. If the Church's Magisterium could err, it followed as a necessary consequence that the Church was not the teacher of truth, as Vatican II had claimed. For, in their opinion, the Church had now grievously erred in the view of the whole world. And no Church that had so dramatically missed the boat on birth control could possibly be thought to "bind" people's beliefs and practices on any other matters, it was decided.

Henceforth many theologians and members of the Church's knowledge class therefore came to believe that *they* now had to become the interpreters and arbiters of what had to be believed and affirmed in the Church. The hierarchical Magisterium had now dramatically failed in the task, in their view, and somebody had to take up the slack. And thus it came to be thought that the many great and controversial questions that concerned and often divided people would now have to be decided on the basis of acquired specialized knowledge and expertise. If that were the case, it was only logical to conclude that the experts and specialists, not the pope and the bishops, would have to be the ones to decide henceforth.

In addition to this Neomodernist approach to Church doctrine, the experts and specialists, along with many educated Catholics generally, also took a new approach to society and to the world. At Vatican II, to repeat a common comparison, the Church "opened up the windows" to the world. Pope John XXIII and the Council Fathers probably intended this action to allow the light of Christ to shine out, as *Lumen Gentium* declares. In practice, however, most people have interpreted it as meaning that the winds from the world and from the culture should blow in, and this is exactly the position most of the members of the theological and catechetical establishments have adopted.

In conformity with this secular outlook, they now equate social activism with Christian action; they are better-worlders. Following Vatican II, they decided that building a better world was the real point of Christianity, and hence they have quite consciously tried to move away from Christianity as salvation from sin and happiness in heaven and move toward social activism and building a better world. This is yet another reason why they are impatient with "mere" doctrinal questions, as they see them.

The principal task of religious education in the new perspective they have adopted is precisely to move people away from their old preoccupations with avoiding sin and saving their souls, considered self-centered, and to orient them toward better-world activism. Suddenly, in this new perspective, even the notions of sin and wrong-doing, thought to have been laid aside along with other hidebound doctrines, have suddenly been revived in a new way and once again represent something to be eschewed and shunned: sin and wrong-doing are now equated with "conservatism" or "traditionalism"—usually equated simply with "extremism". People with "extremist" views do *not* believe in a better world. That is why it is possible to be "judgmental" about *them*; they have transgressed the bounds of what is now acceptable to modern enlightened progressives.

The idea of building a better world, of course, has been the core idea of a number of modern ideologies virtually since the time of the eighteenth-century Enlightenment. Some of these ideologies have had ample opportunity to show what they could do toward actually bringing a better world into being. Nevertheless, as everybody knows, the world has not become noticeably better. Nor does it seem that anything that post-Vatican-II liberated Catholics are likely to add to the mix will contribute significantly to a world that really is better. However, people who have been taken over by ideologies are sometimes not notably discouraged by a lack of any real results.

However that may be, these are the kinds of basic attitudes, as we have seen, that pervade most of the commentaries on the *Catechism* that we have studied and cited in this book. These attitudes have become so general in the current theological and catechetical establishments that for the most part they are no longer even argued. They are now simply taken for granted, along with the really basic idea that it is now the trained experts who have to decide for Catholics, where formerly the pope and the bishops decided. This attitude was already well established among the Church intelligentsia long before the *Catechism* came along. The new theologians and the new catechists, almost in direct proportion to their formal theological training, seem utterly convinced of it and have long since been acting upon it.

But they are wrong. The Church has not ceased to be "the pillar and bulwark of the truth" (1 Tim 3:15). The Magisterium of the Church has not ceased to teach this same truth. The Magisterium has been right all along, in fact, and was so in *Humanæ Vitæ* as well. It is the modern world that is now visibly afflicted, is possibly even dying, of the disease identified by Pope Paul VI in this encyclical: the belief that the use of sex can be artificially separated from its natural life-giving potential. Today's virulent epidemics of divorce, abortions, fatherless families, sexually transmitted diseases consequent upon promiscuity, including and especially AIDS—all these modern plagues stem directly from the erroneous modern belief that the human sexual faculty can be electively used as people today decide they want to use it, while its procreative dimension is suppressed by artificial contraceptive means (and by abortion if and when these means fail, as they regularly do).

For the moment, the modern world has completely bought into the belief in the necessity and efficacy of contraceptives; and one of the other results of this belief is that among most Western, formerly Christian, formerly Catholic, nations, the birth rate has now fallen below replacement levels, so that the very future of the world—and the Church—is going to be very different from the past.

Pope Paul VI warned in *Humanæ Vitæ* of the catastrophic consequences that would follow upon the general separation of the procreative dimension of sexuality from its unitive dimension. These consequences have not failed to follow in the modern world at large just as the Pope predicted. The encyclical *Humanæ Vitæ* has proved to be one of the watershed events of our times. Meanwhile, though, the defection of a substantial part of the Church's educated knowledge class over the encyclical meant that these Catholics were abandoning the Church for the world at the very moment when the world was entering upon a perhaps irreversible slippery slope of moral corruption and bankruptcy.

Many of these same members of the Catholic knowledge class still remain in a 1960s time warp. For them the only thing that Pope Paul VI's encyclical supposedly proved was how badly the Church's Magisterium could err. This is pretty much where many of them stand today as far as the *Catechism* is concerned: If the Magisterium can err, the *Catechism* can err, and it is up to them, therefore, to say the way things should be. If the *Catechism* can err, then the task is to read it "critically", rather than accept it gratefully as a gift from Christ's Church. And many of these same experts believe that the *Catechism* has erred in important ways, as we have noted in some of the texts we have reviewed.

Obviously this current problem of the *trahison des clercs*, or "treason of the intellectuals", with regard to the *Catechism*, is far more serious than any mere question of variant "theologies" or "methodologies". It turns out that some "theologies" are simply incompatible with the faith that has been handed down and is now set forth in the *Catechism* (some "methodologies" are incompatible with it too, for that matter). As a result of the *trahison des clercs*, it is now to be feared that the Church is faced with an enormous problem, perhaps one on a much more serious scale than dissent from *Humanæ Vitæ*, since, with the *Catechism*, we are dealing with the Church's statement of her own basic faith.

Dissent from this *Catechism* would seem to place someone strictly outside the bounds of Catholicism. Yet many who do dissent from it are the very people who are supposed to be primarily responsible for its implementation. How is the Church ever going to resolve this dilemma?

Our contemporary culture tells us that we must generally not be "judgmental" about people, even when they err. This common contemporary viewpoint, by the way, is *not* the same thing as the old Christian idea of loving the sinner while hating the sin. (For one thing, our contemporary culture no longer appears to hate the sin all that much.) In its common "Christian" or "Catholic" version today, this modern attitude against being judgmental is frequently equated with being "charitable". And being thought guilty of "uncharitableness" today, in fact, soon effectively removes people from having their views even taken into consideration.

Today's strong cultural reluctance to be judgmental (except in the case of "extremists" who flout the accepted *Zeitgeist*) very often means in practice that people within organizations can no longer really be disciplined for failing to follow the organization's line; they are sincere, after all, and who is to judge them? This phenomenon is by no means confined to the Church. It is, we repeat, a strong feature of our contemporary culture, and people often act in accordance with it without entirely realizing they are doing so; it just seems to be the natural and logical thing to do.

We should learn to recognize the sources of this attitude in the contemporary secular culture, however, and we should not imagine or be persuaded that it arises out of some Gospel imperative of "charity" toward those who are out of line. The fact is that both justice and truth can be denied when people come to be automatically excused out of charity, no matter what they do.

This reluctance of our culture to judge the actual behavior of people is matched in importance today by another one of our contemporary culture's strong imperatives, namely, the idea that substantive matters must normally be left to "the experts in the field". Heads of organizations are not supposed to meddle in the "technical details" (such as, for instance, what is actually in the new religion books or actually being taught in the classroom). This almost reflexive confidence in professional expertise can be combined with yet another idea also considered almost beyond dispute in our era, namely, that the one in charge of an organization must first choose the right people, then delegate responsibility to them, and give them their head. Attempting to "micro-manage" what they do is considered counterproductive, as is failing to defend them against criticisms that come from the outside. Americans in particular are inveterate "delegators" in this fashion, as they tend also to be belligerent defenders of "their people".

If we take only these three common contemporary cultural factors—the reluctance to be judgmental, the reliance on experts in the field, and our typical contemporary practice of delegating and automatically backing those to whom responsibility is delegated—we will come very close to explaining the difficulties we currently face with regard to the proper implementation of the *Catechism of the Catholic Church* in the United States.

At many levels in the Church's religious-education structure, bishops, pastors, school principals, and DREs at both the diocesan and parish levels have generally been content to appoint people with the proper degrees or training to the varied tasks involved in teaching the faith. Then they have simply left them to carry out those tasks as they saw fit. More, they have generally reacted almost reflexively to any criticism of anything amiss in religious education by vigorously defending those who are now their "own people", and hence they have been quick to dismiss the critics as troublemakers and especially as "uncharitable" ("troublers of Israel"). To give credence to such critics would automatically call into question their own selection and delegation procedures.

We surmise that it is probably a rare bishop or pastor who has ever responded to criticisms of what was going on in religious education by, for example, actually sitting down and reading through—forming his own personal judgment about—many of our contemporary religion texts (or sex-education texts!).

We also surmise that it has probably been equally rare for a bishop or pastor really to *listen* to what many of the critics have been trying to say about these contemporary religion texts. By and large critics have been effectively dismissed simply by accepting the contention of the new catechists that any possible critics would necessarily have to be people not wanting to implement Vatican II or, most likely, people "hung up" on the old *Baltimore Catechism* methods by which *they* once learned the faith—people who are, in short, "extremists" by definition in the contemporary understanding of things.

Thus, in this kind of climate, any religion books complained about have simply been passed back for evaluation to the same people trained by the same current catechetical establishment that was responsible for these defective books in the first place.

Yet nearly everyone is prepared to agree in general that religious education in the postconciliar era has not been particularly successful. It is only when someone attempts to get to the specifics of *why* it has not been successful that the system suddenly seems to break down and end in inaction, suspicions, and recriminations. Yet it would seem to be a transparently simple idea to take some of the products of the current catechetical establishment and determine, first, *if* these products adequately contain and convey the faith and, if not, *why* they do not.

Pursuing this very elementary idea, the present authors, in order to write this book, simply sat down and went through a few of the books recently published in English supposedly commenting on or implementing the *Catechism of the Catholic Church*. What we discovered, of course, was a persistent *pattern* of not very carefully concealed dissent from Church teachings and defiance of Church authority on the part of many in the same professional Church circles that should be most directly involved in implementing the *Catechism*. Indeed, a veritable *culture* of dissent and of doing one's own thing appears to exist in the Church's current theological and catechetical establishments where the *Catechism* is concerned.

Nor is this the first time in history that a specialized class or elite, or bureaucracy has broken loose from the authority structure over it and tried to go it alone, charting its own distinctive path. It is a consistent feature of modern *revolutions* from 1789 on, as a matter of fact, that a segment of the elite or knowledge class revolts against, declares its independence from, and tries to usurp the functions of those in authority. The well-known expression *trahison des clercs*, which we have employed, vividly describes the recurring reality of what happens in this kind of revolutionary situation.

Moreover, this same sort of thing has occurred before in ecclesiastical settings. Dramatic examples of it can precisely be seen in the evolution of some modern mainline Protestant churches from orthodoxy to Modernism in recent times. Lacking an episcopacy or papacy, the leadership of some of these churches has sometimes been unable to resist the influence of liberalizing and modernizing elements.

A common feature in such Modernist revolutions (or take-overs) has been launching a crusade against perceived "fundamentalists" in the name of the latest scholarship. These "fundamentalists", meanwhile, have usually included anybody continuing to hold to the communion's orthodox rule of faith. Nor have the "moderates" in these controversies ever proved very helpful by going around counseling moderation and even appeasement lest irreconcilable positions permanently damage the communion; such moderate positions have usually just facilitated the liberal takeover.[16]

The typical result of victories by the Modernists and the liberalizers in such contests has generally been the evacuation of any real meaning and truth from the basic Christian revelation preserved in sacred Scripture. "Liberal theology can really have no meaning," writes one Calvinist author, "since every liberal theologian speaks only for himself." In one such case, some New England Congregational churches, which had abandoned orthodoxy, asked for a statement of the things they now believed and even threatened to depose a minister for believing something else besides what they had been contending for. They were loftily rebuked for this by William Ellery Channing ("the first American humanist"), who logically pointed out that "liberality and tolerance was [sic] now their creed. Progress was to be the life and end of [their] movement."

Channing objected to any creed, as still found in the evangelical churches, because, he wrote:

> They separate us from Christ; because they are skeletons, freezing abstractions, metaphysical expressions of unin-

---

[16] See, for example, Bradley J. Longfield, *The Presbyterian Controversy: Fundamentalists, Modernists, and Moderates* (New York and Oxford: Oxford University Press, 1991).

telligible dogmas; because Christian truth is infinite and cannot be confined within the limits of human creeds; and because the very idea of a creed involves the idea of Church authority, and this [hinders] the simplicity of individual religious faith and life.[17]

Dr. Channing was correct about the next to the last part: "The very idea of a creed involves the idea of Church authority." This is a truth that some of our Neomodernist new theologians and new catechists seem to understand instinctively—and hence they immediately enter the lists to combat it. This paragraph by Dr. Channing could surely have been composed, for example, by any one of a number of the commentators on the *Catechism* whose work we have considered in previous chapters; we have quoted some comparable sentences and paragraphs that some of them *did* write, as a matter of fact.

# III

Theologians or religious educators who have evidently come to disbelieve in the Church's teachings as set forth, for example, in the Church's creeds and now, in considerable detail, in the *Catechism of the Catholic Church*, might in one sense normally be expected to want to leave the Catholic Church. The Church, after all, no longer represents or accepts what they *do* now appear to believe. We have now reviewed the work of a number of theologians and religious educators professedly engaged in explaining or implement-

---

[17] Winfield Burggraaff, Th.D., *The Rise and Development of Liberal Theology in America* (New York: Board of Publication and Bible School Work of the Reformed Church in America, 1928), 79–80.

ing the Church's new authoritative *Catechism*. On the evidence of their own statements, some of these people frankly appear to disbelieve some, or much, of what the *Catechism* nevertheless declares to be true and to be the normative belief of the Church, incumbent upon all those who profess the Creed, if they are really going to remain Catholics in the full sense.

Why do people who have reached this point in their faith life stay in the Catholic Church? The Church has now, in the *Catechism*, definitively come out with a version of the faith they evidently do not accept, again on the evidence of their own words in their commentaries on the *Catechism*. At the same time, the Church has rejected, at least by implication, the versions of the faith many of them think should be the wave of the future in the brave new Church they envisage. In this situation, must it not finally be considered rather futile if not actually dishonest for them to continue going through the motions of professing or propounding a faith they do not, in fact, believe in or accept?

It would seem so. Nevertheless, the fact that theology or religious education may still be their profession, or, indeed, their *life*, does not make it easy for them to move on. Anyway, many voices among their professional colleagues still continue to repeat, against the evidence, that it is the Church that is going to be transformed by the new theology and the new catechesis. For such people it is thought to be just a matter of waiting.

"We are everywhere", repeat the voices of the revisionist faith (which, however, did *not* get written into the new *Catechism*!): "We still control the theological faculties and edit the theological journals. We make the decisions about academic appointments and tenure; we write the textbooks; we train the teachers; we tell the bishops and pastors how things are supposed to be done in religious education today", these same voices go on. "We are also the ones who keep any critics, preconciliar in their outlook, at arm's length. We continue, in short, to *run* religious education today."

"All that has to happen", these same voices keep telling each other, "is one single puff of white smoke. One of *ours* will eventually be elected pope; he will take the name of John XXIV; and he will then proceed to ratify, finally, all that we have been doing and saying over the past thirty years. At that point nobody will have to worry any longer about aging Italian popes with hang-ups from the past— or about 'conservative' popes from Poland who simply do not 'get it' about how the brave new Church needs to accommodate itself to the modern world. At that point, too, nobody will ever have to take the *Catechism of the Catholic Church* off the shelf again—off that shelf where we have meanwhile made sure it is placed."

It is an interesting scenario. Pope St. Pius X already understood why the original Modernists wanted to stay in the Church in his day, in spite of the fact that the Church certainly did not seem to be moving very fast toward adopting any of their new beliefs or agendas, anymore than the Church is moving in that direction today. The saintly Pope, implacable foe of the Modernists, wrote: "It is necessary for them to remain within the ranks of the Church in order that they may gradually transform the collective conscience."[18]

Thus, some who may have come to disbelieve in the Church, as she continues to declare herself in the *Catechism* to be, do not leave the Church because it is evidently their intention to stay and try to *transform* her from within.

---

[18] Pope St. Pius X, encyclical letter *Pascendi Dominici Gregis*, September 8, 1907, no. 27.

The Church cannot be transformed from within, they reason, *unless* they remain within her. In some ways, this idea of remaining within the Church in order to transform her from within can even take on a certain plausibility. A recent fund-raising letter from a group of progressive Catholic activists, for example, assures potential contributors that:

> Your voice is needed to speak out for change. . . . Make no mistake about it: whether change comes with John Paul II or after his tenure, it will be the incessant and resounding chorus of Catholic voices from the grassroots that sends the message of renewal to church leadership, including those who will elect the next pontiff.[19]

But this is not going to happen. The fact that the *Catechism of the Catholic Church* has now been written and issued constitutes perhaps the largest single contemporary proof that Christ's promise to the Church has not failed and will not fail. For over thirty years, a significant portion of the Church's intellectual class has been pressing very hard to get modified or dropped certain Catholic doctrines held to be incompatible with a Neomodernism itself believed to be the wave of the future for a Christianity "reunited" on the basis of a lowest common denominator of "faith", and also reconciled in other important ways to the typical imperatives of the modern world. Indeed, some of the members of this revisionist intellectual class in the Church have sometimes talked and acted as if this desired "transformation" of the Church had *already* taken place.

Instead, the Church has come out with a *Catechism* expressly reaffirming every single Catholic doctrine that the new theologians wanted and expected to be changed. Typical

---

[19] "Catholics Speak Out", a program of the Quixote Center, Hyattsville, Md., July-September 1995.

"expectations" in *their* camp have turned out to be "flawed" —just as the Church's expectations that her theologians would stand behind the new *Catechism* as a matter of course have proved to be flawed. It turns out that the Pope and the bishops themselves are the "fundamentalists" whom the progressives and revisionists are obliged to combat.

But they cannot win. The real battle for the Church's faith, in fact, is already over and won: the *Catechism* has been issued in its present form containing an authentic statement of the faith in its fullness. Henceforth this will be the undeniable *standard* by which questions of the faith will have to be judged. As the years go by, the *Catechism* will be used and accepted even more widely than it is already, and simply because it is there. Meanwhile, it is safe to predict, the kinds of commentaries and parodies of the *Catechism* we have been looking at in this book will surely soon be *forgotten*.

Those who reject the *Catechism* are the ones who stand self-condemned. They, along with the audiences and adherents they so often manage to find only because of the positions they unfortunately happen to occupy within the Church's educational structure, will become increasingly irrelevant in a Church that, meanwhile, will be moving forward on the right path in very great part on the basis of the new impetus provided by the *Catechism*.

It is not that these people have not done, and will not continue to do, damage. They have done a lot of damage, as we have unhappily had to document in these pages. Many of them still continue to occupy positions where they can go on inflicting damage. But let us say it very plainly: *They have no hope whatsoever of ever transforming the Church.*

They have no hope of transforming the Church because the Pope and the bishops remain firmly in charge of the Church and continue to enjoy the help of the Holy Spirit in the promulgation of the true faith, in spite of all the considerable efforts that have been made to undermine and supplant their authority. This, indeed, is where the Catholic Church differs from those Protestant churches that *were* successfully subverted and transformed by Modernists and liberals working within them. But this is never going to happen to the Catholic Church. The issuance of the *Catechism* itself is one of the principal contemporary proofs of it: against all the odds, the Church has instead once again reaffirmed her authentic faith.

Therefore, it is the continuing effort to secure the proper reception and implementation of the *Catechism* that has to go on; it has to go on in the face of whatever current obstacles and difficulties may exist. Now that we have what Pope John Paul II has so insistently called the great "gift" that the *Catechism* represents, why should we not try to make use of it for all it is worth?

# APPENDICES

# The Translation of the Catechism

## I

On December 10, 1992, Pope John Paul II officially promulgated the *Catechism of the Catholic Church*, the first "universal" Catholic catechism in over four hundred years. Seven years in preparation by a drafting committee composed of bishops from various parts of the world, the new *Catechism* was presented to the world by the Holy Father in a moving ceremony in Rome in which he called it "a sure and certain standard for the teaching of the faith".

The *Catechism* had already attracted considerable attention in the course of its preparation. Following its promulgation, it quickly became, in the United States at any rate, one of the most popular of all themes for articles, speeches, conferences, symposia, and the like, and the months following its promulgation saw a steady stream of expositions and

This article, originally entitled "The Translation of the *Catechism*", appeared under varying titles in *Crisis*, November 1993 (United States), *AD2000*, November 1993 (Australia), *Le Temps de l'Église*, December 1993 (France), *Challenge*, January 1994 (Canada), *Brandsma Review*, January 1994 (Ireland), and *Faith*, January/February 1994 (United Kingdom). It is reprinted here as written.

explanations and appreciations of the new *Catechism*. Few ecclesiastical subjects have attracted more attention over the past year or so, as a matter of fact, than this particular document. One anomaly, however, considering all the attention steadily being focused upon it, has been that, as week followed week and month followed month after its promulgation, there hasn't really *been* any "document".

That's right. The official text of the *Catechism* has not been available in English. Nor, as of the time of this writing, is it yet known when an English version will be available. All of those who have written or spoken about it have had to work from the French text, which was the official text promulgated by the Holy Father. The document was originally written in French, apparently, because that proved to be the best common medium for the bishops from various countries who were writing it. It was expected that translations into all the major languages would quickly follow the publication of the French text, and this has proved to be the case for such languages as German, Italian, and Spanish. A common English version for the whole English-speaking world was known to be in preparation as well.

By the summer of 1993, however, no English translation had yet made its appearance, prompting the American bishops themselves to urge Rome to approve an English translation expeditiously. But it seemed that Rome was not to be hurried in the matter. Although public indications were sparse, several news stories did appear, confirming rumors that the English translation was being held up—in the Congregation for the Doctrine of the Faith, no less.

Considering all the fanfare and ballyhoo which had accompanied the preparation and promulgation of the *Catechism* worldwide, its continued nonappearance in English could not help creating something of an anticlimax, if not constituting an embarrassment. In some quarters, the continuing delay even gave rise to the expression of various "anti-Roman" sentiments, since the CDF was neither releasing the translation now known to exist, nor was it issuing statements or calling press conferences, American style, to explain what the hold-up was all about. The whole affair could thus be viewed as one more example of Rome adopting the stance of "never apologize, never explain", meanwhile leaving everybody hanging.

## II

The writers of this article have both been professionally engaged, among other pursuits, in translating books on Catholic subjects from French into English. Both of us have also long since had the occasion to go over the entire *Catechism of the Catholic Church* in French. As a result of our perusal and study of this document, we are entirely in agreement with Pope John Paul II that this new *Catechism* is "a precious, splendid, profound, and timely gift for all". We yield to none in our eagerness to see this magnificent document made available in English; and, especially, made the new basis of the teaching of religion in Catholic religious instruction at all levels in this country.

However, we have now also been in a position to read and study the translation of the *Catechism* that was made for English-speaking Catholics—the one still being held up by the CDF in Rome as we write. Regretfully, we have not been reassured by what we have found in this translation.

Speaking primarily as translators—although also as educators, another pursuit in which we have both long been professionally involved—we are obliged to judge this translation to be a very bad one. If this translation had been successfully foisted off on the English-speaking world as the *Catechism of the Catholic Church*, in the form in which we have studied it and in which apparently it went to the CDF for approval, we believe it would actually have brought discredit upon the whole *Catechism* enterprise, to the detriment of the faith and the Church.

In our opinion, the CDF will be seen to have performed an outstanding service for the Church by insisting upon holding this translation up. The text of it is in very serious need of correction on not a few points, and many not unimportant ones. Whatever the embarrassment flowing from the long delay, the embarrassment of coming out with an English version of the *Catechism* reflecting so imperfectly the text which the Holy Father actually approved would have been a very much greater embarrassment. The principal aim of the present article is to bring this out.

Without pretending to be able to deal comprehensively with the translation and its defects within the compass of a single article, we believe that the publication of at least some varied and salient examples of just where and how the translation falls short can and will contribute to greater public understanding and acceptance of what has already proved to be a very long delay in bringing out a usable and acceptable English version of the *Catechism of the Catholic Church*; but it is a delay that will prove to have been justified if the appropriate corrections and revisions are made.

Dozens and even hundreds of other examples of errors in the translation could be cited than the ones we are going to cite in this article. Many of them, individually, no doubt represent small points. Nevertheless some of them do *not* represent small points; and, cumulatively, they do all add up —dismayingly, in fact. Besides, why *not* get the thing right?

It is not an impossible task; and English-speaking Catholics deserve no less.

In the translation which went to the CDF for approval, then, we have found numerous cases where words and phrases have simply not been translated correctly. There are other cases where the English version is evidently not complete; things that are found in the French are not found in the English. There are other cases where things have been added into the English version, apparently on the translator's sole authority. In yet other cases, these "translation" problems turn out to be no mere translation problems; they possess theological and doctrinal significance as well, sometimes major doctrinal significance.

Finally, there is in this translation what turns out to be the simply enormous problem of the so-called "inclusive language" that was unfortunately used in it. Inclusive language is the contemporary term used to describe the avoidance of using "man" or "men", or "he" or "him", when what is meant is "mankind", "everybody", "people in general", "both men and women", "the human race", and so on. Ideological feminists today claim that women are not "included" if "man" or "he" is used in a generic sense; hence language must now be used which, in their view, does "include" them. No longer can we affirm, for instance, that "all men are brothers"; apparently we now have to say that "all men and women are brothers and sisters"—but then what about children, who are neither men nor women? Are *they* left out when contemporary "inclusive language" is used?

This contemporary "inclusive language" is believed by some to be necessary today in spite of the fact that the English language and its Anglo-Saxon ancestor have been using "man" and "he" and the like in a generic sense for well over a thousand years; but that, apparently, does not cut any ice, either with today's ideological feminists or with those fellow travelers of theirs who imagine that these feminists somehow "represent" women and constitute the wave of the future, when everybody will presumably always naturally and automatically say "he and she", "him and her", and so on.

*The Funk and Wagnalls Standard English Dictionary*, published in 1967, defines "man" as: (1) a member of the genus *Homo*; (2) the human race; (3) anyone, indefinitely; and (4) an adult male, as distinguished from a woman or a boy. Today's radical feminist claim amounts to saying that this last definition of "man", given only in the *fourth* place in a standard, recent English dictionary, is the only valid definition. As late as 1986, *Webster's New World Dictionary* was still defining "man" as (1) a human being; (2) the human race; and—in third place this time—(3) an adult male human being. Thus "man", as the English language has always viewed him and still does view him, *already* includes "woman" when used in specific contexts—and the meanings, according to these contexts, are always perfectly understandable by everybody, by the way.

Unfortunately, however, under modern ideological feminist influence, some dictionaries such as *The Random House College Dictionary*, published in 1985, have now taken to listing the definition of "man" as "an adult male human being" as the *first* definition enumerated. But this represents a major, unprecedented novelty. Nor is it necessarily something that is going to last. Moreover, even such dictionaries as the Random House one are nevertheless obliged to list the *other* definitions of "man" as legitimate too—while the call for "inclusive language" implies, precisely, that these other usages of the word "man" are *not* legitimate; otherwise why is it necessary to switch?

The dictionaries could scarcely omit these other meanings, however, since these other meanings do reflect the way English continues to be used, regardless of the preferences of the ideological feminists—who, defying reality, thus refuse to recognize as legitimate the *majority* of those uses of the word "man" which *every* dictionary necessarily does continue to recognize.

Now the problem, for our present purposes, is that French, like English, uses *"l'homme"*, "man", in the same generic way that English does; and the official version of the *Catechism of the Catholic Church* is therefore replete with many hundreds of cases, beginning with the very first numbered paragraph of the document, in which "man" is used precisely in the way that stirs up ideological feminist ire: for the text of this first paragraph of the *Catechism* declares that "God . . . freely created man" (*"l'homme"*)—which the English translation under consideration here renders "God . . . freely created the human race." This same first paragraph goes on to affirm that God is "close to man". The translation gives this as "close to *us*". The passage goes on to affirm that "He gathers all men" (*"tous les hommes"*)—which, as anyone can guess by now, the translation then renders as "God gathers the human race" (note not "He" but "God").

Thus does it appear that the translator, apparently acting in response to the ideological feminist imperative—certainly no principle of translation would ever justify it—has laboriously and relentlessly gone through the entire text of the *Catechism of the Catholic Church* changing "men" to "people" or "humanity" or something of the sort—and adding "sister" wherever "brother" happens to appear—and even repeating the nouns "God" or "Christ" in order to avoid using "He" or "Him" for them as much as possible

—everywhere that such changes are thought to be necessary.

When the *Catechism* teaches (CCC 402) that "all men are implicated in Adam's sin", this becomes, in this translation, "all humanity is implicated in Adam's sin." Later, in the same paragraph, "all men" becomes "all people". In paragraph 543, exactly the same French expression, *tous les hommes*, becomes "everyone". And so on.

This kind of alteration aimed at adding "inclusive language" into the text of the *Catechism* was apparently believed necessary by the translator even in the case of many of the passages quoted from papal and conciliar documents, from the Fathers of the Church, and even from Scripture itself; such a proceeding goes far beyond what could ever be justified as a "translation"; rather, it is an ideological statement.

Nor are the results happy. The text generally ranges from banal through awkward to jarring. Sometimes the results are downright deplorable; other times they are merely absurd. Occasionally the almost maniacal concern which is evident to avoid generic language at all costs can lead to actual distortions and misstatements of Christian revelation and essential Catholic doctrine.

The upshot of all this is that, in the case of this translation, "the Catholic faith that comes to us from the apostles", finds itself joined in a rather crude and uneasy *mésalliance* with a brand of feminist ideology that comes to us from the American sixties. Such an outcome would seem to be a terribly high price to have to pay, apparently in order to attempt to appease a school of contemporary ideological feminist thought, which, for the most part, is bitterly anti-Catholic and hence unappeasable anyway. It is hard to imagine how anyone not blinded by this reigning feminist ideology could ever consider this translation as suitable for the *Catechism of the Catholic Church*.

The CDF should thus clearly not be blamed for holding up this particular translation; the CDF is only doing its plain duty in this instance. Responsibility for the delay belongs rather to those who ever presumed to put forward such a translation as this as anything that could possibly be acceptable for English-speaking Catholics.

## III

There are many words and phrases in the translation which are not correctly translated. *"La plus pure"* does not mean "supreme" in English, as this text translates it (CCC 64); it means "the purest" or "the most pure". A *"différend"* in French does not mean "difference" (CCC 247) but a "point of disagreement". Nor does *"sollicitude"* in French mean "supervision" (CCC 303), but rather the same thing that its cognate means in English. The French verb *"se dévoyer"* basically means "to go astray"; to translate it (CCC 311) as "to become corrupted" is much too strong for the normal usage of this word. French *"services"*, again meaning roughly the same thing as its cognate word in English, is unaccountably translated "ministries" in paragraph 794, while in paragraph 1509, "ministry" is the English word used to translate the French *"charge"* (meaning being made responsible for something). *"Schismes"*, which means exactly the same thing in French as it does in English, is blandly translated "divisions" (CCC 1206); *"symbole"* is wrongly translated as "emblem" instead of "symbol" (CCC 1220). *"Opéré"* is translated as "achieved" instead of "effected" in paragraph 1221, while "achieved" in paragraph 1275 turns out to stand for yet another word, *"s'accomplit"*, which, again, is not the proper rendering. *"Signifier"* does not mean "to express" (CCC 1333) but "to signify".

In paragraph 1532, *"passage"* to eternal life becomes "passover", which is simply ludicrous in English (although *"passing* over" would no doubt be acceptable). *"Offensé"* is translated "attacked" instead of "offended" (CCC 1469). *"Clément"* becomes "gentle" instead of "merciful" or "clement" (CCC 2086). *"Révèle"* does not mean "portray" (CCC 2259); it means "reveal". Nor does *"promesse"* mean "sign" (CCC 2347); it means "promise". In paragraph 1334, *"définitif"* is translated as "conclusive", while in paragraph 1340, the same word is translated as "ultimate"—when all the while the English cognate "definitive" could and should have been used in both cases. And *"biens"*, "goods", most certainly does not mean the same thing as "blessings" (CCC 2590).

Paragraph 2238 speaks of the Christian's "right and sometimes [his] duty"—as we are translating the French here—"of making a just protest against that which may appear harmful to the dignity of persons and the good of the community"; in the translation before us, however, the French *"juste"* in this passage is translated "lawful", which could imply that the kind of protests in question would not be legitimate if they were "against the law"—*not* "lawful", in other words. This kind of translation will not do in a society where abortion, for example, now is "lawful"—and regular protests against it are both necessary and just. The translation, however, rather strangely seems to favor "lawful" in a number of cases where it does not precisely fit. Paragraph 2278, for example, on the subject of euthanasia, speaks of *"les intérêts légitimes"*, "the legitimate interests", of the patient; and, again, the translation renders this as "lawful interests"—which will presumably then no longer obtain as soon as euthanasia is made "lawful", as it has apparently already partially been made so in the Netherlands. "Legitimate interests" is clearly the proper translation here.

All these are examples of mistranslated words. Many other examples could be cited. Many French expressions are likewise not rendered correctly considering the context in which they appear. For example, *"toujours actuelle"* does not mean "ever appropriate", as it is translated in paragraph 1351, but rather "current", or "going on now". Similarly, *"dès maintenant"* does not simply mean "now", as in paragraph 1404, but "from now on" or "henceforth". Nor does *"la présentation des oblats"* in any way mean "the preparation of the altar", as it is translated in the text (CCC 1350); apparently, in the context, it refers to the bringing up of the gifts. Speaking of the Mass as both a sacrificial memorial and a sacred banquet, paragraph 1382 of the translation merely says "both", leaving out the French *"à la fois et inséparablement"*, "at once and inseparably".

Whole clauses or sentences are also sometimes wrongly or misleadingly translated. In paragraph 197, for example, it is stated that "the whole Church . . . communicates the faith to us as the matrix of our faith." Besides being almost nonsensical (how is it possible to "communicate faith" as the "matrix" of itself?), this reading fails to translate the French properly; the French says *"l'Église toute entière . . . nous transmet la foi et au sein de laquelle nous croyons."* What this means is: "The whole Church . . . transmits the faith to us, and in her bosom we believe." (It is significant, by the way, that "communicate faith" is preferred to "transmit the faith"; one can communicate whatever one decides upon, whereas one can only transmit what one has received.)

Dealing with a similar subject, paragraph 1253 informs

us that "of necessity, the faith of each believer participates in the Church's faith." However, the French here says *"ce n'est que dans la foi de l'Église que chacun des fidèles peut croire"*; and this means: "It is only in the faith of the Church that each believer can believe."

In paragraph 1350 we read that "in Christ's name the priest will offer . . . the bread and the wine in the eucharistic sacrifice *when they have become his body and blood"* (emphasis added). This translation implies that the priest will offer the bread and the wine only after they have somehow already become his body and his blood. A more correct translation would be a more literal one: "The bread and the wine . . . will be offered by the priest in the name of Christ in the eucharistic sacrifice *where* they will become the body and blood [of Christ]" (emphasis added again). The French reads: *"Le pain et le vin . . . seront offerts par le prêtre au nom du Christ dans le sacrifice eucharistique où ils deviendront le corps et le sang [du Christ]."*

In paragraph 2009, the translation says that "as God's adopted children, justified and given a share in the divine life by God's free gift, we can truly merit." The French for this says something quite different, however: *"L'Adoption filiale, en nous rendant participants par grâce à la nature divine, peut nous conférer, suivant la justice gratuite de Dieu, un véritable mérite."* This sentence would be much better translated by the following: "Filial adoption, by making us participants through grace in the divine nature, can confer on us, following God's justice freely accorded, a true merit." Now it is simply not the same thing to say that *we* can freely merit, which is what the translation says, instead of saying that God can "confer . . . a true merit" on us by filial adoption, which is what the original French text says.

Or, again, speaking of confirmation, paragraph 1288

speaks, rather weakly, of "the fulfillment of Christ's wish", whereas the French text has *"pour accomplir la volonté du Christ"*, which is to say, "to fulfill the *will* of Christ."

Paragraph 517 tells us that Christ's whole life is a mystery of redemption [including] "in his Resurrection by which he justifies us"—*"dans sa Résurrection par laquelle il nous justifie"*. The translation of this clause, however, gives "in his Resurrection *because* he justifies us", which could imply that Christ's Resurrection is a "mystery" only in that he justifies us. Also, for those modern theologians who see the Resurrection not as an actual historical occurrence but rather as some kind of a "faith event", the Resurrection would logically flow from the fact of our justification. But, of course, it is precisely the other way around, as the original French text makes abundantly clear.

We could go on. At length. Not a few of the passages in this English translation are marked by inexactitude and imprecision. Admittedly some of them do involve rather difficult texts which any translator might have difficulty with; and many of them may concern only fine points. Nevertheless the fact remains that there are far too many such mistranslations in this text; on these grounds alone, it must be considered to be wholly inadequately translated.

Moreover, some of the mistranslations can seem to be inexplicable, even frivolous—as if the translator was not paying close attention. For example, in paragraph 1446, there is a quotation from Tertullian speaking about "the second plank [of salvation] after the shipwreck which the loss of grace is"—*"la seconde planche [du salut] après le naufrage qu'est la perte de la grâce"*. In the translation this passage becomes "as the shipwrecked grasp the support of a plank", without any reference to the subject of grace at all, or apparently any understanding that the word "plank" here really means something like "the second item" relating to salvation.

Or, again, there is Paragraph 2125, quoting Vatican II's *Gaudium et Spes* (no. 19), which the Flannery translation of the Vatican II documents renders, "Believers can have more than a little to do with the rise of atheism"; the French for this is: "*Les croyants peuvent avoir une part qui n'est pas mince . . . dans la diffusion de l'athéisme.*" The text before us, however, translates this same passage as "the rise of atheism is *largely attributable* to believers" (emphasis added).

Finally, in paragraph 484, the translation renders Luke 1:34, quite arbitrarily, it would seem, as: "How can this be since I am a virgin?" Even though it is presumably not doctrinally wrong to have Mary affirming her own virginity, it is not what the French original says; nor is it what the Gospel of Luke says. They both say: "How can this be since I do not know man?" No translator can legitimately take such liberties with a text, even if what he says happens to be true.

# IV

As already noted above, there are many instances in this English translation of the *Catechism of the Catholic Church* where things have either been left out or have been added in. In this single article we can supply only a few illustrative examples of these omissions and additions; but there are plenty more where these came from for anyone who wants to take the trouble of comparing the English translation with the original French, as we have done.

*Omissions.* One fairly regular omission appears to be the dropping, even when quoting Church documents, of words like "sacred" in expressions like "sacred council", or of words like "Holy" and "Mother" from the expression "Holy Mother Church" (CCC 1203, CCC 1667). The translator seems to have an aversion to the idea of the Church as a "woman" or a "mother", in fact; this would seem to be the necessary obverse of the radical feminist demand for so-called "inclusive language". Like the latter, it does not enhance the literary style of the translation, though.

Other omissions include such things as paragraph 425's omission of *"d'abord"*, "first of all", or "primarily", from the sentence declaring that "the transmission of the Christian faith consists in proclaiming Jesus Christ"; for although the transmission of the faith *does* consist in proclaiming Jesus Christ, it does not consist *only* in that. Similarly, paragraph 469 in the translation omits "inseparably" from the statement that the Church "confesses that Jesus is both true God and true man".

Paragraph 1205, quoting in part Vatican Council II's Constitution on the Sacred Liturgy (no. 21), states that "the liturgy, above all, that of the sacraments, 'is made up of immutable elements, divinely instituted, and of elements subject to change' "; but the translation omits here an important phrase in the French that "the Church is the guardian of the liturgy." Paragraph 1174, speaking of celebrating the Liturgy of the Hours "in the approved form", also leaves out the intelligence that this approval is something given "by the Church".

Paragraph 1467, discussing the secrecy of the confessional, drops the adjective "absolute". In paragraph 1567, where it is stated that priests owe their bishops "love and obedience", the word "love" is dropped in the translation, and the same sentence in English instead reads "obedience and respect". In paragraph 2039, the translation arbitrarily

drops the adjective "fraternal" coming before "service"—
probably for reasons that by now we should have no difficulty guessing.

Paragraph 2366, quoting Pope Paul VI's encyclical *Humanæ Vitæ* (no. 12) on the inseparable connection between
the unitive and procreative meanings of conjugal intercourse
leaves out the encyclical's important statement that this
teaching has "often been expounded by the Magisterium
of the Church". In fact, the translator would seem to have
a thing about "the Magisterium". On occasions too numerous to enumerate, the translator regularly uses the phrase
"teaching authority" to translate the French *"Magistère"* (for
example, CCC 2036). Why not "Magisterium"? It is true
that this word *means* the "teaching authority" or "teaching
office" of the Church—an "authority" and an "office" that
have existed in the Church since Christ first pronounced the
words contained in Luke 10:16 addressed to his apostles. But
the word "Magisterium" has appropriately come into wide
use in relatively recent times in order to reenforce the claim
that the Church does, precisely, teach truth (cf. Vatican II,
*Dignitatis Humanæ*, no. 14; *Sacrosanctum Concilium*, no. 16)
—as opposed, for example, to those Christian communions
who apparently hold that "truth" emerges from the "private
judgement" of the believer reflecting on Scripture or whatever; and, especially, in an era and in a culture that strongly
tend to deny that truth—what the Church does objectively
teach—can even be knowable at all. In any case, the language of the *Catechism*, in the original, regularly reflects
this established and valid modern use of the word "Magisterium". So why not just translate it?

*Additions.* Paragraph 1313, indicating that the ordinary minister of confirmation is the bishop, goes on to say that the

bishop "may, for serious reasons, delegate to the priest the faculty of confirming *children baptized in infancy*"—the italicized phrase, again, has been added into the English without any warrant in the French text to do so. Paragraph 1371, speaking of the faithful departed who have died in Christ, once again adds, without any warrant, that these faithful departed "*are therefore assured of their eternal salvation*".

In paragraph 1069 concerning the liturgy, the text adds "whole" before "the people of God" and in paragraph 1071 it adds "effective" before "visible sign" for no apparent reason in either case. In paragraph 1210, the word "chrismation" is added as a synonym for "confirmation", although this is surely a word most speakers of English have never even heard; nor is it to be found in a couple of the standard desk dictionaries we consulted at random. The text of paragraph 2263, speaking of "legitimate defense", adds "deliberate" before "murder", although murder is by definition deliberate; and the text of paragraph 2278, speaking of medical procedures, adds "unnecessarily" before "burdensome".

A systematic review of the text of the translation would reveal numerous other additions of this same type. Again, some of them may well involve minor matters. Nevertheless, their occurrence can only serve to undermine confidence in the integrity of the whole translation—both the process and the product.

V

It should be apparent from a number of the examples already cited that some of the mistranslations, omissions, and additions to be found in the English translation of the *Cat-*

*echism of the Catholic Church* are not without doctrinal significance. This is unhappily the case. In too many instances —it should, of course, be "in *no* instances" where a "catechism" or simple compendium of the faith is concerned— this translation evidences a definite *parti pris* with regard to some of the theological controversies that have raged in the Church over the past generation. This *parti pris* can surface even in such seemingly small things as the title "*Constitution Hiérarchique*" to be found directly above paragraph 874; the translation gives "Hierarchical *Structure*" for this particular title. But it happens to make a difference whether the Church's sacred hierarchy is part of the Church's organic "constitution", as the latter was originally established by Christ himself, or not; or whether the hierarchy is just another one of those hated Church "structures" which we read about in *The National Catholic Reporter* and which the editors, writers, and no doubt also the readers of that popular journal appear to imagine could be swept away, perhaps any day now, on some new and progressive wave of modern enlightenment.

Similarly, the language of the translation in such passages as the last two sentences of paragraph 1577, concerning who is able to receive sacred ordination, can be of some doctrinal significance; the translation here reads: "The Church considers itself bound by [the] choice of the Lord. For this reason the ordination of women is not possible." But this translation could imply that, since the whole question is merely something that the Church "considers", then the Church might well sometime equally be brought to "*re*consider" the question, especially if feminist pressure in the matter continues to be as effective as it has proved to be in apparently persuading some that the Church needs "inclusive language" in the English version of her universal *Catechism*.

The French in this text says, however, that *"l'église se reconnait liée"*, that is, "the Church recognizes [the reality] that she is bound", and that therefore, the implication of this retranslated text is, no change in the matter is ever going to be possible.

Comparable loose wording is found in the translation of paragraph 2382, where it is stated that "the Lord Jesus insisted upon the original intention of the creator who willed that marriage *should* be indissoluble" (emphasis added). The question immediately arises: Maybe it should be, all right, but *is* it? Given one of the very common meanings of the word "should" in English, this translation might well be interpreted by some to mean that what the Creator willed was merely the *desirability* of a marriage bond that is permanent and unbreakable. However, the French in this sentence is very clear: *"Le Seigneur Jésus a insisté sur l'intention originelle du Créateur qui* voulait *un mariage indissoluble"*; that is: "The Lord Jesus insisted on the original intention of the Creator who *willed* marriage to be indissoluble" (emphasis added).

The translator also apparently has problems with both the word and the essential theological idea of "the Fall". In paragraph 410, the sentence, "After his fall, man was not abandoned by God" (*"Après sa chute, l'homme n'a pas été abandonné par Dieu"*), comes out in the English translation as: "God did not forsake our first parents after their *sin*" (emphasis added). In the sentence following this one, "lifting [man] up from his fall" (*"le relèvement de sa chute"*), becomes, again, "removal of their *sin*", that is, Adam *and* Eve's sin. Similarly, in paragraph 289, the triad "creation, fall, promise" (*"création, chute, promesse"*) once more becomes "creation, *sin*, promise" (again emphasis added). In paragraph 385, where the word "fall" *is* used, it is placed, significantly, within quotation marks (even then, it comes out as the "fall" of "humanity", not of "man"—this for "*chute de l'homme*" in the French). Why this aversion to the very word "fall"?

Consistently for this translation, the word "hell" is another no-no, as so many fashionably dissenting theologians have been so quick to suggest in recent years. Whereas the French text, speaking of the descent of Christ "*aux enfers*", that is, "into hell", the translation prefers to speak of Christ descending "to the dead" (for example, CCC 631, CCC 634). In paragraph 633, where the word "hell" is found in the English version, it is placed between quotation marks. In paragraph 634, where the French text actually does use the expression "*séjour des morts*", "abode of the dead", the translation again gives, invariably, "to the dead". (After awhile, the question inevitably does arise of what kind of games the translator thinks he is playing with these kinds of variations.)

More serious yet is the way the whole notion of sin is treated in this translation. Although the *Catechism of the Catholic Church* carefully delineates the Church's traditional understanding of mortal and venial sin (CCC 1854–64), the translation nevertheless succeeds in rather thoroughly obfuscating that distinction—just as it thoroughly obfuscates the distinction between "grave" and "light" matter in moral questions. Generally, it tries to avoid using the term "light" entirely, substituting "not grave" for it (for example, CCC 2073). In many other places, "*péché grave*", "grave sin", is translated instead as "serious sin" (for example, CCC 1385, 1457); "grave sin", in fact, appears to be a distinctly unpopular notion in this translation.

There is method here, though, not just muddle, since "serious sin" is not only the most frequently mentioned type of sin recognized in the translation; it is also, instead of "mortal sin", sometimes explicitly contrasted with "venial sin" (for example, CCC 2480), not only implying thereby—for this *is* the implication—that venial sin is *not* all that serious; but also, more importantly, explicitly recognizing the categories of sin postulated by the so-called "fundamental option" theory. This modern moral theory introduces between the traditional categories of venial and mortal sin another category of sin which it styles, precisely, "serious sin". For the fundamental-option people, a sin may be "serious" but not necessarily "mortal"; for them a sin is "mortal" only when the sinner has explicitly decided to reject God in the process of acting against his will.

Now the fundamental-option theory, of course, has been expressly rejected by the Magisterium of the Church (cf. CDF, *Personæ Humanæ*, no. 10, 1975; John Paul II, *Veritatis Splendor*, nos. 65–67, 1993). Thus it would seem to be a rather singular thing that its characteristic moral terminology should nevertheless suddenly resurface here in this translation of this compendium of authentic Catholic doctrine which the *Catechism of the Catholic Church* is supposed to be. If not corrected, the kind of language used here to characterize sin could well dispose some of those being catechized from the *Catechism* in the future to be influenced by the superficially plausible but erroneous fundamental-option theory. This kind of theory is exactly the sort of thing that does appeal to our dominant secular "culture" today (this "culture" is hard enough to fight without having a Catholic catechism come along seeming to lend it further credence!).

We can only wonder whether there is not some desire at work here, conscious or unconscious, to try to accommodate the harsh world in which we are obliged to live today. The same kind of question arises when we see dropped in the translation, as we do see dropped, the word "all" in the *Catechism*'s paragraph concerning "the moral evil of all procured abortion" (CCC 2271). For its part, the particular world we are obliged to live in today finds the Catholic view of morality and sin excessively rigid; and so the temptation perhaps to try to meet the world halfway is always strong; but it is not a temptation to which a catechism aiming to transmit the integral faith of Christ can afford to yield.

Far be it from both of us, however, to insinuate motives other than what the translator was charged to produce. Nevertheless there are certain perceptions which have arisen in the course of our examination and analysis of the translation. We have merely sought to allow our observations to assist tens of thousands of English-speaking Catholics here and abroad in understanding some of the reasons for the protracted delay in the publication in English of the *Catechism of the Catholic Church*.

# VI

In spite of all of the above, the fact remains that the most serious deficiency in this English translation of the *Catechism of the Catholic Church* is still its almost all-pervasive use of so-called "inclusive language"—its conscious rejection of what is clearly a fundamental part of the original French text, namely, the use of "man", "men", "he", "his", and "him" used in a generic sense to mean "men and women", "the human race", "everybody", and so on. Nor are the results of the decision to adopt the radical feminist idea of what kind of language is acceptable today happy results for a compendium of Catholic doctrine. These results are so bad, in fact, paragraph after paragraph, page after page, chapter after chapter, that the only conceivable merit of publishing the *Catechism* in its present form in English would be that it might very quickly convince all but hard-core feminist ideologues that today's attempt to introduce so-called "inclusive language" into Catholic teaching and worship can never end in anything but failure.

One occasionally hears in discussions concerning the fate of this English translation—still being held up in Rome as we write—that it employs "inclusive language" only "horizontally", that is, only when referring to human beings; never "vertically", that is, when referring to God. And what, some ask, is so bad about that?

One of the things that is bad about it is that it is not true. We saw in the very first paragraph of the *Catechism* how the word "God" had to be unnaturally and awkwardly repeated in order to avoid using the term "He"—even when applied to God! Once the feminist premise about language is accepted, it would seem, the feminist bias steadily resurfaces.

For example, the simple title above paragraph 203, which in French reads *"Dieu Révèle Son Nom"*, becomes in English the much more bland and abstract "The Revelation of God's Name". In the same paragraph, the exposition suddenly shifts from the third person singular to the first person plural—"a name expresses *our* essence" for *"le nom exprime l'essence"*—evidently in order to be able to avoid using "his" later on in the passage when referring to the name of God. As we remarked above, this is game-playing; and it is not amusing when what is involved is the truth of God.

In paragraph 212, *"hormis Lui"*, "besides Him", becomes, gratuitously, "besides YHWH". In paragraph 221, in the sentence, "God is an eternal exchange of love, Father, Son, and Holy Spirit, and has destined us to share in that exchange", the "He" that is included in the French text indicating Who has thus "destined" us is quietly dropped, as is surely the case hundreds of times in the course of the translation. In paragraph 383, the scriptural text of Genesis 1:27 itself is changed in response to the feminist imperative, and "he created them" has to be made to read "God created them." If there is conflict between what Scripture says and what the feminist imperative demands, it would be unwise to bet on the former and against the latter as far as this translation is concerned. In paragraph 442, Galatians 1:15, "He who set me apart", again becomes "*God* who set me apart". And so on.

These few citations represent only a few examples of how feminist assumptions dictate the translation, not only of "horizontal" language referring to human beings, but also of at least some "vertical" language referring to God and to Christ. It is astonishing, in fact, that anyone should think that these feminist claims and assumptions should be accepted as justification for changing the words of Scripture itself. Who has the right to change Scripture? Anyone?

What these feminist locutions do for normal language most of us have now long since had sufficient experience of, and therefore we do not need to provide extensive examples. What typically happens, though, is that an expression such as "*péché des hommes,*" "sin of men", comes to be [mis]translated as "sinful humanity" (CCC 211). "*Les anges et les hommes*", "angels and men", become not just "angels and human beings", but, absurdly, "people and angels" as well, all within the confines of the same paragraph (CCC 311). Another passage speaking of "the love that finds in each man a neighbor, a brother"—"*la charité qui trouve en chaque homme un prochain, un frère*"—gets translated in a way that first substitutes "person" for "man", and then, compul-

sively, has to add "and sister" after "brother" (CCC 1931).
What about "cousin"?

Even those who are perhaps not particularly bothered by
how clumsy and even jarring such phrases and locutions can
be should nevertheless be able to realize that they are simply
*not English!* A translator is supposed to render as faithfully as
possible in his target language what has actually been said in
his source language—not deform what his source language
says in his translation in response to the dictates of a highly
debatable modern ideology.

More than that, however, some of these inept substitutions for natural English actually alter the *meaning*, sometimes profoundly, of the text. Paragraph 383, for example,
alters Scripture (Genesis 1:27) in order to say that "God . . .
did not create the human person to be a solitary." "Human
person", of course, is substituted here for the word "man"
(*adam*) which is actually found in the Bible. However, the
two terms are not equivalents. For example, Jesus Christ
was a man—but he was not a "human person".

Again, paragraph 364 asserts in the English version that
"humanity . . . [is] a unity of body and soul." But this is not
true. "Humanity" has neither body nor soul; humanity is an
abstraction. Only individual men have bodies and souls, as
the French text clearly says in speaking of how "*l'homme*"
is "*vraiment un*" though possessing "*corps et âme*". In paragraph 659, the same abstract word, "humanity", is used to
translate Christ's "*body*", glorified at the Resurrection; indeed, according to this passage, it was Christ's "humanity" which was taken up into heaven! Quite apart from the
questionable theological implications here, this is the kind
of writing that wouldn't pass freshman English.

Oblivious to all other considerations in its single-minded
determination to imprison the *Catechism* within the cheer-

less walls of "inclusive language", then, this translation even proves capable of changing the inspired phrase in Romans 8:29 familiar to every Christian, "the first-born among many brethren", into—can this even be believed?—"the first-born within a large family". This absurdity appears not just once (CCC 381), not just twice (CCC 501), but at least three times (CCC 2790).

Enough then! How much easier it would have been simply to bow to the millennium-old fact that the word "man" is *already* "inclusive". More could be said, of course; many more examples could be adduced. But enough has now surely been said to indicate the utter folly of trying to bring out the *Catechism of the Catholic Church* in feminist-influenced "inclusive language". The translator of the *Catechism* should have stayed away from this minefield as surely as Adam and Eve should have passed up the forbidden fruit in the beginning.

In view of all the deficiencies of this "Englished" version of the *Catechism of the Catholic Church* that we have been examining, then, it is surely devoutly to be hoped that the protracted sojourn of this translation in the Congregation for the Doctrine of the Faith in Rome *means*—that it is in the process of being thoroughly revised and corrected.

# *The* Catechism *in English: The Art (or Artifice?) of Translation*

I

Catholics in the United States are generally aware that the official translation into English of the *Catechism of the Catholic Church* has continued for many months as of now to be held up in Rome. The new *Catechism* received considerable publicity even while it was still in preparation—in this country in large part because of a widely perceived crisis in the teaching of the faith over virtually the past two decades, a crisis for which the *Catechism*, at long last, was finally supposed to provide the remedy.

When the Holy Father, Pope John Paul II, promulgated the officially approved version of the *Catechism* in French in December 1992, it was expected that the English version would shortly be available. The continued nonappearance

This paper was delivered by coauthor Whitehead at the annual conference of Women for Faith and Family held on November 5–7, 1993, in St. Louis, Missouri, and then printed as it appears here in the *Fellowship of Catholic Scholars Newsletter*, December 1993.

of an approved English translation nearly a year later has thus been more than just a little bit anticlimactic.

Why the hold-up? Evidently Rome found a number of things wrong with the translation of the *Catechism* submitted for its approval and has thus presumably been in the process of revising and correcting the translation before approving it. At least I hope so. For I have had the opportunity to go over this English translation and compare it at numerous points with the French original approved by the Holy Father.

The experience has not been reassuring. Msgr. Michael J. Wrenn and I have even prepared an article-length critique of the translation for *Crisis* magazine, detailing some of the things we found wrong with the translation, including mistranslations of words, phrases, and entire passages, additions to and omissions from the French version, and even renderings which sometimes appeared to misstate or distort what seemed to us important doctrinal points.

I do not intend to repeat here any of the criticisms already set forth in the article by Msgr. Wrenn and myself. Read the article in the November 1993 *Crisis* magazine.[1] Here I want to deal with a number of other important points concerning the translation of the *Catechism*, including especially some of the criteria which the translator has stated he followed in making the translation; and also, very briefly, some of the criteria our bishops are currently accepting concerning Church translations.

One important theme that runs through almost everything I will be saying here today—and which is of special interest to Women for Faith and Family—is the degree to which this translation of the *Catechism* is gravely flawed

---

[1] See Appendix One *supra*.

and marred—I believe even fatally so—by the use of so-called "inclusive language", that is, language which self-consciously avoids using the words "man" or "men", or the masculine pronouns, in a generic sense to mean such things as "everybody", "the human race", "men, women, and children", "people in general", and so on.

The English language, of course—like the French language from which the *Catechism* has been translated—does use the words "man" or "men" and the masculine pronouns in precisely such a generic way. English has been doing this virtually since Anglo-Saxon times more than a thousand years ago. Today, however, the ideological feminist movement has risen up to claim that women are not "included" when such generic language is used—hence a presumed new need to use language and expressions and locutions which specifically do "include" women.

Unfortunately, many have been persuaded by this feminist claim. Acceptance of the need for inclusive language is even supposed to indicate special sensitivity to women's concerns —as if the ideological feminists truly represented "women". Attempts, some of them strenuous, are even being made in our culture to get this new inclusive language accepted as standard English usage. Most such attempts, however, have neither been very successful; nor have they enjoyed universal approval. Far from it: not rarely these attempts provoke ridicule; some people even find them offensive.

For the fact largely remains true, in spite of intense feminist efforts and pressures, that hardly anybody at all really writes or speaks in the stilted, clumsy, and highly artificial way that consistent inclusive language would impose upon all of us. Inclusive language is *not* standard English usage. Even pro-feminists do not normally speak this way unless they are consciously thinking about it.

Nevertheless the fact that inclusive language is not really standard English did not prevent an unwise decision from being made that the *Catechism of the Catholic Church* should be translated into English using this inclusive language— just as plans have long since been underway to try to impose the same dubious and unnatural kind of language on the liturgy and worship of the Catholic Church in English.

What the decision to translate the *Catechism* using inclusive language has really entailed, however, is this: the stated aim of the translation itself, in the words of the editorial committee for the *Catechism* in English quoted by the translator himself, namely, "to convey the real meaning of the text in idiomatic English which does not in any way distort that meaning", has proved to be *impossible of realization*! Yes. It has proved to be impossible of realization for the simple reason that inclusive language is *not* "idiomatic English"; nor is it possible to *avoid* distorting meanings when using inclusive language.

The text of the translation sadly provides literally hundreds of examples verifying both of these statements. Only a few selected ones of these examples can obviously be provided within the compass of this single presentation. Anyone interested in finding more of them can easily do so by comparing the English translation with the original French text.

One benefit that may nevertheless stem from the fact that inclusive language has been drearily though unsuccessfully employed throughout all the 2865 individual numbered paragraphs of this translation of the *Catechism of the Catholic Church* is this: Rome, having seen the dismal results of this misbegotten ideological experiment, has now been given the opportunity to see in a very concrete way that inclusive language simply *won't work*! It won't work for the liturgy any more than for the *Catechism*. Having now been obliged to hold up the translation of this *Catechism*, perhaps Rome will now also begin to see the necessity of taking another look at some of our recent Scripture translations into English and at some of the language being proposed for our new lectionaries and sacramentaries as well.

*Speremus.* Let us hope.

## II

The main things that I want to address today concerning the English translation of the *Catechism of the Catholic Church* are some of the stated "criteria" that were employed in the preparation of this translation. Examination of some of these criteria will quickly enable us to identify more than one probable reason why it is that the translation has been held up in Rome. The translator himself, one Fr. Douglas Kent Clark, pastor of St. Anne's Church in Richmond Hill, Georgia, has conveniently provided us with a list of such criteria in an article he published in the summer 1993 issue of the USCC Department of Education's quarterly religious education review, *The Living Light*.

In this article, entitled "On 'Englishing' the Catechism", Fr. Clark explains that, while he worked with two editorial committees in making the translation, one in Britain and one in the United States, and also enjoyed both the services of a research assistant as well as advice and counsel from other experts, the decision was early made that a single translator should perform the task of translation, "in order to ensure a consistent style and a relatively quick translation".

Much of what Fr. Clark says in his *Living Light* article

concerning the problems of translation in general and of translation from French into English in particular few translators would disagree with. It is quite true that translation involves considerably more than, as it were, rote word-for-word substitutions; choices and judgments constantly have to be made. I must admit that I was initially quite impressed with Fr. Clark's exposition of all the problems posed by this particular translation the first time I read it—but that was before I saw the translation itself. In the light of the product, it seems pretty clear that some of the translation criteria employed were at the very least questionable; and more than one of them have turned out to be, in my opinion, grossly erroneous criteria.

In fairness to Fr. Clark, it should be pointed out that he was not himself responsible for all the criteria employed; they appear to have been decided collectively; he was working under direction with his editorial committees and such. Nevertheless that does not make everything right. Committees can make mistakes too. Now that I have looked at the translation in some detail, compared it to the French original, and then have subsequently gone back to ponder the stated criteria used in producing it, I seriously wonder whether any translator could have produced an entirely acceptable translation using such criteria.

Let us examine some of them.

# III

*Scripture.* The minute we get into the translation's handling of Scripture, we immediately sink deeply into the morass of the problems created by the original decision to go with inclusive language. It is virtually impossible to read even a

page of this translation without running into such renderings as the one in paragraph 146 from Romans 4:11, where
Abraham, as "the father of all who believe", becomes instead "the *ancestor* of all who believe"; or the one in paragraph 205 from Exodus 3:15, where "the God of your fathers" becomes "the God of your *ancestors*". The statement
in Acts 4:12 that "there is no other name under heaven given
among men by which we must be saved" becomes in paragraph 452 of the translation "among *mortals*". The phrase
"in the likeness of men" from Philippians 2:7 becomes in
paragraph 461 "in *human* likeness". Acts 5:29 records Peter
and the apostles saying, "We must obey God rather than
men." Paragraph 2256 changes "men" here to "*human authority*".

In the paragraph following, to a quotation from Matthew
5:21 beginning, "But I say to you, everyone who is angry
with his brother . . .", we are not even surprised by this time
to find the translation adding: "and sister". And so on. You
get the idea.

Now at the simplest level it must be recognized that, quite
apart from the motives of the translator, all these renderings do not represent what the original text *says*. To state this
may strike some as simplistic; nevertheless it remains true,
and truth ought to count for something, especially where
Scripture translations are concerned.

Reading this translation, though, it seems that Scripture
itself is simply being arbitrarily changed to fit the feminist
mold wherever this is thought to be necessary. But *who* has
ever been authorized to change sacred Scripture in this fashion (or in any fashion)? To alter the very words of Christ
and then give out the alteration as if it issued from Christ?
This is a form of falsification. Is anybody at all authorized
to do this?

But then in our present case it turns out that all these renderings are not just the banal fabrications of the translator of the *Catechism*; it turns out they are all taken from a new and highly touted *published translation* of the Scriptures, the so-called New Revised Standard Version of the Bible (NRSV), which Fr. Douglas Kent Clark, in discussing his translation criteria, describes as "the premier scholarly English translation used on both sides of the Atlantic". I fear some of us might wish to demur about that particular judgment.

However, the fact that we are talking about an actual, supposedly standard new translation of the Bible, and not just some arbitrary proceeding of the translator, does put a somewhat different light on the problem. Moreover, as Fr. Clark hastens to point out, this NRSV has not only been approved for liturgical use in the United States (in November 1991); this approval by the American bishops of this version of the Bible has also been confirmed by Rome's Congregation for Divine Worship and Discipline of the Sacraments (on April 6, 1992).

What kind of a translation is this NRSV? We have already encountered some of its renderings as used in the *Catechism* translation. In fact, it is only too easy to imagine how the NRSV handles many other passages. For example, we read in Mark 1:17: "And Jesus said to them, 'Follow me and I will make you fish for people.'" Or take John 2:24–25: "But Jesus on his part would not entrust himself to them because he knew all people and needed no one to testify about anyone; for he himself knew what was in everyone." Such a stilted, flaccid sentence as this provides an immediate illustration of how the Gospel message is inevitably distorted by using inclusive language to avoid saying: "But Jesus did not trust himself to them, because he knew all men and needed no one to bear witness of man; for he himself knew what was in man."

Many more examples could be given, but I will spare you. The realization that our American bishops, after some two decades of imposing the mediocre New American Bible on us, have now approved *this* translation, and are apparently contemplating its universal use, is dispiriting if not dismaying. Nor does it help that the NRSV is a so-called "project" of the National Council of Churches, an organization that long ago would seem to have abandoned strict gospel imperatives in order to pursue leftist politics (is the NCC going to get the royalties on all the sales to Catholics too? What a prospect! The Catholic Church helping to subsidize the National Council of Churches!).

We truly must hope that the hot water in which the *Catechism* translation currently finds itself in Rome will spill over into the liturgical area, and that the current Roman approval of this new NRSV translation will be revisited. We must hope that our own hierarchy will also decide that this decision has to be revisited. Eventually it *will* have to be revisited. It is incompatible with the faith that has been handed down.[2] And the health and strength of that faith on these shores, if not in other English-speaking countries, could be at stake for years to come.

Meanwhile let us call things by their true names. This New Revised Standard Version of the Bible is *not* a "translation". It is an ideological adaptation. Jesus did *not* say, "I

---

[2] On July 27, 1994, Archbishop Geraldo Agnelo, secretary of the Congregation for Divine Worship in Rome, wrote to Archbishop William Keeler of Baltimore, president of the National Conference of Catholic Bishops, withdrawing the earlier Roman permission to use the NRSV Bible in English for Catholic liturgical use.

will make you fish for people." The Greek is: *poiesu umas genesthai aleeis anthropun:* "I will make you become fishers of *men*"! To impose the supposed demands or prejudices of our age and our culture upon any text transmitted from antiquity, not just a Gospel text, is a falsification (and this assumes that inclusive language *is* what our age really wants).

Nevertheless, this is what this translation of the *Catechism* would now involve the Church in English-speaking countries in: falsification. It is a high price to imagine we have to pay in order to appease ideological feminists whose dedication or commitment to the Catholic Church is hardly the most salient thing about them that might ever strike anybody.

And it is all so unnecessary. From the point of view of faith, for example, the scriptural passage Genesis 1:27 already *demonstrates* that God's creation of "man" expressly *included* "woman": "So God created man in his own image, in the image of God he created him; male and female he created *them*." The switch to the plural here is precisely intended to make clear that "woman" *is* included in "man" in the general sense, regardless of how the feminists may grouse. Genesis 5:2 goes farther; it goes on to say: "Male and female he created them and he blessed them and named *them* 'Man' when *they* were created" (emphasis added). Scripture is absolutely clear on the matter. Why is this so hard for some people to understand?

"What is man that thou art mindful of him, and the son of man that thou dost care for him?" This invocation from Psalms 8:4 is familiar to all Christians. The NRSV renders it: "What are human beings that you are mindful of them, mortals that you care for them?" Here the important biblical phrase "son of man", in Hebrew *ben adam*—especially important in view of its later extensive use by our Lord—is actually translated "mortals" in the NRSV. This is a wholly arbitrary translation; the question of man's mortality in no way arises in connection with this text; and it seems to be an especially arbitrary choice when we recall that *the* Son of Man came, among other reasons, in order to overcome our mortality.


## IV


So much for the translation of Scripture in the *Catechism*. Let us go on now to review, at least briefly, some of the other translation criteria mentioned by Fr. Douglas Kent Clark, the *Catechism* translator, in his article in the summer 1993 issue of *The Living Light*.

*Liturgical Texts.* Fr. Clark explains that where liturgical texts appear in the *Catechism* translation they were taken from the approved ICEL translations from the Latin currently in use in English-speaking countries. Strictly as a criterion, of course, it does make sense for these liturgical texts to be uniform in both the *Catechism* and the Missal—quite apart from what we may think of some of the ICEL's handiwork.

Fr. Clark adds that the currently approved liturgical texts "were not changed in the *Catechism*" even when different in some respects from the French. Again, this is all right in principle. Unfortunately, however, what he says does not appear to be entirely true; once again the feminist imperative raises its head, apparently overriding every other consideration. For in paragraph 380, for example, the current Fourth Eucharistic Prayer of the Mass is quoted as: "Father . . . you made us in your own image and set us over the whole world." But the currently approved text of the Fourth

Eucharistic Prayer actually reads, as Mass-going Catholics will recall: "Father . . . you formed *man* in your own likeness and set *him* over the whole world" (emphasis added). Thus, the currently approved ICEL translation *was* apparently changed in this case—in order, once again, to avoid those dreaded words "man" and "him".

No doubt the translator in this case was simply "anticipating" the new ICEL translations with inclusive language which are presumably expected to be approved; but if this sort of thing keeps going on, pretty soon we men are going to start feeling "excluded" too. We will have to start demanding inclusive language for *us*!

*Ecclesiastical Writers and Magisterial Documents.* Fr. Clark explains that the numerous quotations from these sources were not simply translated from the approved French text. "Patristic and older magisterial documents for which no official translation exists were translated directly from the original texts and not from those texts in French translations", he explains. This may sound impressive and may even seem like a perfectly reasonable criterion.

What it allows the translator to do in practice, however, is, once again, to refashion the text in the feminist image. The result is, in such texts as paragraph 2783, to make such substitutions in a citation from St. Ambrose as "O mortal" for "O man"; and "child" for "man". (Again, though, that is not what St. Ambrose *said*; a translator who alters what his author said in accordance with extra-translation considerations is no longer really a translator.)

Also, compare the following text of the *Catechism* found in paragraph 1458 based on an important teaching of St. Augustine, which bears not only upon the topic of sin but upon that of the God-man dichotomy. I give my own fairly literal translation from the French first, and then the translation using inclusive language:

| MY TRANSLATION | INCLUSIVE-LANGUAGE TRANSLATION |
|---|---|
| The one who confesses his sins already acts along with God. God accuses you of your sins; if you accuse yourself, you join yourself to God. The man and the sinner are, so to speak, two realities; whenever you hear tell of the man, this is what God has made; whenever you hear tell of the sinner, this is what man has done. Destroy what you have done so that God may save what he has done (St. Augustine, *In Jo. Ev.*, 12, 13). | Whoever confesses his or her sins already cooperates with God. God rebukes your sins; if you also rebuke them, you are united to God. The person and the sinner are, so to speak, two realities; when you hear "person"—this is what God has made; when you hear "sinner"—this is what the person has done. Destroy what you have done so that God may save what he has done (ibid.). |

Quite apart from the fact that the important scriptural theme of the God-man dichotomy is obscured here, by using "person" instead of "man", the inclusive-language translation inescapably distorts the meaning in a more fundamental way; the text no longer conveys what St. Augustine said. This is true for the simple reason that "person" is not equivalent to "man". God is a person, for example; Jesus is a person; are they also "sinners"? Did they "make" sinners? The questions answer themselves.

If this is how "ecclesiastical writers" are treated according to these translation criteria, what about "magisterial documents"? A crucial—and I believe fatal—decision was made when the translator decided not to use any of the existing standard English translations of the documents of Vatican II for the literally hundreds of citations from the Council that the *Catechism* includes. This decision was made, Fr. Clark tells us, because his "editorial committee discovered errors and infelicities of style" in the existing Vatican II translations. This may well be, but the translator's decision to make his own Vatican II translations can scarcely be said to further the aim of "the development of a common theological and catechetical vocabulary for English-speaking Catholics"— which, elsewhere in his *Living Light* article, Fr. Clark had indicated to be one of the principal aims.

The principal advantage of doing his own Vatican II translations, though, was no doubt so that—you guessed it!— he could also present Vatican II in inclusive language, along with everything else! Certainly the existing Vatican II translations in current use today in English-speaking countries would not help him much there. As it is, he has a field day. In paragraph 541, for example, he changes what in the Flannery Vatican II translation of *Lumen Gentium* (no. 3) is "raise men" to "raise human beings"; in paragraph 1701, what in the Flannery translation reads "the very revelation of the mystery of the Father and his love fully reveals man to himself" becomes instead "the mystery of the Father and his love fully discloses what it means to be human." Again, you get the idea. You could do this yourself. You don't need to be either a theologian or a French translator.

*Gaudium et Spes* (no. 13), in the Flannery translation, informs us that "man, enticed by the evil one, abused his freedom at the start of history." The *Catechism* translation instead renders this in its paragraph 1707 as "humanity was beguiled by the evil one and abused its freedom at the dawn of history." But "humanity", an abstraction, did no such thing, either at the dawn of history or at any other time; only individual human beings with will and intellect would be capable of doing such a thing, and so, once again, the inclusive-language translation distorts the true meaning of the text.

*Lumen Gentium* (no. 11) in the Flannery translation specifies that the faithful, "reborn as sons of God . . . must profess *before men* the faith they have received from God through the Church". In paragraph 1270 of the Catechism translation, we find instead the rendering, "reborn as children of God" —the French text also specifies "through baptismal regeneration" here—"the baptized are in duty bound to profess *publicly* the faith they have received from the Church." Elsewhere in his *Living Light* article the translator specifically defends this rendering—the use of "publicly" in place of the expression "before men" so often found in Scripture— as being perfectly valid and adequate. In this he is surely mistaken; "publicly" simply does not mean the same thing as "before men", as even the NRSV recognizes, translating such passages as Matthew 10:32—"Everyone who acknowledges me before men, I also will acknowledge before my Father who is in heaven"—by saying "before *others*".

*Recent Magisterial Documents.* Still discussing his translation criteria, the translator declares that "all recent (post-Vatican-II) documents of the Holy See for which official English translations exist are quoted from the official Vatican translations"—but not, apparently, without adding such things as "or hers" to "his" where considered necessary in such texts as the quotation from the CDF's Instruction *Donum Vitæ* found in paragraph 2375. Inclusive language, like *amor*, always *vincit omnia*, apparently.

*Code of Canon Law.* The translator notes under this rubric in his *Living Light* article that the American CLSA translation of the new 1983 Code of Canon Law was used by common agreement on both sides of the Atlantic. A similar decision should have been made regarding a single standard Vatican II translation. Many of the problems with this translation would never have arisen if available standard translations of Church texts had simply been uniformly used.

Yet even here consistency would appear to be lacking. In paragraph 2102, for example, if we compare the Canon Law Society of America's actual translation of Canon 1191 §1 with the way in which our Catechism translation apparently modifies (and garbles) this same Canon, we find the following discrepancy:

|  CLSA VERSION | CATECHISM TRANSLATION VERSION |
| --- | --- |
| A vow is a deliberate and free promise made to God concerning a possible and better good which must be fulfilled by reason of the virtue of religion. | A vow is a promise deliberately and freely made to God concerning some good which is possible and good. The virtue of religion requires that it be fulfilled. |

Now how can a possible "good" simply be—"good"? The *Catechism*'s translation of this Canon is tautological. The CLSA version properly distinguishes that what is at issue is a *better* good—the object of a religious vow. We are always obliged to do good and avoid evil; but vows "which must be fulfilled by reason of the virtue of religion" involve, precisely, a "good" which is "better".

How much easier it would have been if only the translator and his editorial committees had been willing to utilize existing and surely acceptable English translations of the hundreds and hundreds of quotations in this *Catechism* taken from popes, councils, Fathers and doctors of the Church, the

Code of Canon Law, and so on. But no: once the decision was apparently made to try to *improve* the product, particularly with regard to modern feminist imperatives, instead of merely translating it—which it was really their responsibility to do—they inescapably entered upon that well-known slippery slope in which the only direction they could henceforth go was downhill.

V

What we are dealing with in the case of this translation of the *Catechism of the Catholic Church* is not a translation at all; it is no more a translation than the New Revised Standard Version of the Bible is a translation. Neither document aims to render in English what its original text says, no more, no less. Both documents are ideological adaptations consciously made in order to serve the ends of what has aptly come to be called today "political correctness".

It is startling, in fact, to realize how much more important modern political correctness appears to be for the artificers of both documents than does the proclamation of God's authentic revelation and his plan for man. This divine revelation and this divine plan constitute the essence of what is truly to be found in the Holy Bible—as it is similarly to be found in the *Catechism of the Catholic Church*. The translators of both documents had an obligation to render *these things*—the divine revelation and the divine plan—which should have automatically overridden all other considerations whatsoever.

But no: having set forth his principal translation criteria, Fr. Clark, in his *Living Light* article, then goes on to state quite plainly what is only too glaringly evident from his product in any case, namely, that what really appears to have driven this translation effort, from beginning to end, is nothing else but insistence upon using inclusive language. "So-called inclusive language reflects a concern that is almost overwhelming in the United States", Fr. Clark declares in his article. Whether this assertion is his own idea, and he convinced his editorial committees of it, or whether, as he indicates, he was "directed" by them to proceed in the way that he did is immaterial. The dismal result is the same.

We can only wonder who the people are such Churchmen talk to when they assert that the demand for inclusive language is "overwhelming" in the United States. Fr. Clark actually claims that what he calls the primary and secondary acceptations of the word "man" have been "reversed over the past half-century, so that one can no longer say 'a woman is a man' and be understood."

I dare say there was *never* a time when anybody ever said anything like that; such an artificial example does not reflect how generic language is normally and characteristically used in English. Moreover, judging from my own random unscientific survey, I think Fr. Clark might be hard-pressed to find a standard English dictionary older than, say, *ten* years, which lists the primary definition of the word "man" as "an adult male human being". And I suspect he will not be able to find any dictionary at all which drops or excludes the meaning of "man" as "the human race", "men, women, and children", and so on, in the way that inclusive language wants and tries to exclude this meaning of "man". For the fact is that the generic use of "man" still is used in English and still is legitimate. To imagine that the language has somehow been evolving along feminist lines over the past "fifty years" is not true to the facts.

Ideological feminism is a product of the last couple of

decades at most; and there is not only no assurance that characteristic feminist demands are going to be adopted by society as a whole; there is already strong and growing evidence that many people are turning away from radical feminism already. Of all possible institutions the Catholic Church is surely the last that should ever have gotten involved with this particular ideological fashion. The only result that is likely to come of it will be to see realized once again the old adage that marrying the *Zeitgeist* usually makes for early widowhood.

## VI

One final point needs to be touched upon in this discussion of ecclesiastical translations, and that is the unhappy fact that, at the present time, our bishops do seem to have been sold the inclusive-language bill of goods. In 1990 they even issued a set of "Criteria for the Evaluation of Inclusive Language Translations of Scriptural Texts". In point of fact, there shouldn't be any such criteria for the simple reason that there shouldn't be any such translations.

As is usually the case with episcopal statements, however, these particular criteria are very carefully framed and on their face appear to be very moderate and reasonable. What could possibly be amiss? In the criteria the bishops note that "some segments of culture have become increasingly sensitive to 'exclusive language', i.e., language which seems to exclude the equality and dignity of each person." *Does* it exclude them, or not? *What* segments of "culture" are even concerned? Is the concern *legitimate*? The bishops do not say. They nevertheless go on to legitimate inclusive language anyway, regardless of whether or not it is really called for, by the very fact of issuing their criteria.

But what a tenuous foundation on which to base what amounts to a veritable revolution! The bishops assume what needs to be demonstrated.

The bishops' criteria go on to say that "impromptu efforts at inclusive language . . . have . . . offended". I would add, on the evidence of the translation of the *Catechism* alone, that *not only* "impromptu efforts" have "offended"! Yet the mere fact that impromptu efforts go on appears to be one of the principal reasons why the bishops found it necessary to issue their criteria in the first place. Apparently it never occurred to anyone—or was perhaps thought too difficult if it did—to do what a young priest in my own parish recently did when he told the lectors who were indulging in their own "impromptu efforts at inclusive language": "You have no right to change the words of sacred Scripture", he said. "So *don't*." The result? Some of the lectors in question have simply not reappeared at the lectern to read; but nobody is changing the Scriptures any longer, either! Many of our other problems today might perhaps be susceptible of solutions as simple as this if it were not, perhaps, for so many moistened fingers being held up to test today's *Zeitgeist* "blowing where it listeth".

The bishops do go on to point out in their criteria such things as that "not everything in Scripture will be in harmony with contemporary cultural concerns" and that language referring to God and to Christ in particular cannot be inclusive; masculine references must continue to be used for them. The upshot of this is supposed to be that only so-called "horizontal language" referring to human beings can be inclusive, while "vertical language" referring to God and Christ cannot be inclusive.

At first sight it may seem that a knotty problem has been solved by making such a distinction. Many people sincerely see nothing wrong with making horizontal language inclusive. On the evidence of the translation of the *Catechism*, however, it turns out that the distinction between horizontal language cannot be that easily maintained in practice. Once caught up in the feminist logic, it would appear, it is impossible not to be affected in more ways than one. Examples of this abound in this translation, beginning with the very first paragraph of the *Catechism*, and continuing, where we find such things as repeating the noun "God" in order to avoid using "He" or "Him" to refer to God; or dropping the pronoun "He" entirely, even when it is present in the French original and stylistically or syntactically should be in the English as well. Later on we find turgid sentences such as the subtitle just above paragraph 469—"How God's Son Is Human"—that are framed so unnaturally that, again, they appear to have been written only in order to avoid having to say that God's Son is a man.

Moreover, there are not a few instances where inclusive language creeps in anyway, even when the reference is supposed to be vertical. For example, paragraph 659 uses the term "Christ's humanity" to translate the French "*corps du Christ*" which means the [physical] "*body* of Christ". Have we reached the point where it is considered insensitive or indelicate to speak of Christ's physical body because it is male?

Similarly, in paragraph 2214, "*la paternité divine*", "the divine paternity"—or "*father*hood"—is translated into English as the "divine *parent*hood", apparently, again, in order to avoid having to say the word with a masculine reference, "fatherhood". Now this is vertical language referring to God; yet the feminist imperative once again rules the translation, contrary to the express criteria of the bishops. In any case, we have surely traveled very far down the wrong road when perhaps the major single fact about God's revelation of himself to us, namely, that he is a "Father", has to be avoided in deference to the imagined sensibilities of "women".

Other examples of this kind of thing could be cited from the text of the translation; they are probably inevitable in the nature of the case, once inclusive language has been accepted.

Furthermore, insistence on inclusive language can distort the meaning of the text, sometimes seriously, even when the bishops' criteria are being followed. Paragraph 480, for example, tells us in translation that "Jesus Christ is true God and true man in the unity of his divine person; for this reason he is the only mediator between God and humanity". But Jesus is not the only mediator between God and "humanity". God, of course, is joined to humanity in and through Jesus (*his* humanity!); it is for this reason, that is, the fact that he is "true man" at the same time that he is "true God", that he is the only mediator between God and *men*—that is, between God and all individual men, women, and children (not *between* God and "humanity"!). The French text gets it exactly right by unselfconsciously using "*les hommes*", "men", in a generic sense in this passage.

This translation, in using "humanity" to translate the French "*les hommes*", is in this case in conformity with the bishops' criteria, since the substituted word "humanity" is supposed to refer to us and not to God or Jesus. Yet the use of this word "humanity" here nevertheless does distort both the real reason why Jesus is the only mediator between God and men and what his relationship is as mediator to individual men, women, and children. These are not fine points. What this kind of example shows is that inclusive language does not really work and cannot work. This is a fact that has to be faced by English-speaking Catholics confronted with such a translation as this.

After all, since Jesus had no human father, the only sense in which it is really possible for him to be a "son of man" —the designation by which he most frequently referred to himself in the Gospels—is: *as* the son of Mary! No other way for him to be the Son of Man! It follows as a necessary consequence that Mary is "included" in "Man" in the term "Son of Man" as used by Jesus in the Gospels. Indeed this is surely a prototypical example of the legitimate generic use of the word "man".

If "man" truly means something "exclusive" of women, as our modern feminists pretend, then Mary, the Mother of Jesus, the Mother of God—his only human parent—is the first woman who has to be excluded. Can such a prospect even be *contemplated* in any scheme of things that is truly *Catholic?* I think not.

We must pray to Mary, conceived without sin—our whole country is dedicated to her under her title of the Immaculate Conception, after all—that she urgently intercede for us in this as in all the things for which we pray.

# Comparative Translations

## I

*French Original*

I. La vie de *l'homme*—connaître et aimer Dieu

1. Dieu, infiniment Parfait et Bienheureux en Lui-même, dans un dessein de pure bonté, a librement créé *l'homme* pour *le* faire participer à sa vie bienheureuse. C'est pourquoi, de tout temps et en tout lieu, Il se fait proche de *l'homme*. Il *l'*appelle, *l'*aide, à Le chercher, à Le connaître et à L'aimer de toutes *ses* forces. Il convoque *tous les hommes* que le péché a dispersés dans l'unité de sa famille, l'Église. Pour ce faire, Il a envoyé son Fils comme Rédempteur et Sauveur lorsque les temps furent accomplis. En Lui et par Lui, Il appelle les *hommes* à devenir, dans l'Esprit Saint, ses enfants d'adoption, et donc les héritiers de sa vie bienheureuse.

---

These comparative translation samples have been reprinted from *The Catholic World Report*, June 1994.

*Initial Translation*

I. *To Live* Is to Know and Love God

1. God's own perfection and happiness are infinite. In the plan of his good pleasure, the Father freely created *the human race* to share his blessed life and so is close to *us* at all times and in all places. He calls *us* and helps *us* seek, know, and love him with all *our* strength. God gathers *the human race*, scattered and divided by sin, into the unity of his family, the Church, through his Son, whom he sent in the fullness of time to redeem and save *us*. Through Christ and in the Holy Spirit, the Father invites *us* to become his adopted sons and daughters and heirs to divine happiness.

*Approved Translation*

I. The Life of *Man*—To Know and Love God

1. God, infinitely perfect and blessed in himself, in a plan of sheer goodness freely created *man* to make *him* share in his own blessed life. For this reason, at every time and in every place, God draws close to *man*. He calls *man* to seek him, to know him, to love him with all *his* strength. He calls together *all men*, scattered and divided by sin, into the unity of his family, the Church. To accomplish this, when the fullness of time had come, God sent his Son as Redeemer and Savior. In his Son and through him, he invites *men* to become, in the Holy Spirit, his adopted children and thus heirs of his blessed life.

## II

*French original*

## CHAPTER ONE: *L'HOMME* EST "CAPABLE" DE DIEU

I. Le désir de Dieu

27. Le désir de Dieu est inscrit dans le cœur de *l'homme*, car *l'homme* est créé par Dieu et pour Dieu; Dieu ne cesse d'attirer *l'homme* vers Lui, et ce n'est qu'en Dieu que *l'homme* trouvera la vérité et le bonheur qu'*il* ne cesse de chercher:

> L'aspect le plus sublime de la dignité humaine se trouve dans cette vocation de *l'homme* à communier avec Dieu. Cette invitation que Dieu addresse à *l'homme* de dialoguer avec Lui commence avec l'existence humaine. Car si *l'homme* existe, c'est que Dieu *l'*a créé par Amour et, par Amour, ne cesse de *lui* donner l'être; et *l'homme* ne vit pleinement selon la vérité que s'*il* reconnaît librement cet Amour et s'abandonne à *son* Créateur.

*Initial Translation*

## CHAPTER ONE: THE *HUMAN* CAPACITY FOR GOD

I. The Desire for God

27. The desire for God is written on the *human* heart, for God has created *us* for himself and never ceases to draw *us*

to himself. Only in God can *we* find the truth and happiness *we* constantly seek:

> *Our* calling to communion with God is the most profound basis of *our* human dignity. As soon as *we* come into being, God invites *us* to converse with him. For *we* would not exist unless God had created *us* out of love and also out of love continued to keep *us* in existence. Nor can *we* live fully in the truth unless *we* freely acknowledge that love and entrust *ourselves* to *our* Creator.

*Approved Translation*

## Chapter One: *Man's* Capacity for God

### I. The Desire for God

27. The desire for God is written in the human heart, because *man* is created by God and for God; and God never ceases to draw *man* to himself. Only in God will *he* find the truth and happiness *he* never stops searching for:

> The dignity of *man* rests above all on the fact that *he* is called to communion with God. This invitation to converse with God is addressed to *man* as soon as *he* comes into being. For if *man* exists it is because God has created *him* through love, and through love continues to hold *him* in existence. *He* cannot live fully according to truth unless *he* freely acknowledges that love and entrusts *himself* to *his* Creator.

# Biographical Note

MONSIGNOR MICHAEL J. WRENN is pastor of St. John the Evangelist Church in New York City. He was the founder and for a decade the director of a graduate catechetical institute awarding the Master's Degree in Religious Studies, and he continues today to serve both as a special consultant for religious education to Cardinal John J. O'Connor and as a board member of another catechetical institute. He has translated a number of books from French into English, and is the author, notably, of *Catechisms and Controversies: Religious Education in the Postconciliar Years* (Ignatius Press, 1991). He has written and spoken widely on religious education and related theological topics in the United States and other countries.

KENNETH D. WHITEHEAD is a former career diplomat and a former U.S. assistant secretary of education. He now works as a writer and translator in Falls Church, Virginia. He has translated some twenty books from French, German, and Italian and is the author, *inter alia*, of *Catholic Colleges and Federal Funding* (Ignatius Press, 1988). He has served as the chairman of the board of directors of a graduate catechetical institute. He is married to a full-time professional parish director of religious education (DRE), and he and his wife have four grown sons.

# Index

*413*